D0229738

ML

ANDERSONIAN LIBRARY
★
WITHDRAWN
FROM
LIBRARY
STOCK
★
UNIVERSITY OF STRATHCLYDE

A Stake in the Future

Also by John Plender:

That's the Way the Money Goes, André Deutsch

The Square Mile (with Paul Wallace), Century Hutchinson

Bib. 561764

A Stake in the Future

The Stakeholding Solution

John Plender

NICHOLAS BREALEY
PUBLISHING

LONDON

First published by
Nicholas Brealey Publishing Limited in 1997

36 John Street
London
WC1N 2AT, UK
Tel: +44 (0)171 430 0224
Fax: +44 (0)171 404 8311

17470 Sonoma Highway
Sonoma
California 95476, USA
Tel: (707) 939 7570
Fax: (707) 938 3515

© John Plender 1997
The right of John Plender to be identified as the author of this work
has been asserted in accordance with the
Copyright, Designs and Patents Act 1988.

ISBN 1-85788-175-3

British Library Cataloguing in Publication Data
A catalogue record for this book is available from the British Library.

All rights reserved. No part of this publication may be reproduced,
stored in a retrieval system, or transmitted, in any form or by any means,
electronic, mechanical, photocopying, recording and/or otherwise without
the prior written permission of the publishers. This book may not be lent,
resold, hired out or otherwise disposed of by way of trade in any form,
binding or cover other than that in which it is published, without the prior
consent of the publishers.

Printed in Great Britain by Biddles Limited.

D
658.4
PLE

Contents

Preface

*A*n occupational hazard of being a leader writer for a newspaper like the *Financial Times* is that constant exposure to politicians, civil servants and businesspeople results in your being overtaken from time to time by an acute sense of unreality. The political and economic debate suddenly seems disconnected from what is happening and increasingly remote from the things that matter. I was particularly conscious of this as I began thinking about this book, at a time when there was growing evidence that, despite a modest economic slowdown, the British economy was in surprisingly robust shape. The chattering classes were nonetheless fixated with the notion that Britain was enmeshed in a cycle of waning competitiveness and relentless economic decline.

This was a strange paradox when Britain shared with the United States most of the advantages of robust market capitalism without suffering from the same extremes of urban violence. It was enjoying a rate of economic growth that seemed tantalizingly beyond the reach of the Germans, French and Italians. For the first time in decades the British economy was even outgrowing the Japanese. And the political sleaze that so concerned the Fourth Estate was at a level that would have delighted the electorates of most other developed countries by its relative innocence.

Opinion polls nonetheless painted a picture of gloom and insecurity across the country. There seemed to be fear everywhere – fear of crime, fear of Asian competition, fear of global market forces, fear of corporate downsizing. There was anger, too, over the boardroom fat cats who lived in an Alice-in-Wonderland world where you could give yourself a warm financial pat on the back regardless of corporate performance or the sensitivities of downsized workers.

If the anger was understandable, most of the fears appeared to me to be misconceived. The figures for property-related crime were behaving rather well. There was little in the labour-market statistics that appeared to justify the general sense of insecurity. Global capital had delivered the British from a fate worse than death in the European exchange-rate mechanism. Yet many of those who were complaining that sovereign governments were impotent in the face of global markets were also in favour of a European monetary union which promised to surrender Britain's monetary policy to unaccountable central bankers, while committing fiscal policy to the strait-jacket of a German 'stability' pact.

Just to cap it all, in January 1996 Labour leader Tony Blair proclaimed a new and powerful intellectual justification of the left-of-centre position with his speech on stakeholding, only to retreat from the whole area in a matter of months. Here the sense of unreality could at least be rationalized by invoking the iron law of modern politics which says that no party can hope to win office without first draining the political debate of serious intellectual content. But it still felt a little bizarre.

The cure for leader writer's syndrome is to distance yourself from the grind and pinch yourself, so to speak, in writing. This I did in the summer of 1996 by putting together this book, in between working on a documentary series for BBC television on the history of privatization. As I talked to politicians, businesspeople and others around the country, my belief that the economy had been substantially transformed since 1979 was reinforced. Yet it was clear that economic growth was failing to deliver the psychological dividend to which everyone felt entitled.

There was a palpable sense that the unrestrained individualism of the Thatcherite counter-revolution had outstayed its welcome. Once-radical policies looked irrelevant in the face of growing inequalities of income and over-indebtedness in housing. The related business culture, with its very nineteenth-century emphasis on ownership, its autocratic managers and its heavy reliance on takeovers, appeared out of place in a world where competitive advantage stemmed more and more from the intangible values embodied in human and social capital.

In ruminating on these things, I became increasingly convinced that the vacuum left by the demise of conventional left–right politics would be filled by a lasting debate over the respective claims of economic liberalism and of stakeholding. The stakeholder concept speaks very directly to contemporary fears, even if it could not be allowed to do so too loudly before a general election. But as well as a resonant political language it has serious economic substance, which is why the idea will not go away. In the form developed by American and British business academics, stakeholder theory seems more relevant to the modern information economy than the unreconstructed shareholder model on which Anglo-Saxon capitalism currently relies.

This book is an exploration of the stakeholder idea for the general reader who is keen to make sense of the evolving political and economic debate. It looks at the main areas of the political agenda from a slightly unusual perspective that draws extensively on economic history to show how our political and economic perceptions have become curiously distorted. It also tests the assumptions of economic liberalism and of stakeholding against what is happening on the ground in industry and the City. This leads to the conclusion that stakeholding could be used to bring greater transparency and legitimacy to the wealth-creation process – qualities that are signally lacking at present.

A Stake in the Future is an optimistic book. A recurring theme is that the obsession with competitiveness and decline is absurdly masochistic when the British economy now delivers a higher absolute standard of living than at any point in history; and when Britain's competitors have as many or more problems of their own. These obsessions also distract us from more important non-material values. Too much of our political debate is devoted to chewing over half-digested borrowings from the dismal science. I shall also warn of the risks of early participation in a monetary union with continental European partners who have hitherto enjoyed stakeholder-type values on the cheap.

All journalists make their living partly by pilfering other people's ideas. The difficulty is to remember which ones are pilfered and from whom. It is easy and pleasurable to acknowledge a substantial debt to my friend Brian Reading of Lombard Street Research, who continues to generate more ideas in a month than most people do in a lifetime. The spark for many of the thoughts in this book came from him. I am equally indebted to my colleague Martin Wolf of the *Financial Times*, who will probably disagree with much of the argument of this book. He is exonerated from reading further, but should know how much I have appreciated the constant stimulus of his conversations in and out of the FT.

Much of my thinking in the chapters on corporate affairs has been developed in the course of a long and fruitful dialogue with Anne Simpson and Alan McDougall of Pensions and Investment Research Consultants (PIRC), to whom I am very grateful. Michael Brett, an adviser to PIRC and a master of computer technology, has given me helpful comments and invaluable support, as he has done with previous books. So too with Paul Beranek, whose advice was much appreciated. I am glad to be able to thank Robert Bischof for taking the trouble to show me the operations of the Boss Group and for much of the material in Chapter 6. I am also grateful for input to the chapter on privatization from John Gau, Chris Powell and Heather Forrester of John Gau Productions, who made the often gruelling business of television production an enjoyable as well as a rewarding experience. Friends who have offered generous advice and assistance include Stephanie Flanders, Sean McPhilemy, Oliver Marriott, Garry Arnott and Adrian Wyatt.

Others who may detect traces of their influence in parts of the text include Geoffrey Owen of the London School of Economics, many of whose judgements I have come to share, even if I reach them by a rather different route. I have to acknowledge a particular debt to Samuel Brittan of the *Financial Times*. Although a vociferous opponent of stakeholding, he remains the most stimulating of colleagues, not least because his constant and rigorous defence of market liberalism forces those of opposing views into a better understanding of their own position. My friend and former colleague Anthony Harris, now a columnist on *The Times*, has left an indelible mark, while David Hale of Zurich Kemper Investments has given me both leads and ideas. I personally retain an exclusive stake in all errors and omissions.

To those who have granted me interviews, many of whom prefer to remain anonymous, I extend my thanks. I apologize for omitting titles, which is not intended as a slight, but the peculiarities of the British honours system sew confusion when titles change and the chronological complexities of pre- and post-ennoblement quickly become an authorial nightmare, as well as a bother for the reader. I have made an exception for peers, when acting in an executive or judicial capacity in the Lords, because it somehow seemed natural to do so.

To my publisher Nicholas Brealey I am profoundly grateful for an unending stream of fertile ideas, encouragement and enthusiasm. To my former publishers, who have yet to reply to a proposal for this book which they received many months ago, I cock a snook in the (probably forlorn) hope that they will live, in their anonymous American-owned fastness, to regret it. Not for the first time, I express my gratitude to Richard Lambert, editor of the *Financial Times*, with whom it remains a pleasure to work. But my most heartfelt thanks go to Stephanie, without whom nothing much would have reached the page, and whose love and support command my eternal gratitude.

Part One

The Declinist Tendency

1

Reinventing Politics

*N*ever in history has the political and conceptual map of the world been destroyed as suddenly and decisively as after the fall of the Berlin Wall. With Marx dead and his critics so overwhelmingly vindicated, the left has been haunted by the obvious but obdurate question: where to find an alternative to Liberalism Triumphant?

So far, left-of-centre governments across the world have failed to deliver a convincing answer. The most striking feature of the international political landscape is simply that the old polarity between right and left is as moribund as Marx. Consider the state of the political dialogue in the leading industrialized countries. In continental Europe there is little to choose, in policy terms, between the parties of either stripe. To the extent that the Germans, Italians and Swedes are retreating from corporatist or leftist habits, it has less to do with ideological revisionism than fiscal pragmatism. The difference between political leaders in France seems to owe as much to the cut of their suits as to the substance of their policies. Everywhere the debate is about means, not ends. There could be no better definition of the death of politics.

In the United States the days of the Clinton administration's ill-fated early experiment in Great Society-style healthcare reform are long gone. In their place has come a bipartisan commitment to balance the budget, with Bill Clinton proposing budget cuts that make the fiscal demands of the Maastricht

Treaty look profligate by comparison. The Democrats' campaign rhetoric before the presidential election of 1996 was all about personal responsibility, toughness on crime and the distinction between the deserving and undeserving poor. As an alternative to what Clinton called 'brain-dead' politics, the New Democrats offered a vision of the nineteenth century.

As for Japan, its people have been too busy since 1945 building the developed world's second largest economy to have had time for a genuine political debate. After the brief retreat from single-party democracy in the recent recession, consensualism quickly returned as the Liberal Democrats reasserted their dominant influence. Bureaucrats and businessmen have anyway played a greater part in the running of post-war Japan than have politicians. Moves towards a more meaningful political dialogue will thus be slow. In Australasia, meantime, the left has long since abandoned conventional leftist policies and chosen instead to steal the clothes of the radical right. No country has ever privatized, deregulated and pruned public expenditure with as much enthusiasm as New Zealand in the days of Labour leader David Lange and his finance minister Roger Douglas, eponymous inventor of 'Rogernomics'.

In the absence of a convincing new-left alternative, the extreme proponents of *laissez faire* have become increasingly strident. Right-wing thinktanks in the English-speaking world pour out blueprints for unmixing the mixed economy and uncoupling welfare from the state. American thinkers such as Robert Nozick have turned the libertarian individualism of John Locke and David Hume into a glorification of selfishness, while James Buchanan's public choice theory offers a wholly cynical view of human motivation. The egalitarian and redistributive instincts that used to temper the workings of liberal economics are increasingly regarded as coercive, reflecting the waning of Keynes's star and the return to fashion of the libertarian Austrian school of economists, whose leading lights include Friedrich Hayek and Ludwig von Mises. Yet right-of-centre governments still maintain levels of public spending far in excess of those that prevailed in the 'socialist' 1960s. And there is little sign that electorates outside the US have much appetite for right-wing radicalism. Collectivism may have been vanquished by market liberalism, but most ordinary people in Europe continue to feel, with the late Ernest Gellner, that government intervention in economic life is a condition of decency, just as its partial absence is a condition of liberty.[1]

Miserable post-Marxists

Nowhere is this more true than in Britain, where the public is beset by a profound sense of insecurity in an economy that is richer, in absolute terms, than ever before. In the full-employment, manufacturing-intensive society of the 1960s it was fashionable to talk of the sense of powerlessness and frustration that afflicted people in large corporations – the Marxist concept of alienation. Today, with manufacturing's share of employment in all industries and services down to 18 per cent, alienation is a broader phenomenon.[2] While in the 1960s there was a high degree of income equality, combined with an extreme division of labour between the interesting and the meaningless tasks in industrial production, we now have more striking inequalities in income both inside the company and in the wider, increasingly casualized, labour market. Fat-cat directors are the conspicuous winners, unskilled workers the most notable losers. The burden of deindustrialization appears to have fallen very heavily on employees, while shareholders – who, in liberal economic theory, are the residual risk takers in the capitalist system – have enjoyed exceptional returns for more than two decades.

There is also a widespread concern that the globalization of markets is eroding the power of governments and threatening the living standards of British workers as fast-growing Asian economies pose a growing competitive threat. Meanwhile both Labour and Conservative politicians have played on the fear that high unemployment and the collapse of community values could lead to crime rates and family breakdown to rival the United States, where one-eighth of all black males between the ages of 25 and 34 are in jail and three out of five black American households with children are headed by a lone mother.[3]

Britain does not yet have anything to rival the US crime problem but, as we shall see in Chapter 2, the structure of the British labour market is beginning to provide the underprivileged with a powerful incentive to regard crime as a career opportunity. As for the family, nearly a fifth of all British families with dependent children now have lone parents; and, if the divorce rates of the mid-1980s continue, 37 per cent of marriages will end in divorce.[4] The market, which has triumphed over communism, appears impotent in the face of urban destitution and family breakdown.

In the aftermath of the Thatcher experiment there are many who feel that self-interest, the motivating force of economic liberalism, has been allowed excessive play in society's affairs and that unbridled individualism has been given too free a rein in the City and in the boardroom. Despite the enormous increases in economic efficiency that have resulted from the privatization programme, Margaret Thatcher's 'public bad, private good' equation has found no great purchase with the British public. A Mori poll before the privatization of Railtrack showed, astonishingly, that a majority appeared to be in favour of a general policy of renationalization.

No doubt this reflected the unpopularity of the more difficult later privatizations such as water, rail and nuclear energy. But it may also have contained a message about the priority accorded to the interests of shareholders, as against consumers and employees, in the very narrow proprietorial version of capitalism espoused by the Conservatives. Milton Friedman's pronouncement that the social responsibility of business begins and ends with increasing profits plays less well in the 1990s than in the heyday of Thatcherism. Another Mori survey has shown that 87 per cent of people in Britain now believe that large companies should have a wider responsibility to the community.[5]

Among the themes that will emerge in the course of this book are that Britain is not in a state of inexorable economic decline; that anxiety in the workforce over the instability of employment is only partly justified by the evidence; that governmental impotence in the face of globalization is a myth; and that the threat to British workers posed by the dynamic economies of Asia is manageable provided that we avoid egregious policy errors, especially within Europe. Yet in politics, perceptions matter. Nor can there be any escape from the fact that national income is being shared very unequally when compared with the 1960s.

It has been widely observed that the United States and continental Europe suffer two separate but related labour-market afflictions. While the US has preserved its ability to generate jobs, it has done so at the cost of hugely increased inequality of earnings: the real pay of the unskilled in the US has been falling steadily for two decades. In contrast, continental Europe has escaped significant increases in income inequality but failed to generate many new jobs. The UK, as so often, comes somewhere in between, but there is no escaping the fact that unskilled male workers' pay has failed to rise much in real terms. Unskilled males have thus increasingly been excluded from any participation in the growth of the economy.

Nationalism confronts liberal orthodoxy

No matter which form the labour-market disease takes, it creates a climate in which the prevailing liberal orthodoxy does confront a serious practical challenge in the political marketplace. There is a clear and pressing demand for a form of politics that promotes values of inclusiveness and fairness, of social responsibility and social cohesion. One way in which the demand can be satisfied is through a destructive retreat into nationalism, whereby cohesion is won at the cost of excluding people, goods and services of foreign origin. The anti-immigrant policies of Le Pen's National Front in France, for example, assert a racist version of national identity which promises Gallic inclusion at the expense of Arab and other immigrants. This has yet to find much of an echo in the rest of Europe, but it is not difficult to see how it might do so in future. In eastern Germany the response to the disintegration of the economy of the old German Democratic Republic takes the form of xenophobia and anti-semitism. In Italy fascism has been given a face lift. In Spain a policy of bribing North Africans to stay at home is likely to run into ever-greater fiscal constraints. History tells us that nationalism is contagious, especially when unemployment is high.

Increasingly, however, nationalism takes an economic form, with demagogues such as Pat Buchanan and Ross Perot in the US and Jimmy Goldsmith in Europe calling for protectionist policies to deal with the supposed threat from cheap labour in the Third World. Part of the appeal of such policies is that they appear to address directly the problems of labour-market exclusion by claiming to protect the real wages of the unskilled through increasing the cost of foreign imports. For countries like France they also provide a means of asserting national identity in a world where the growth of international trade in services such as films, television news and recorded music is deemed by politicians to pose a threat to domestic cultural values which the consumer cannot be relied on to address responsibly.

It would be ironic indeed if, just at the point where Russia, China, India and Latin America have abandoned the habits of autarky and economic nationalism that have contributed to their impoverishment, the West were to adopt a remedy which at best is irrelevant to its problems and at worst would reduce the living standards of its people. Yet it would be foolish to underestimate the appeal of populist trade policy when insecurity is so rife, especially where protectionism has strong roots as in the European Union. If no

mainstream Western political party has yet adopted this full-scale protectionist agenda, many governments increasingly pursue weaker and more
'respectable' forms of economic nationalism by seeking to create a sense of
economic purpose around the idea of competitiveness. Instead of protecting
their economy from imports, they actively promote exports and inward investment by fostering a business-friendly environment for internationally mobile
capital and offering flexible labour markets, low corporate taxation and up-to-
date infrastructure.

While this nationalistic pursuit of competitiveness is often described as
the 'Singapore model', its advocates range from left-of-centre Conservative
proponents of inward investment such as Michael Heseltine in Britain to US
Democrats like the Clinton Administration's Robert Reich. Inward investment has a number of economic attractions. As well as bringing new employment, multinational companies can help raise productivity to international
standards. But they also downsize and delayer, which means that low-key
economic nationalism of this kind offers only low-key reassurance for an
insecure electorate. It does not do much for the sense of national identity or
social cohesion.

The stakeholding solution

So what is the alternative? If there is a way of offering hope amid the prevailing insecurity in the English-speaking economies and attacking the intellectual basis of individualistic liberalism, it almost certainly lies in promoting the
values of community. That implies a domestic agenda which seeks to extend
the language of inclusion to the workplace and the welfare state and to the
ownership of capital; an agenda which emphasizes collective obligations as
well as freedoms. And if any politician can claim to have come up with a
blueprint that fits this description, it is Britain's Labour leader Tony Blair. In
the course of a fact-finding mission to Singapore early in 1996, Blair gave a
thoughtful and much publicized speech in which he developed a vision of
what he called the Stakeholder Economy.[6] The core of his thesis merits
extended quotation:

> The creation of an economy where we are inventing and producing goods
> and services of quality needs the engagement of the whole country. It must
> become a matter of national purpose and national pride. We need to build

a relationship of trust not just within a firm but within a society. By trust I mean the recognition of mutual purpose for which we work together and in which we all benefit. It is a Stakeholder Economy in which opportunity is available to all, advancement is through merit and from which no group or class is set apart or excluded. This is the economic justification for social cohesion, for a fair and strong society, a traditional commitment of left of centre politics but one with relevance today, if it is applied anew to the modern world...

We need a country in which we acknowledge a collective obligation to ensure each citizen gets a stake in it. One Nation politics is not some expression of sentiment, or even of justifiable concern for the less well off. It is an active politics, the bringing of a country together, a sharing of the possibility of power, wealth and opportunity. The old means of achieving that on the left was through redistribution in the tax and benefit regime. But in a global economy, the old ways won't do. Of course a fair tax system is right. But really a life on benefit – dependent on the State – is not what most people want. They want independence, dignity, self-improvement, a chance to earn and get on. The problems of low pay and unemployment must be tackled at source.

The economics of the centre and centre left today should be geared to the creation of the Stakeholder Economy which involves all our people, not a privileged few, or even a better off 30 or 40 or 50 per cent. If we fail in that, we waste talent, squander potential wealth-creating ability and deny the basis of trust upon which a cohesive society, One Nation, is built. If people feel they have no stake in a society, they feel little responsibility towards it and little inclination to work for its success...

Successful companies invest, treat their employees fairly and value them as a resource not just of production but of creative innovation. The debate about corporate governance in Britain is still in its infancy and has largely been focussed on headline issues like directors' pay and perks. We cannot by legislation guarantee that a company will behave in a way conducive to trust and long term commitment. But it is surely time to assess how we shift the emphasis in corporate ethos from the company being a mere vehicle for the capital market to be traded, bought and sold as a commodity, towards a vision of the company as a community or partnership in which each employee has a stake, and where a company's responsibilities are more clearly delineated.

Singapore (with apologies to the reader for a brief digression) was a rather curious place for a Labour leader to look for new ideas and expound the stakeholder alternative to unreconstructed market liberalism. Apart from economic dynamism, the 'isms' customarily associated with the South East Asian city state include a thoroughly unattractive authoritarianism, a high degree of paternalism and a Confucianism whose values are among the few things in Singapore which cannot be readily and efficiently exported to the West. These values find their most obvious expression in a compulsory savings rate of 40 per cent – 20 per cent each from employers and employees – payable into the Central Provident Fund that administers the city state's welfare system.[7]

That said, the Singaporean model has numerous admirable features including rapid economic growth and exceptional social cohesion. The crime rate is very low, whether as a result of authoritarian flogging or innate Confucian virtue. More to the point, Tony Blair made it clear that he was not in Singapore to borrow the model wholesale, but to learn from the locals while expounding his Big Idea for the people back home. And the stakeholder thesis certainly had both a suitable pedigree and political resonance.

Origins and theses

The core of the idea is that the electoral franchise alone is not enough: a real sense of participation in the nation's future is impossible without the support of a more tangible stake. And the proposition that each and every member of the population should have such a stake goes back at least as far as the eighteenth century and to the works of the revolutionary thinker Thomas Paine. Paine shared Adam Smith's belief in the value of private property and the efficacy of the market economy, while deploring extremes of inequality in income and wealth. In *Agrarian Justice* he proposed a basic guaranteed income for every citizen to be financed out of death duties on land and property.[8] Part of the logic of this redistributive justice was that if people enjoyed monetary independence, it could no longer be argued that those without property should be denied the vote on the ground that they would be too afraid of their masters to exercise the franchise responsibly.

Paine's proposal thus incorporates a firm stakeholder concept, albeit with a reversal of the causal logic. In the late eighteenth century it appeared necessary to argue for a stake in order to make the case for the majority vote; today the majority has the vote but needs a stake to enjoy what Blair calls 'a

sharing of the possibility of power, wealth and opportunity'. But Paine's prescription is a clear antecedent of Blair's conception of a welfare system which
'holds the commitment of the whole population, rich and poor', although it
might fall short of satisfying today's demand for adequate work incentives.

The impact on the political fraternity of the Labour leader's description
of this modern version of stakeholding was in no way diminished by the teas-
ing theft in his speech of the old One Nation rhetoric of an increasingly
divided Tory party. And as a socialized alternative to the individualistic Tory
commitment to wider share ownership, which has done little since privatization to enhance the possibility of power, wealth and opportunity for many people, it cannot easily be stolen by the right. With its emphasis on community
and welfare universalism, Blair's speech was enthusiastically welcomed by
many members of Labour's old guard like Roy Hattersley, whose commitment
to equality remained a central tenet of their socialist credo. References to
'independence, dignity, self-improvement, a chance to earn and get on' were
well pitched for potential middle-class recruits to Labour's cause.

As for broad economic policy, Blair offered no fiscal hostages to fortune.
Part of the attraction of a concept that emphasized trust, community and self-
improvement was presumably that it carried a hint that the high-spending role
of the state was being downgraded. More positively, Blair's placatory references to business and his view of the firm as a community in which human
capital provides a key to competitive advantage looked a well-judged retreat
from Old Labour's hostility to business.

Although short on detail, the Labour leader's opening outline of a
stakeholder alternative certainly offered a potent language with which to
address the concerns of the electorate. There were, however, some snags. The
first was that the Stakeholder Economy was not, in itself, a slogan with much
tabloid appeal. But no matter. That could equally have been said of the Social
Contract, *Reflections on the Revolution in France*, or *Das Kapital*. The second
was that the shadow chancellor Gordon Brown did not share Blair's enthusiasm for the idea. A final and wholly unpredictable caveat arose from the fact
that the most vocal proponent of a stakeholder economy in Britain was Will
Hutton, author of the bestselling book *The State We're In* and an associate editor, at that time, of the *Guardian* newspaper.[9] Under the unwitting influence
of this engaging and enthusiastic advocate, the Big Idea suddenly started to
shrink.

Huttonomics frightens the horses

The State We're In, which contained an impassioned plea for a reformed constitution and a stakeholder economy, was the publishing phenomenon of the mid-1990s. It was that rare thing – a serious tract on political economy in the tradition, so its author claimed, of Keynes, Polanyi, Galbraith, Friedman and others, which reached the bestseller list and stayed there for month after month. It was also a notable contribution to a characteristically English genre, the literature of decline, belonging to the subform which worries about a shrinking manufacturing base and attributes economic decay to the presumed dominance of finance over industry. This is a very durable tradition which goes back more than a hundred years. Its peculiarity is that it continues to thrive despite the British economy's unyielding propensity, boom and bust notwithstanding, to grow in peacetime at a long-run rate of around 2 per cent a year in real terms.

The obsession will be explored further in subsequent chapters, but in essence it is an occupational hazard of having started the Industrial Revolution. A country that has been the world's economic top dog is condemned to relative decline as other countries grow, even in the midst of prolonged absolute growth in incomes and living standards. The result is that excitable commentators experience a similar feeling to people in a stationary passenger train who are convinced that they are moving backwards when they see another train pull out of the station.[10] This is not to deny the acuteness of many of the insights into the workings of the economy and the City in Hutton's book. But his depressed view of British economic prospects drove him to advance a multiplicity of proposals which smacked heavily of Old Labour nostrums and reflected a passionate admiration for the more interventionist, subsidizing habits of Germany and Japan – countries where the stakeholder model is generally perceived to be running into trouble.

Looked at from a Labour perspective, this was an unhappy recipe for frightening the horses before a general election, which was the last thing that its author would have wished. Trade unions seized on the idea with alacrity, since it appeared to provide an opportunity to win back power and influence under the new guise of stakeholding. For the Tories this was a heaven-sent gift. They quickly realized that Hutton's instinctive suspicion of the free market, his unreconstructed enthusiasm for public spending and his unconstrained assault on the City of London could be used to embarrass Labour.

As one Tory politician after another quoted Huttonomics as if it were Labour policy, Blair felt obliged to retreat from his original vision. The stakeholder economy dissolved into woollier statements about the stakeholder society, as Labour spokespersons started to emphasize that their interest lay in 'political' stakeholding, as opposed to stakeholder economics.

This was unfortunate, because stakeholding amounts to precious little if it is deprived of its economic dimension and it remains the most coherent and constructive alternative to liberal orthodoxy. Moreover, in this book I will put a case that the very specific problems of the English-speaking countries – pervasive insecurity and income inequality – can best be addressed by adopting stakeholder principles that owe little to the Germans or the Japanese; indeed, that there is much about continental European stakeholding, especially when combined with the move to monetary union, that could be very damaging to Britain. It will suggest that the strength of the idea derives not only from its promise of a more inclusive society, but from its ability to provide a workable alternative to the very narrow and abrasive Anglo-Saxon version of capitalism which threatens to turn creative destruction, the great strength of capitalism, into mere destruction.

The economics of trust

To put the arguments in context, a brief excursion around the recent history of the stakeholder concept is necessary. To the extent that stakeholding constitutes an explicit theory, it was initially developed at the level of the firm, not of society or the economy, in the United States in the 1960s. It does not, so far as I have been able to establish, have a single originator or a definitive original statement, but the Stanford Research Institute in California played an important part in fostering the theory at a time when Americans were showing a growing interest in the question of business's responsibility to the community. Those at Stanford who played a significant role included two former managers at Lockheed Aircraft Corporation, Robert F Stewart and Otis J Benepe, and the Swedish management theorist Eric Rhenman. In essence, the theory is a set of ideas revolving around a critique of the conventional notion of a company as a bundle of property rights in which the various constituents – shareholders, managers, employees, customers and suppliers – conducted their relations through a nexus of private contracts, with the pre-eminent participants, the shareholders, delegating responsibility for running the business to professional managers.

Stakeholder theory proposed instead a view of the managerial role which came closer to trusteeship, where the trustees' role was to balance the interests of the various constituencies in the business and to recognize a wider responsibility to society. Its essential insight was that the market liberals' conventional description of corporate life was out of touch with events. In the modern world, large professionally run companies more closely resembled social entities in which investors enjoyed few rights of possession and control, and failed to exercise many of those rights that they did have. Other stakeholders, such as managers, employees, customers, bankers and suppliers, were providing support without which the business could not survive. This, indeed, was how many businessmen had long seen things. As Robert Reich has pointed out, the chairman of Standard Oil Company of New Jersey, Frank Abrams, gave an address in 1951 in which he said: 'The job of management is to maintain an equitable and working balance among the claims of the various directly interested groups – stockholders, employees, customers and the public at large.'[11]

What gave the stakeholder concept additional marketability was that it coincided with a realization that the success of the Japanese owed much to stakeholder values. Most large Japanese companies are run primarily in the interests of employees; secondarily in the interests of stakeholders such as suppliers and banks; and lastly for shareholders, whose interests have rarely, until recently, been given a second thought. Impetus also came from the realization that more and more of the value in the modern corporation lay in human capital and in the nature of the relationships with employees and suppliers. The success of Japanese car firms, to take the most obvious example, rests on mass-production techniques whereby management places huge trust in the employees to ensure smooth running and high quality. Devices such as just-in-time inventory control also require close cooperative relationships with suppliers. These relationships are governed not by contractual arrangements but by mutual agreement; and in the case of the suppliers they are cemented by cross-shareholdings on which the dividend return is regarded as unimportant.

Human capital is of growing significance in the more sophisticated service industries, as well as in high-technology areas. As Stanford professors Paul Milgrom and John Roberts have pointed out, employees in these newer areas of business often make a costly investment in knowledge and skills that are specific to the firm and not transferable if they change jobs.[12] The decisions taken by the firm therefore put the employees' human capital at risk in much the same way as investors' capital is at risk There is thus an enhanced moral as well as economic case for taking the employees' interests into account in the firm's decision making. The attempt to make firms accountable to wider stake-holding constituencies is not without its dangers, as we shall see later. But state law in the US increasingly acknowledges the reality of the employee 'stake' in the firm. And writers such as Margaret Blair at The Brookings Institution in Washington – no relation of the Labour leader – have looked at ways of incor-porating the stakeholding concept into the practice of corporate governance, the rather cumbersome phrase which describes the rules under which man-agers run the company and are held accountable for their stewardship.[13]

Civic-minded elks and scouts

Academic work on the stakeholder concept of the firm coincided with the development of a loosely related set of ideas to do with the role of trust and civic engagement in society and the economy. The notion of 'social capital' was propounded by the American sociologist James Coleman and, with much greater éclat, by Harvard academic Robert Putnam. According to Putnam, social capital arises from those features of social life such as networks, behavioural norms and trust which enable people to work more effectively towards common goals – intangible qualities referred to by legal theorists as relational contracting and known in economics as implicit contracts. In his book *Making Democracy Work*, Putnam researched the cultural differences between regional government in the north and south of Italy and concluded that the north's far greater success derived from its sense of civic engagement, which stemmed from an ingrained tendency to form small associations.[14] The south's capacity for democratic self-government and economic growth had been inhibited by the hierarchical, authoritarian structure imposed on the society centuries earlier by the Normans. The south thus provided arid ground for the growth of social capital.

This seemingly recherché work was another rather unlikely publishing success story – and more. 'Here,' said *The Economist*, 'is a book that mas-querades as a routine study of Italian regional government but is actually a great work of social science, worthy to rank alongside de Tocqueville, Pareto and Weber.'[15] How well that euphoric verdict will stand the test of time remains to be seen. But the anonymous reviewer was right in identifying a clear echo of de Tocqueville's view that American democracy derived immense strength from the way in which 'Americans of all ages, all conditions, and all dispositions constantly form associations'.[16] And what gave Putnam an edge – and the ear of Bill Clinton – was that he combined this academic work with a more populist thesis of decline. The United States, as befits a top nation under-going the psychological strain of adjusting to increased competition from Japan, has followed the UK in spawning a lively declinist literary tradition, albeit with an angst that has a more strident and less resigned quality about it. Much of the anxiety centres on homelessness, urban blight and rising crime. These, Putnam argued, were the direct result of a loss of civic-mindedness.

On the basis of 'time-budget' studies of how individual Americans spent their day, and of membership records of organizations such as The League of Women Voters, the Red Cross, unions, parent–teacher associations, the Elks, scouts and bowling leagues, Putnam concluded that social capital and civic engagement had declined sharply over three decades. He attributed this to the decline of a 'long civic generation' that had acquired cooperative social habits in the stressful circumstances of the 1930s Slump and the Second World War; also to the toll taken on people's social lives by television. The final ingredient of Putnam's success lay in the horror quotient of his thesis. For in suggesting that southern Italy's modern plight was attributable to the destruction of its social capital by the Normans, he implied that social capital was extremely difficult to recreate; and that an absence of civic virtue going back over decades or centuries might make it impossible for countries that were struggling to construct a new, liberal society to establish a crucial build-ing block of democracy. The fearful implications for the former communist bloc need no underlining.

In the hands of Francis Fukuyama, author of the controversial tract *The End of History and the Last Man*, the concept of social capital has been used to provide an explanation for wider divergences in well-being and economic per-formance between countries.[17] Part of Fukuyama's thesis is that where a coun-try's culture permits firms to rely on trust rather than private contract to manage their affairs, there are large benefits to be had from lower transaction costs. Lawyers, accountants, audit trails and paper bureaucracy become redundant because implicit contracts based on trust are just that: implicit. As we shall see in Chapter 6, Fukuyama rationalizes the relative failure of the Chinese to develop large corporations, and the ability of the Americans to do so, by reference to the contrast between a familistic Chinese culture, which is distrustful of non-family members, and the trustful American habit of civic engagement, which lends itself to the kinds of cooperative behaviour that are needed to make large corporations work.

Culture vultures

The concept of social capital is by no means an American monopoly. It has much in common with ideas of the German school of economists loosely known as 'institutionalists', who believe that the competitive success of firms in markets for goods and services depends on restraining or guiding the markets for labour and capital.[18] Many echoes are also to be found in Britain. The economist Mark Casson, for example, has developed a critique of orthodox economics in which he argues that economic performance directly reflects the level of trust in an economy, which in turn depends on culture.[19] The economist and management theorist John Kay, some of whose arguments are explored in later chapters, has written extensively on trust and is Britain's most cogent advocate of stakeholding.[20] Among left-of-centre politicians, Frank Field has proposed a reform of the British pension system which incorporates a stakeholder view of ownership.

The view of corporate activity held by the business guru Charles Handy makes him an honorary member of the stakeholding club. And the Royal Society for the encouragement of Arts, Manufactures and Commerce (the RSA) has propounded a practical version of stakeholding in its influential *Tomorrow's Company* report, which argues that competitive success in future will increasingly depend on inclusive criteria of the kind normally associated with stakeholder theory.[21]

The concept of social capital, with its emphasis on trust, is a central part of the stakeholder canon. It is a train of thought that emphasizes the distinction between the legal and political institutions of the state on the one hand and those of civil society on the other, a category that includes all forms of association which are spontaneous, customary and not necessarily dependent on law, such as companies, unions, churches, clubs, charities, pressure groups and so forth. The suggestion is that the robustness of the political and economic system is heavily dependent on a multiplicity of such intermediate institutions, whose existence usually reflects a strong tradition of civic engagement. In the post-Cold-War climate, a thesis of this kind has obvious appeal for the left, since its focus is specifically on the middle ground between the respective preserves of the discredited state and the unrestrained individual.

The intellectual ancestry of sociologists such as Putnam and Fukuyama does not lie on the left of the political spectrum. If anything, they have more in common with the tradition of Edmund Burke, in his criticism of individualism and his emphasis on the family, social norms, continuity and order. Burke likewise whispers in the ear of such communitarian thinkers as Charles Taylor and Amitai Etzioni. Their belief is that libertarians have promoted the values of individual freedom and profit at the expense of social life, while socialists have wrongly assumed that the state can compensate for the social fragmentation that results from the disruptive forces of economic change. Etzioni's communitarianism has been another influence on the thinking of Labour under Tony Blair.

At first sight, it may seem extraordinary that the intellectual baggage of a British Labour leader should be stamped with the label of a conservative Whig such as Burke. Yet Blair has clearly understood a fundamental appeal of conservatism, which stems from its claim to satisfy the yearning for certainty, order and stability. And this underlines an even more extraordinary truth about current politics in the English-speaking countries. In a world where the intellectual underpinnings of the left–right political debate have collapsed, where technology and trade are causing huge upheavals in industry and commerce, where crime appears to be increasing inexorably and where unemployment is an intractable problem, the left is unelectable beyond all hope unless it wholeheartedly embraces the more reassuring values of conservatism.

This is precisely the attraction of stakeholding for left-of-centre politicians. It provides an unembarrassing cloak for their entrée into conservative territory. By proposing a form of conservatism which is genuinely distinct from the prevailing liberal orthodoxy, with a wholly different economic and social agenda, it allows the left to steal the some of the best clothes of the right. That is one of many reasons that the idea is likely to prove politically durable despite Labour's retreat from its initial enthusiasm.

The missing 20 per cent

Part of the attraction of the economic side of stakeholding is that it speaks directly to concerns about the market liberals' one-dimensional view of human beings as 'rational personal utility maximizers'. Samuel Brittan, no friend of stakeholder theory, has frequently pointed out that Adam Smith did not expect the 'invisible hand' doctrine of benign self-interest to be applied without the exercise of moral restraint; a functioning market presupposes a basis of trust which is itself a form of social capital.[22] Since the eighteenth century, welfare economics, the branch of the dismal science that deals with the distribution of production and the efficiency with which resources are allocated, has sealed itself off from the disciplines that consider wider ethical issues. In consequence it is oddly silent about the rules, inhibitions and instinctive reflexes that modify the pursuit of uninhibited self-interest. It does not provide answers to a host of important questions.

By way of example, asks Brittan, is it legitimate to try to monopolize a market in the absence of strong laws against restrictive practices? If there are such laws, should we cooperate actively or merely conform? If the labour market is clearly malfunctioning, is an employer who deliberately tries to provide more jobs a social benefactor? Or is he meddling in matters outside his influence, so that society would benefit more if he simply confined himself to promoting shareholders' financial interests? On questions such as these a stakeholder advocate will frequently arrive at different answers to a Chicago liberal, placing greater emphasis on individual responsibility. To put it in Fukuyama's terms, there is a missing 20 per cent of human behaviour about which neoclassical economics can give only a poor account, because that 20 per cent concerns the customs, morals and habits of the society in which it occurs – in a word, culture.

A more practical attraction of the stakeholder theory is that it contains an implicit injunction to adjust market mechanisms to take account of social costs and benefits, for example in relation to the environment, that are not explicitly priced in today's marketplace. This is not at all inconsistent with economic liberalism. It is more in their insistence on the importance of 'shareholder value' that market liberals fall into the trap of placing too much emphasis on what is easily quantifiable by conventional accounting, instead of the important intangible values that can only be captured in softer data.

As Margaret Blair puts it, the primitive model of the corporation in which shareholders are seen as earning all the returns and bearing all the risks is a throwback to an earlier time when the typical company owned and operated simple undertakings such as a canal, a railway or a physical plant. For enterprises that still fit that model, it may make sense to give shareholders as much control as possible on the basis that this will both maximize wealth and increase the welfare of society as a whole. For the many enterprises that do not, a commitment to shareholder value may, as we shall see in due course, destroy wealth rather than help create it.

In their support for the concept of shareholder value, market liberals also implicitly adopt a simplistic and one-dimensional view of human behaviour that parallels, in economics, the blinkered view of public choice theory, which sees politics as a market process whereby politicians trade policies in exchange for votes and seek to exploit public office for private personal gain. They assume that executives are out to maximize their personal utility at the expense of shareholders and that they must therefore be subjected to very narrow financial oversight if the value in the company is not to be eroded. As with public choice theory, there is a basic insight here which has some validity. Many executives do seek to milk the company and there are many more who are incompetent. That said, the great majority are honest people who want to do a decent job. The problem is that if all executives are cynically assumed to be bent on maximizing personal utility rather than balancing the interests of the various constituent parties in the enterprise, the narrow discipline required to keep the supposed milkers and maximizers in check tends to become a very disruptive constraint that encourages short-termism. This mirrors the problems that arise from the public choice theorists' advocacy of constant referenda over taxation. It sounds plausible in theory, but referenda have proved a mixed and disruptive blessing in California, the great adventure playground of public choice theory.

From small picture to big

It will be apparent by now that the stakeholder concept operates at several levels. At the level of the firm, it asserts the need to recognize the value in a much wider set of relationships than those acknowledged by the conventional principal–agent model of capitalism, with its heavy emphasis on property rights. Those relationships, whether described in the sociologist's language of social capital or the economist's jargon of implicit contracts, are an all-important element in the competitive advantage of firms. It is the job of the manager to foster them in the long-term interests of the company and the wider interests of society. The emphasis on the cohesive nature of the relationships between the various economic actors does not preclude shareholders' exercise of discipline over management. But it does imply a different definition of objectives and thus a different approach to monitoring, of which more in due course.

At the level of the nation, a stakeholder economy is one which derives competitive strength from a cohesive national culture, in which the exercise of property rights is conditioned by shared values and cooperative behaviour. The emphasis on shared values is important because economic performance depends heavily on what economists call transaction costs – the costs of monitoring relationships such as those between management, employees and all the other actors that contribute to the wealth of the enterprise; and of ensuring that these relationships work in an orderly and productive fashion.

In highly individualistic societies a heavy emphasis on the exercise of private property rights greatly increases such transaction costs. More people are needed to keep an eye on employees where there is no trust between management and workers. More human capital is diverted into economically unproductive activities such as the law, as people seek constantly to define their rights *vis à vis* others, in and out of court. The state responds to the excesses of individualistic behaviour with excessive legislation and costly regulation. Trading in property rights, notably in the financial markets, exceeds what is needed to fuel the workings of the wider economy. For fear of poaching, employers are more reluctant to invest in training for their employees. Those who are excluded from employment more readily resort to crime.

No absolute definition of a stakeholder economy is possible, since all countries have some cohesive and some less cohesive elements in their national cultures. There is a spectrum. At one extreme are those countries in Africa where loyalty to the family and the tribe makes cooperative economic behaviour in a capitalist framework extraordinarily difficult. At the other is Japan, where capitalism has acquired a collectivist ethos that bears a surprising resemblance to communism. In the middle come countries such as the United States, with a destructive individualism in the urban ghettos, a constructive individualism in such high-tech corporate giants as Microsoft and a strong tradition of civic association which helps condition the behaviour of the middle Americans who work so productively in so many large organizations. Britain, with its combination of innovative individualism, craft-based unionism, a divisive educational system and an instinctive belief in fair play, is hard to place on the spectrum. But it is probably – marginally – on the African as opposed to the Japanese side relative to the United States.

The historic success of stakeholder economies such as Germany, Switzerland or Japan is partly explained by their lower transaction costs, both inside and outside the firm. The cooperative ethos of German and Swiss culture, for example, encourages a universal commitment to investment in training. In Japan it leads to a legal profession that is tiny by the standards of the rest of the developed world; and the Japanese do not have to fear for their safety if they walk the Tokyo streets late at night, which means that law and order impose a lesser burden on the national budget. The penalty for antisocial opportunism in such societies is not a legal but a social one, on a scale that ranges from disapproval to social ostracism.

Finally, at a political level, stakeholding offers a language in which the criterion of inclusion represents a central yardstick. Much of this book will be devoted to exploring the extent to which the institutional infrastructure of Britain meets that criterion and addressing the question of what should be done where it falls short. But if the political language is potent and the economics of stakeholding is effective, why, it might be asked, are the Japanese and German economies encountering difficulties in the present decade? And why are the these countries starting to move closer to the Anglo-Saxon shareholder model?

Flawed foreign models

The extent to which the Japanese and Germans are retreating from the stakeholder model can be greatly exaggerated. Under the pressure of economic forces they are merely picking and choosing selectively from an Anglo-Saxon model which is itself beset with problems. The point is rather that these countries' versions of stakeholding have become flawed in current circumstances because the interests of the various constituents have become very unbalanced. Investors and depositors have historically been financially disadvantaged in relation to the other stakeholders. This was because the heavily regulated and bank-dominated financial systems of Japan and Germany were intentionally designed to deliver a low cost of capital to industry.

The bias was sustainable and sensible in the early decades after the Second World War, but the justification for a penalty on returns to capital no longer exists now that the Germans and Japanese have become rich, their populations are ageing and their economies are growing more slowly. Indeed, the penalty has become destructive. In Japan the low returns accorded to investors have exacerbated the Japanese banking crisis while contributing to the insolvency of the Japanese life insurance and pensions system. This is because the banks and insurance companies are themselves among the country's biggest investors in their capacity as stakeholder members of the informal *keiretsu* groupings through which big Japanese companies do business. They are being forced to reduce their cross-shareholdings in these groups not because they want to, but because they need to restore their profitability and capital to stave off bankruptcy.

In Germany the systemic problem is more a case of managing the huge bill for one of the world's best-upholstered welfare systems, which has been greatly increased by German unification. The bill falls disproportionately on business, which finds it harder to compete against low-cost competition in Eastern Europe and elsewhere. Some German businesspeople also argue that the large role accorded to the unions is beginning to reduce the flexibility of German companies in confronting big structural adjustments in the economy. What is clear is that, with Japan and Germany both now operating in highly competitive global markets for goods, services and capital, it becomes increasingly difficult for them to sustain uneconomic subsidies at home from one group of stakeholders to another.

A far bigger potential criticism of these foreign stakeholder models is in fact political and social. Stakeholder societies derive much of their strength from their high degrees of income equality, which help provide glue for the social structure, especially at times of economic adversity. They also appear to be much better than individualistic societies at doing those things like education that are best done collectively. It is necessary only to recall the damage done by Margaret Thatcher to the British educational system with her vilification of public-sector employees – unthinkable in Germany or Japan – to see the truth of this. But it is equally true that much of the social cohesion of Germany and Japan derives from a sense of self-definition that is hostile to foreigners, immigrants and underprivileged or outcast groups.

A down on outsiders

Foreigners have always come low in the Japanese estimation and Japan's instinctive economic nationalism remains largely intact despite the benefits it has derived in the post-war period from international trade. Its labour market is kind to the élite who enjoy lifetime employment in large companies; but it can be vicious for those in the small companies which go bust in droves at each downturn of the economic cycle as they are ruthlessly squeezed by larger corporate customers. Lower down the scale, the Japanese are exceptionally harsh in their treatment of their Korean underclass and of the *burakumin* caste – Japan's equivalent of India's untouchables. In a society that prides itself on its homogeneity, even the handful of remaining ethnic Japanese, the Ainu, suffer indignity under a government that refuses to acknowledge their ethnicity.[23] And now social cohesion is threatened in a different way. Even in large companies, the salaryman's 'One Nation' sense of commitment has been undermined by inflated land values, especially during the 'bubble economy' period in the 1980s, which have ended up excluding even some company chairmen from any prospect of home ownership.

Germany has a more humane culture than Japan and has treated foreigners with much greater respect since the war – witness the contrast in the countries' respective attitudes to apologizing for war crimes. But Germany, too, is prone to exclude outsiders. It has, for example, traditionally allowed the burden of adjustment in recession to fall on Turkish guest workers. And the terms of German unification were such that the exchange rate for D-marks and Ostmarks left Germans in the east with incomes much higher than was justified by their underlying productivity at work. Real wages there were higher than in the United States and Japan. So while west German jobs were protected from eastern competition, employment in east German agriculture fell by three-quarters, while manufacturing employment fell by two-thirds.[24] The 'Ossies' were priced out of the global labour market for the foreseeable future. Switzerland is even more dependent on foreign workers and even more xenophobic about them. They are admitted as seasonal workers for nine months of the year, but cannot join the mainstream workforce until they have completed four seasons. Foreign workers constitute the biggest unemployed group in the Swiss labour market.

In many stakeholder societies such as Singapore the commitment to social cohesion is tinged with authoritarianism. Nor is this a purely oriental phenomenon. The cultures of Switzerland and Scandinavia are not without oppressive features. Equally important, stakeholder societies tend to exclude women from participation in the workforce and suffer from higher rates of female unemployment than do the English-speaking economies. The risk of being in a low-paid job is particularly high for women in Germany, Japan and Switzerland.[25] As David Soskice, a director of the Wissenschaftzentrum in Berlin, has pointed out, the logic of these systems is that long-termism in industry calls for long-term loyalty and continuous availability of employees, especially managers. They depend either on large numbers of unpaid mothers or elderly relatives to look after children at home, or on female employment in the public sector to do so, as in Sweden.[26]

The recent crisis in the Swedish welfare model (and the wider fiscal crisis of the state elsewhere) does, then, raise fundamental questions for the politics of inclusion. Is it really possible to address the problems of the unemployed and the poor without spending big sums on housing, childcare and skills? And will a younger generation sufficiently share the values of the old to pay the taxes necessary to finance such expenditure when demographics are moving in an unhelpful direction? Can the sense of community be

enhanced when memories of shared hardship in wartime and of a common
enemy in the Cold War are receding?

Right and wrong turnings

In reality, a stakeholder society can exist perfectly well without external enemies or an internal underclass to sustain its sense of cohesion. But it is important not to make excessive claims for the idea. Some advocates of political
stakeholding, especially those with a strong moral conscience, have an un-
realistic view, both in social and fiscal terms, of what can be achieved by
encouraging the growth of intermediate institutions and the role that might be
played by a reinvigorated church. As Anthony Sampson has remarked in his
book *Company Man*, the corporation has long since taken over from the
church as the main outside social polarity in people's lives.[27] It is, rather, in the
workplace that stakeholding can make its real contribution to our sense of
well-being. And outside the company it could be argued that the characteristic intermediate institution of the post-Enlightenment age is not the church
but questioning, anti-establishment organizations like Greenpeace, Amnesty
International or even the National Childbirth Trust, which has successfully
challenged the orthodoxies of a male-dominated medical establishment.

Liberals such as Samuel Brittan also argue, with some historic justification, that many of the worst atrocities have been perpetrated when people
have abandoned self-interested liberalism and identified their interests with
grandiose visions of state, society or religious creed. Society is a word that has
frequently been used by the reactionary, nationalist right as a weapon with
which to beat liberal utilitarians. Yet the fear of violence perpetrated in the
name of the nation state looks anachronistic in a post-Cold-War Western
European context. The more plausible wrong turnings for a stakeholder society are excessive authoritarianism, of which there is a strong hint in the writ-
ings of communitarian thinkers such as Etzioni, and economic nationalism.
It is at times like the present, when unemployment is high and insecurity is
rife, that these threats are most potent.

The political paradox of the post-communist world is that while liberalism is triumphant, its non-ideological values remain as non-inspirational as
they have always been. In place of righteousness, liberalism offers the tepid
qualities of utility, tolerance and humanity. That is the whole nature of liberalism, its weakness and its strength. The economic paradox is that the growing

sense of economic dispossession means that the value of a vote to the more insecure members of the electorate is increasing. All it requires is for a populist demagogue to make people sufficiently aware of this to put it to use.

The risk, then, is that the vacuum that has opened in the political landscape after the demise of traditional right–left politics and the fall of the Berlin Wall could soon be very unattractively filled; and that the big divide on the political map will be between a liberalism of weak appeal and a populist and authoritarian economic nationalism that speaks (as ever, with a forked tongue) to the dispossessed. That includes not only the unemployed and unskilled, but those in all walks of life who live in fear of losing their jobs or seeing their incomes decline. And as we shall see in Chapter 11, the risk could be greatly increased by participation in a European monetary union that includes member states that have yet to face up to the real cost of their welfare commitments – states that have, in some cases, been enjoying their stakeholder model on the cheap.

Yet there is an alternative to the politics of nationalism and dispossession. The concept of stakeholding is sufficiently flexible to incorporate the best of market liberalism with a language and commitment to social cohesion that could help pre-empt a lurch into protectionism or worse. It is adaptable enough to offer a framework for rethinking corporate life without having to borrow from the Germans or the Japanese. (The Swiss version of stakeholding, for example, entails a very lightly regulated labour market and much lower social security contributions than in Germany.[28])

This book will explore the claim of stakeholding to engage human beings more constructively in society and to contribute to a more competitive economy. It will offer several suggestions as to where the principle can be usefully wedded to existing Anglo-Saxon practice. But first we need to look more directly at the prevailing psychological malaise that seems to affect people of all classes regardless of the economic environment. Why is it that people feel so insecure?

2

High Anxiety

*I*f the condition of the British nation had been subjected to analysis by the proverbial Martian at the mid-point of the 1990s, the verdict would probably have been rather flattering. In 1994 the British economy had been growing at an impressively solid 3.8 per cent. Inflation was at its lowest level for 27 years. Unemployment had been falling for two years in a row, while the government's budget deficit, although high, appeared to be coming rapidly under control. Even more surprising, given the economy's historic performance, was that the source of growth was shifting from private consumption to strengthening exports. Apart from a somewhat slow upturn in investment, this was the kind of balanced economic recovery that had eluded the British since 1945.[1]

A similarly encouraging picture could have been drawn of Britain's wider role on the international stage. Since the end of the Cold War, the country had exercised disproportionate influence in world diplomacy and retained its permanent seat on the UN Security Council. It was playing an important part in global peacekeeping and the prowess of its armed forces was a source of envy even to the French. As for the quality of life, the exceptional number of American, German and Japanese executives who made Britain the first choice for inward investment in the European Union rated it excellent. The arts in London flourished with exceptional vigour.

The difficulty, in this extraterrestrial audit, would have been to rationalize the contemporary political debate, since it scarcely reflected the more benign features of Britain's situation. Labour repeatedly attacked the Conservative government for falling further down the international league table of world prosperity, while vigorously pursuing the themes of short-termism, underinvestment and continuing national decline. Even the Tories, riven with dissension over Europe and plagued by a wafer-thin majority, appeared unconvinced by their own rhetoric and unsure of their country's place in the world.

At a more subjective level, quality newspapers continued to refer to Britain as a medium-sized power whose aspirations ran ahead of its economic strength – a curious perspective on the meaning of medium-sized, given that the British economy was the developed world's fifth or sixth largest, depending on how much of Italy's black economy found its way into the national income statistics. A look at the budget deficits and public debt of the rest of the Group of Seven industrialized countries would quickly have dispelled the notion that Britain was any more prone to overreach itself than the others. Some nonetheless remained convinced that Britain was forever condemned to downward mobility. Much editorial hand wringing accompanied the sale of the Rover group, Britain's last domestically owned car manufacturer, to BMW of Germany.

The discomfiture of the monarchy, as the Prince of Wales appeared to lose the public war of words with his estranged, and then divorced, wife, was widely seen in the press as symbolic of the continuing decline of great national institutions. The opinion polls, meantime, painted a picture of a people not only disillusioned with their monarchy but afflicted with more immediate insecurities. Weighed down by debt, repossessions in housing and the fear of redundancy, the British appeared more than usually obsessed with crime and rising drug use, despite statistical evidence that reported crime had peaked in 1992 and was falling markedly. At the same time the experience of 'delayering', 'downsizing' and 'reengineering' – business's weasel words for firing people – had introduced the middle classes to an experience hitherto confined to manual workers. The Americans, suffering similar treatment, called it 'white-collar shock'. Among the hardest hit were middle managers whose traditional role in filtering and disseminating information around the corporation had been usurped by the increasingly versatile computer.

Small wonder that the public, in an attempt to fill the void left by the absence of a so-called 'feelgood factor', spent nearly £100 million a week on the new national lottery.[2] It was ironic that a Tory government dedicated to

privatization had succeeded in inventing a monopolistic nationalized industry whose success rested on its ability to offer people a dream of escape from
the status quo. The management was subcontracted to the appropriately
named Camelot, whose spiralling profitability rested on offering wretchedly
unfavourable odds to punters who pursued the unholy grail. It may not have
been stakeholding, but it was at least a distraction from the consequences of
Tory policy.

The other natural outlet for the feelings of shocked white-collar workers in mid-decade was to rail at fat cats in the British boardroom, which was
one of the few places in the economy where inflation remained rampant.
Public hostility to business was probably greater than it had been since the
early 1970s, when the Conservative leader Edward Heath had pronounced
anathemas on 'the unpleasant and unacceptable face of capitalism'. Perhaps it
was greater, even, than at any time since the Slump of the 1930s. This was, to
say the least, paradoxical, given that the demise of the former Soviet Union
had cast capitalism in a more flattering light than at any time since the onset
of industrialization. All things considered, our Martian would have been entitled to feel puzzled that the British appeared bent on a zestless *fin de siècle*, to
be crowned by a Millennium Commission whose idea of a good time was
embodied in a plan to spend £42 million towards a 2500-mile cycle route
around the country – a scheme tailor-made to appeal to worthy Fabian socialists of a century earlier.

The happiness deficit

This snapshot of the way things looked and felt in the mid-1990s encapsulates
no more than a single point in time. Within a year the economy was looking
less healthy, as it paused for breath before the usual pre-electoral pump prim-
ing. But it nonetheless underlines an important point about general perceptions – namely, that if the upheavals of the Thatcher years had actually done
something to halt the process of national decline, the fact had not impressed
itself in the slightest on the national psyche. Surprising numbers of people, in
the midst of an economic recovery where unemployment had fallen un-
expectedly quickly, were still convinced that the country was in recession. In
their punch-drunk, post-Thatcherite state, they were highly receptive to Will
Hutton's argument, in *The State We're In*, that Britain was locked in what he
called 'a self-reinforcing downward spiral'.[3]

Even the experience of white-collar shock appeared to be rooted partly in misconceptions about job insecurity. Between 1984 and 1993 there was virtually no change at all in the length of time for which male employees held on to their jobs; and almost two-thirds of men aged 30–49 had held their job for more than five years, a statistic little changed from 10 years earlier.[4] For women the number of short-duration jobs even fell somewhat. The question is why, in the midst of Britain's unexpected success, were public perceptions and expectations so depressed? And how can we explain the national psychosis whereby so many seemed blind to the rather impressive performance of the economy?

One part of the answer is obvious enough. Behind the improvement in the government's budgetary position lay a swingeing increase in the taxes borne by the British people. In successive budgets Norman Lamont and Kenneth Clarke had presented the bill for the Tories' pre-electoral promises and for the increase in social security payments necessitated by Britain's longest post-war recession. It was also hard for a nation conditioned for so long to think of the economy as a recalcitrant mule to adjust to the idea that it might have turned into a sleek thoroughbred – especially when the people making this claim were the same politicians who had just put the country through the trauma of recession and increased taxes.

Equally important, the performance of an economy is not easily captured in simple statistics. Labour's league table, based on gross domestic product per head after adjusting for purchasing power in the respective countries, is an entirely respectable yardstick of competitiveness. Yet it needs interpretation. If it shows the country falling further down the scale it is chiefly because dynamic economies in the Far East, such as Hong Kong and Singapore, have leapfrogged Britain. But these Asian economies have also leapfrogged Germany, France and Italy, which are arguably more relevant comparisons for the British citizen. And if Britain is compared with those European countries on the basis of growth, productivity and employment, it is not difficult to put a case that the country has, since Margaret Thatcher started her reign in Downing Street in 1979, put an end to its relative underperformance.

Real gross domestic product grew marginally faster in Germany between 1979 and 1994. Yet in per capita terms it grew rather faster in the UK. Given that the period took in Britain's longest and deepest post-war recessions, while Germany experienced the one-off economic boom from reunification, that is quite something. As for the UK's performance against other leading competitors, it has been little different from that of the United States,

France and Italy over the same period. The most decline-obsessed commentators frequently base their case on a comparison with rates of growth in the period before the oil crisis of 1973. Yet global growth has slowed down since then; and there has been a tendency, in the aftermath of the twin oil shocks of the 1970s, for rates of growth in the developed world to converge. Among the larger industrialized countries, only Japan has performed significantly better since 1979 than its main competitors including Britain, and Japan has significantly underperformed the UK since 1990.[5]

As for employment, the British economy managed to generate two million new jobs between 1983 and 1994. Both in terms of job creation and the level of unemployment, its record looks markedly better than that of the main continental European economies whose labour markets are less flexible. In business productivity, Britain since 1979 has completely outpaced every other member of the Group of Seven industrialized countries including Japan. The economist Walter Eltis, who advised Michael Heseltine when the latter was President of the Board of Trade, has shown that three-quarters of the gap between UK manufacturing productivity and that of its trading partners was closed between 1979 and 1993, while nearly all of the gap with Germany was eliminated.[6] In addition, the high-technology content in British manufacturing was on a par, in percentage terms, with Japan, lagging only behind the United States.[7]

In view of the central role attributed by most economists to poor productivity in explaining sluggish post-war growth and investment in Britain, these are not trivial statistics. Indeed, it is hard for the dispassionate observer to escape the conclusion that the Thatcherite experiment really did transform the British economy and arrest its relative decline. Yet this momentous change seems not to have been translated into any great sense of material improvement. There appears to have been a breakdown in the transmission mechanism that leads from economic growth to happiness.

This apparent malfunction in the normal linkages between the economic, the social and the psychological is at the heart of the current policy debate. It is precisely to this condition that the idea of a stakeholder society makes its appeal. Yet some will immediately object that it is naïve to assume any connection between growth and happiness. Policy across the industrialized world is nonetheless based universally on this presumption – and for good, practical reasons. Even an Anglican bishop would surely accept a weaker version of the case, expressed in the form that happiness is harder to achieve in circumstances of economic deprivation. And as a common-sense observation, we all know when a 'feelgood' factor is present or missing. Harold Macmillan's statement in 1959 that 'you've never had it so good' caught a buoyant public mood that was sustained throughout the 1960s.

No doubt the absence of a feelgood factor in the mid-1990s partly reflected cyclical considerations which could be expected to disappear over the course of the rest of the decade. There were pre-electoral tax cuts in the pipeline and windfalls to come from building society flotations and mergers. But, even allowing for some improvement in economic conditions after the slower growth that followed a buoyant 1994, the conventional wisdom is that there will be no immediate return to the low levels of unemployment of the 1960s and early 1970s. And as we shall see in due course, the discontents of the mid-1990s were rooted in something more complex than the level of unemployment alone.

The boom in the Slump

The disconnection between economic growth and a wider sense of well-being is not a uniquely modern phenomenon. History has some instructive parallels which suggest that a 'feelbad' factor often coincides with a very specific and poisonous economic cocktail that includes extreme fluctuations in the price level, big structural changes in industry, collapsing asset prices and major policy mistakes. In the past 150 years there have been two periods which very clearly fit that description, where contemporary perceptions were unusually and similarly depressed. One was in the 1930s, when the appalling experience of the Slump blinded people to the fact that the decade saw very rapid economic growth.[8] Even now the period is often seen as one of unrelieved economic gloom. Yet from the moment Britain left the gold standard in 1931, the economy started to recover very rapidly behind newly erected trade barriers. Between 1932 and 1937, growth averaged 3.9 per cent a year – the fastest rate of growth in Britain in the century.[9] The country also escaped lightly compared with the other leading economies. The fall in output from peak to trough between 1928 and 1935 was a mere 6 per cent in Britain, compared with 28 per cent in the United States, 24 per cent in Germany, 22 per cent in Austria and 15 per cent in France.[10]

The calculation of unemployment figures over long periods is subject to big uncertainties and discontinuities. Even allowing for this, the number of occasions over the past 150 years in which the percentage of unemployed people in the workforce has risen into double figures, on any basis of calculation, is so small as to be worthy of note. And double-figure unemployment is something that the recession of the early 1990s shared in common with the Slump.[11] Another intriguing similarity with the 1990s is the small dent that increased employment made on the unemployment figures. When the rearmament programme generated around 1.5 million new jobs in the second half of the 1930s, unemployment fell only very modestly because of a big increase in the number of people participating in the workforce.[12]

Equally important, looking back from the 1990s, prices were sending very confusing signals. The overall price level, as measured by the retail price index, fell over the course of the inter-war period, with the result that living standards rose for the majority who remained in work during the Slump. At the same time asset prices were plunging during the worst years. From 1929 to the bottom in 1933 prices on the UK stock market fell by 30 per cent.[13] Since the great majority of the shares on the stock market were then owned by private individuals, the impact was more widely felt than it would be in today's more institutionalized world of pension fund investment. In the depressed housing market, less than a quarter of households consisted of owner-occupiers. But there was a counterpart to today's repossessions in the high level of evictions from private rented accommodation.

Yet the comparison with the 1990s should not be taken too far – not least because today's welfare safety net is vastly greater, while the stock market has been buoyant. We have seen nothing to match the 1930s' experience of a sharp contraction of the US money supply, the domino collapse of banks across the world and the general retreat from free trade. Nor is today's unemployment as persistently high in the UK as it was during the Slump. Then, on one of the most respected estimates, the percentage of the workforce that remained idle stayed in double figures in every year between 1930 and 1935.[14]

The Depression that wasn't

A more apt parallel, as the economist Brian Reading has argued, is with the Great Depression of the nineteenth century, which lasted from 1873 to 1896.[15] The use of the word depression here is revealing about contemporary perspectives, because the so-called depression was a myth. As with the UK in the 1980s and 1990s, there were severe fluctuations in output and employment. A noteworthy feature of the perceived slump years of 1876 to 1878 and 1884 to

1886 was a severe policy constraint: the Bank of England felt obliged to hold back economic recovery in its struggle to maintain its gold reserves and stay within the gold standard system.[16] This offers an interesting parallel with the monetary overkill of Margaret Thatcher's early chemistry-set capitalism phase and John Major's equally devastating experiment with the European exchange-rate mechanism in the early 1990s. Yet by historic standards the Great Depression saw a solid economic performance overall, with growth averaging 2 per cent between 1873 and 1896 – much the same as between 1979 and 1995. Even more strikingly, that period in the nineteenth century coincided with the first truly significant rise in the real earnings of the British people since the Industrial Revolution began.[17] Why, then, were people at the time so insecure that they were convinced that the years 1873 to 1896 were a depression?

Part of the explanation for this collective myopia was that prices, both globally and domestically, were falling while output was rising. But the decline in the general price level was slow and thus not fully grasped by people in a period when less attention was given to much scantier economic statistics. In fact money wages fell from a peak at the start of the Great Depression in 1873, even though the falling price level transformed this in due course into a rise in real wages. While unemployment was not consistently high, as it was in the 1930s, the changes in labour-market conditions were abrupt over quite short periods. The best guesstimate of unemployment between 1873 and 1879 shows the numbers unemployed rising from 1.1 per cent of the workforce to 10.7 per cent. Between 1882 and 1886 the rise was from 2.3 per cent to 10.2 per cent.[18] This was far more extreme than anything experienced over the previous 20 years or, for that matter, in the German economy at that time. And in the absence of unemployment benefit, such fluctuations engendered widespread fear. There was also a panic about crime, which had greatly increased following the huge migration of workers from agriculture into the towns as industrialization accelerated.[19]

A more important point was that the psychology of 'declinism' had already set in. Since the Paris Exhibition of 1867 British manufacturers had become acutely aware for the first time that they no longer enjoyed a comprehensive lead in virtually all areas of industrial activity. And by the start of the Great Depression they were confronting serious competition in the global marketplace for the first time. Increased international specialization through trade caused exports of older industries such as iron and cotton yarn to peak in the early 1880s, never to recover. New technologies were having a devastating effect on the labour market. Typical of the way in which technological advance was affecting whole industries and employment prospects was the collapse of freight rates, as ocean-going transport became more efficient and reliable. Between 1873 and 1908 the index of inward freight rates to Britain fell by 73 per cent.[20] This allowed geographically remote countries to compete more directly in the British and European markets; hence the plight of many older industries such as textiles, as they faced more cost-effective competition, and of agriculture.

Yet the onslaught of foreign competition was accompanied by the development of new trades such as the transport of refrigerated meat and the arrival of commodities for the newer products of industrialization such as copper for electric wiring and rubber for bicycle tyres. The problem was that workers in the older industries and regions, although more mobile than today, had similar problems in switching to the new jobs being created elsewhere. New technologies such as ring spinning in cotton textiles led to the replacement of high-paid males by low-paid females. And the British, being less well educated than the Americans, French and Germans, started to lose their competitive edge in this new, more science-intensive phase of industrial development. Foreign competition also added to the insecurity of the workers because it encouraged employers in some industries to attack craft control on the shopfloor – a system which had provided many with a career structure that held out the promise of increasing real earnings over their lifetime. British bosses, especially in engineering, were impressed in 1892 by the forceful way in which Carnegie Steel in the US rid itself of unions.[21]

There is here a very powerful echo of today's labour-market conditions, including the mismatches in skills, the displacement of male by female labour, the erosion of union power and the collapse of stable career structures. In the face of huge structural adjustments in the economy, people had good reason to feel insecure, even if real earnings across the economy were increasing. And the widespread late Victorian conviction that Britain was in relative economic decline was greatly reinforced by what was happening to the rentier class and the agricultural workforce. In the nineteenth century a disproportionate amount of private wealth was held in the form of agricultural land. According to the historian David Cannadine, the British landed establishment in 1880 consisted of around 11,000 families who owned two-thirds of the acreage in the British Isles.[22] In an age when land was still seen by many as a prerequisite of responsible rule, these people enjoyed a stake in society the like of which will probably never be seen again. As well as having an overwhelming influence on the affairs of central, regional and local government, they controlled the livelihood of large numbers of employees on the land and in their homes. The extent of their dispossession, when agricultural prices collapsed and farm rents halved in the Great Depression, was thus momentous. Estates across the country, especially those encumbered with mortgages, were repossessed or broken up.

So there was, in fact, a depression in agriculture and it lasted until the 1930s, by which time land values had fallen to a third of their level in the mid-Victorian period.[23] In a world where the political and social ramifications of land ownership remained overwhelmingly important, it was perhaps not so surprising that perceptions in the Great Depression should have been deeply coloured by the problem. David Cannadine has argued that the development of a global market in agricultural produce marked the beginning of the end of an aristocratic ruling class in Britain. The historian Lewis Namier even declared that the arrival of US wheat did more to change the composition of the House of Commons than did the first two reform acts combined.[24] For ordinary people the collapse in agricultural prices meant either consumer advantage or labour-market disaster. The ones who confronted the long march from the countryside into the urban ghettos of the nineteenth century experienced a feelbad factor of a nature and scale that make today's discontent look wildly self-indulgent by comparison. Between 1860 and 1914 the number of farm labourers shrank by a third.[25]

Home, unsweet home

The relevance of all this for modern-day Britain lies in the explanatory power of the particular combination of circumstances: the confusing behaviour of prices, the extreme fluctuations in economic activity, the grinding adjustments required of industry in the face of global competition and the general, unfounded belief that Britain was in decline. Consider, first, today's property market, where the behaviour of prices has been more than disconcerting. The plunge in house prices of up to 40 per cent in some parts of the country in the early 1990s carries a faint echo of the nineteenth-century fall in agricultural land prices. But whereas there were only 1.44 million houses in owner occupation before the First World War, equivalent to between 10 to 15 per cent of the total housing stock, owner occupation in 1990 extended to 15 million people.[26] No less than 67 per cent of housing was in owner occupation. And for most of those people, the home was their biggest investment.

Between early 1989 and late 1992 the Halifax Building Society house-price index dropped by almost 15 per cent, or around 40 per cent in real terms. What made this collapse in house prices particularly painful in the 1990s was that so many home buyers had based their purchase on the assumption that house prices could only go up and that inflation would continue to erode the value of the mortgage raised to finance the transaction. Yet this rested on a misconception about the workings of the housing market, wrought by money illusion of an equal and opposite kind to that which prevailed in the late nineteenth century – inflation, not deflation. While house prices have borne some relation to the long-run growth in earnings, which has shown a steady upward trend, they have still fluctuated heavily in real terms. Indeed, after adjusting for inflation, the housing market has seen no less than three serious slumps since 1945.[27]

On the first two occasions, which coincided with the recessions of the mid-1970s and the early 1980s, it mattered little to many home owners, and escaped the attention of others, because nominal house prices did not fall at all. Between 1973 and 1977, for example, real house prices fell by 35 per cent, yet in nominal terms prices actually increased by more than 20 per cent. At the same time, the real value of mortgage debt continued to erode thanks to inflation. Here is part of the reason that insecurity was not an important political theme in the deep recession of the early 1980s, despite unemployment that remained in double figures for longer than in the 1990s. Money illusion provided people with some protection.

Hence the shock when house prices were actually seen to fall properly in the third slump in the 1990s. This disinflationary blow to home owners' expectations resulted, at one extreme, in a 'negative equity' trap, as many of those who had recently borrowed up to the hilt to buy their home found that it was worth less than the related mortgage debt. Estimates of the number of households with a negative stake in the housing market ranged, at the worst point in 1993, up to 1.8 million, of which nearly three-quarters were first-time buyers (although this may have been overstated, as we shall see later). A further two million or so were reckoned to have too little equity to be able to afford the costs of moving. And repossessions reached levels unprecedented in the twentieth century. The house-price falls were often worst in working-class areas where buyers were aspiring to middle-class values. So one of the most devastating consequences of the Thatcherite experiment, which liberalized mortgage finance and encouraged the sale of council houses, was that large numbers of these potentially upwardly mobile people were brutally, if unintentionally, thrust back into their proletarian box.[28]

The penalty paid by the middle classes came in the form of the collapse of the housing ladder, whereby people bought larger and more luxurious houses in the course of their working lives with the inflated sale proceeds from their earlier homes. This process was shortcircuited once the belief in perpetually rising house prices evaporated. The depressed state of the housing market was a critical element in the absence of a feelgood factor in the mid-1990s. One of the highest rates of home ownership in the world ended up fostering insecurity instead of a sense of a stake in a prosperous society.

Just-in-time people

There was similar confusion in the world of work. In contrast to the Great Depression, the trouble came from a reduction in the rate of inflation, rather than from a fall in the overall price level. Yet expectations were similarly frustrated. Having become accustomed to the idea that wages went up every year, the workforce suddenly discovered that the pace of earnings growth was slowing and that in some sectors of the economy rises were no longer automatic. But the larger uncertainty concerned the workings of the job market itself.

The existence of a large welfare safety net meant that joblessness was no longer to be feared as it was in the 1880s or 1930s. But in 1995, at around 8 per cent of the workforce, unemployment was still at double its level in 1979 on a broadly comparable basis. Not only was the safety net being progressively cut back as the Conservative government weakened employment protection legislation, the penalty for being unemployed was also rising. In 1981 75 per cent of those who ceased to be unemployed went back to work, rather than giving up hope and opting for economic inactivity or premature retirement. By 1993, a higher proportion of the unemployed were throwing in the towel: only 60 per cent of those who stopped registering as unemployed were going back to work.

This is the chief and disheartening explanation for the more rapid fall in unemployment after the 1990s recession than after the recession of the 1980s. And those who did come back into the active labour force rarely went back to full-time employment with statutory minimum employment rights. Full-time employment had fallen from 55.5 per cent of all jobs in Britain in 1975 to 35.9 per cent in 1993. Pay prospects were also likely to be miserable: real earnings for jobs taken by the unemployed between 1979 and 1991 scarcely increased at all. And as Paul Gregg and Jonathan Wadsworth of the

London School of Economics have pointed out, the typical job filled by people previously out of work pays, at around £110, a mere 40 per cent of the average weekly wage in other jobs. One-third of jobs going to those out of work pay less than £60 a week.[29]

This reflected, among other things, the casualization of a labour force in which the growth of part-time employment and self-employment left more people's living standards hostage to the fluctuations of the economic cycle. For those fortunate enough to enjoy full-time jobs, the Thatcherite assault on the unions nonetheless meant that their bargaining power and job security were eroded. British management, having mastered Japanese techniques of just-in-time inventory control, increasingly treated employees as just-in-time people. Having failed ever to rise above 2.6 per cent in the 1950s and 1960s, the percentage of unemployed in the workforce has been measured since the late 1970s in multiples of that figure. In six of the fifteen years to 1995 unemployment was, according to the government's own data, in double figures – a performance matched only in the 1930s, since reliable figures have been available.[30]

Although overall employment was actually increasing, numbers in manufacturing shrank from nearly 26.5 per cent of the workforce at the end of 1979 to 18 per cent by the end of 1995.[31] All the job generation was in services, where average earnings were lower. Earnings also grew more slowly than in manufacturing. And in the recession of the early 1990s the service sectors were badly hit, which they had not been in the 1980s. Given that services accounted for more than 70 per cent of all employment at the start of the 1990s, this goes a long way towards explaining why insecurity was rife in the second of these two great recessions, but not the first.

Another important feature of the labour market was that the maintenance of family living standards depended increasingly on the growing participation of females in the workforce, who were more likely to be employed part time and without such benefits as sick leave and pension rights. The unskilled male breadwinner was also becoming a rarity. Many unskilled working-class male youths, on whom unemployment fell particularly harshly, were even finding themselves excluded from parenthood in a normal family environment because they were not an attractive prospect to young females. A growing number of unmarried mothers were staying unmarried, not because they wanted to sponge off the state but because they had no wish to commit themselves to economic no-hopers by whom they had become unintentionally pregnant.

The death of paternalism

Middle-class angst had more to do with the death of paternalism and the shock to expectations. The great policy innovation of the 1980s, privatization, brought job insecurity for the first time to managers and employees who had hitherto taken lifetime employment for granted. In the civil service, where security of employment had been deemed a necessary guarantee of objectivity since the nineteenth century, the principle of tenure was abandoned without so much as a Royal Commission or even a serious parliamentary debate on the nature and purpose of a modern professional civil service. Employment was particularly hard hit in the middle-class heartlands of the South East, where joblessness was an unfamiliar experience for the great majority.

Today there is hardly a large company that does not have plans for further redundancies, complete with sinister-sounding 'change management' consultants to advise on the process. Many have scrapped sports clubs, Christmas parties for children of staff and other manifestations of paternalistic employment practice in the interests of aggressive 'human resource management' and short-term 'shareholder value'. Here lies one possible explanation for the lack of change in the length of time for which people held their jobs between 1984 and 1993. While more people were being made redundant, others may have been holding on to their existing jobs longer than in the past out of insecurity.

Britain has never had the precise equivalent of the Japanese lifetime employment system. But in larger companies there was, throughout the postwar period, an identifiable career ladder, often accompanied by seniority-based pay. Redundancies and job changes may have slowed or accelerated progress up the ladder, but most people could reliably expect to go on climbing. Now the career ladder has fallen down, just as the housing ladder has done. And this twin trauma has been accompanied by an unprecedented, and unusually consistent, growth in the inequality of incomes. The Tories' cuts in the higher rates of direct taxation were partly responsible. But the incomes of the poorest had scarcely risen since the late 1960s. The number of people living in households whose incomes fell below half the national average had, in fact, risen from around 5 million over the 1960s to more than 11 million by the start of the 1990s.[32] An OECD study reported in 1995 that the gap in the incomes of rich and poor had grown faster in Britain than in any other country in the developed world. In the post-Cold-War economy, Britain's labour market was seeing a big shift in the balance of power from labour back to capital.[33]

The psychological impact of growing income inequality is profound. People may not worry a great deal about the size of the national income relative to that of other countries, but they are deeply preoccupied with their own income relative to their fellow citizens'. Most derive their sense of a stake in society from their job, which allows them to participate in the prosperity of the nation via the progressive long-run increase in real earnings. It also provides them with a social context in which to win recognition of their status and dignity. Yet the statistics demonstrate that growing numbers are being excluded from a stake in the growth of the economy while nonetheless remaining in employment. Even for the better off, labour-market conditions are disturbing, since unemployment now touches all reaches of society.

This combination of robust growth in the number of jobs and growing income inequality is common to the English-speaking economies. It contrasts sharply with the less flexible labour markets of continental Europe, which are marked by higher unemployment, especially for females, and greater income equality. The United States, for example, has seen the highest rate of employment creation among the larger economies of the developed world, having generated a phenomenal 28 million new jobs since 1980. Its unemployment rate in early 1996 was a mere 5.7 per cent and only 12 per cent of the jobless had been unemployed for longer than a year, compared with 30–40 per cent in much of Europe.[34] Yet public opinion in the US in 1996 was even more obsessed with unemployment and industrial downsizing than in Britain.

Corporate shrinkage

At the top 500 companies in the US, once considered the most stable employers, total employment had declined from 16.5 million jobs in 1979 to 11.5 million. Permanent dismissals in the overall economy accounted for 40–45 per cent of job losses, compared with 30 per cent in the late 1960s. Since most new jobs, as in the UK, were being generated in services and in small businesses that were more prone to go bust, the resulting employment was less secure than in the past. And income inequality was even greater than in the UK.

Chief butt of the US press were the highly paid bosses – dubbed 'corporate killers' by *Newsweek* and others – at companies such as AT&T, the telecoms giant, which announced plans to shed 40,000 mainly white-collar employees early in 1996. These job cuts were greeted rapturously on Wall

Street, where AT&T stock soared on the announcement. The right-wing populist Pat Buchanan milked the white-collar shock story to such good effect
when running for the Republican nomination in the 1996 presidential election that it looked for a brief moment as though he might see Bob Dole off the
field.

In Britain the degree of income inequality is not as great as in the US,
but it nonetheless poses a serious social threat, as we shall see later. The economic malaise is also more heavily coloured in the UK by the experience of
shrinking wealth. For the middle classes, the sense of a stake in society is inti-
mately bound up with rights of ownership as well as employment conditions.
And in the advanced economies there is a natural rhythm in the relationship
between the labour and capital markets which provides a benign stabilizing
influence over the economic cycle. In a recession slower earnings growth and
rising unemployment invariably coincide with soaring stock markets, which
are boosted by surplus liquidity in a weak economy. Stock-market analysts
then rationalize soaring share prices by suggesting that they are anticipating
increased profits from an incipient economic recovery. The perception of
increasing real wealth helps mitigate the pain in the labour market and provides encouragement to consumption.

Yet this has not been happening in Britain, chiefly because stock-market
investments are held mainly through tax-privileged pension schemes and
through life assurance, both of which insulate people from any awareness of
increasing wealth. Most pension schemes are paternalistic. They embody a
curiously intangible form of property right that consists of no more than a
promise to pay a pension, which is normally related to final pay before retirement. This means that nobody has a measurable stake in what is usually the
private individual's second biggest long-term investment after home ownership. Despite the Thatcher government's rhetorical commitment to popular
capitalism in the 1980s, it failed to address this point, preferring instead to
increase home ownership to a level which inhibits labour mobility.

The irony here is that the negative-equity problem in housing is largely
illusory, precisely because so many people have bought their homes via
endowment-related mortgages which are similarly paternalistic. The rise in
their value thanks to the buoyancy of the stock market is not disclosed to the
borrower before the surrender or maturity of the policy. Anatole Kaletsky, the
economics editor of *The Times*, has calculated that if the value of these
endowment-related savings is taken into account, the number of households
with negative equity in the mid-1990s was probably overstated by a factor of

more than two. The wider concern over falling house prices was overdone for similar reasons. The opaque nature of these savings arrangements is thus an important part of the explanation for the depressed state of the national psyche in the mid-1990s. While the stock market was exploring record high territory, few in the British population either knew or had reason to care.

The causes of inequality

Why, after decades in which growth in the industrialized world was accompanied by an increasingly equal distribution of incomes and opportunities, have incomes now become much less equal? In attempting to explain this polarization in the labour market in the midst of widespread industrial restructuring, economists differ on where to place the emphasis. But technological innovation has so far been the most important factor. Today's equivalent of the nineteenth-century collapse in transport costs is to be found in the telecommunications and computing industries. A fall of more than 90 per cent in the cost of sending information and transacting financial business around the world has contributed to explosive growth in the volume of international financial transactions. Microchips have transformed everything from business administration to the inside of a car engine.

Technological innovation has not invariably been associated, in the past, with greater inequality of incomes or rising unemployment. It seems strange that the technologies of the 1980s and 1990s have produced relatively few new end-products like motor cars or aeroplanes which generate both increased consumer demands and a need for accompanying investment in infrastructure such as roads and airports. Those like the microchip have chiefly revolutionized the manufacture of old products, while using much less capital, labour, raw materials and energy than before. Yet what is undeniable in today's high-tech environment is that the returns to education have increased, while the returns to unskilled labour have fallen behind.[35]

A complementary, if less important, explanation for income inequality lies in the increase in global competition as a result of progressive trade liberalization. More specifically, the decline in the living standards of unskilled workers has coincided with unprecedented growth in imports from developing countries. And more than half of those imports now take the form of manufactured goods, compared with a mere 5 per cent in 1955.

This is the great scare story of the 1990s, which touches on the political debate in Chapter 1: the challenge that globalization poses to the Western workforce. It is the modern equivalent of the adjustment faced by the British economy in the final quarter of the nineteenth century, when newly industrializing countries such as the US and Germany started to take on the British in global markets. There is now a single, integrated industrial market across the world for products ranging from T-shirts to microchips. The industrialists' decisions as to where to produce those shirts and microchips are increasingly based on hard calculations of costs on a global basis. In effect, the world has discovered deep new veins of labour, which multinational companies are integrating into the global marketplace. The emergence of this huge new supply of cheap labour is naturally a frightening prospect for the workers of the developed world, not least because imports from the developing world, although sharply up, still represent only a small proportion of the total. Mainstream industries are being exposed to low-tech competition from the cheap labour countries, while high-tech industries are challenged by the smaller dragon economies as they move up market.

The threat of globalization to the British worker is vastly exaggerated, for reasons which will be explained in Chapter 11. Yet it remains true that workers in the economies of the developed world will continue to have to cope with the consequences of big structural adjustments as a result of those twin engines of growth – trade and technology. And in confronting the social strains arising from this process, stakeholder economies such as Germany or Switzerland have the advantage of a high degree of domestic social cohesion and equality. They have preserved a very narrow differential between the incomes of the best paid and the lowest paid. They remain relatively well-ordered, cohesive societies.

The British and Americans, in contrast, have been asked to confront this age of uncertainty against a background of high unemployment and growing inequality in pre- and post-retirement incomes. Their individualistic cultures and flexible labour markets make for a more rough-and-tumble form of capitalism. It is not a coincidence that the feelbad factor has been much stronger in the English-speaking economies than in much of continental Europe, despite the depressing impact on the continental European economies of the budgetary contraction that has resulted from the convergence criteria of the Maastricht Treaty.

Periods of industrial upheaval invariably impose huge stresses on the political system. The climate of insecurity in the Great Depression provided a fertile breeding ground for the rise of Marxism, from which the world is now finally in retreat. In the 1930s, the malign response to unemployment was the rise of Hitler and Mussolini, accompanied by such manifestations of economic nationalism as competitive devaluation and protectionism. Today there is a real risk that protectionism could make a comeback, spurred by the politics of dispossession. Insecurity in Britain and depressed demand in continental Europe make an unholy combination that pulls Europe in that direction. But income inequality also poses another worrying social threat, in the shape of more and faster-rising crime than in cohesive stakeholder societies such as Switzerland, Singapore or Japan.

The magic of the black market

Crime is a subject that needs careful treatment in an economic context. Many common assumptions about it are ill founded. There cannot, for example, be any straightforward correlation between economic deprivation and rising crime rates given the huge increase in absolute living standards since the Industrial Revolution: if there were a positive correlation, the more than nine-fold increase in national income per head in Britain since 1820 would by now have eliminated crime.[36] The statistics, too, need careful treatment. Much crime goes unrecorded; and some criminologists even argue that crime waves are manufactured, with help from the police and the media, by governments seeking to distract the electorate from failed economic policies. Certainly editors throughout the ages have used crime to sell their newspapers. Even *The Times* fomented a wholly unjustified national scare in the 1860s about garotting.

Yet on any reading of the crime statistics there appears to have been a very striking acceleration in recorded crime from the mid-1970s, just as the phenomenon of income inequality and stagnant real incomes at the bottom end of the labour market started to become apparent. The coincidence is suggestive. There also seems, in the recessionary economic cycle of the early 1990s, to have been a clear cyclical pattern to the property-related crimes of burglary and theft. Against that background the insecurity of the 1990s begins to take on a wider social dimension. Indeed, the feelbad factor is a rather good popular description of what the founding father of sociology, Emile Durkheim, called anomie – the disconcerting condition in which people lose their sense of being subject to accepted and binding social norms and codes. That would pass as a fair description of the Thatcher years, in which the values that Britain held in common with the more stakeholder-inclined societies gave way to unrestrained individualism and, at the extreme, to the rise of the 'greed is good' school of capitalism, which percolated all the way down from the New Right thinkers in the US to the yuppies on the trading floors of the City. It also aptly describes the way in which the modern workplace delivers a dwindling sense of community.

In a classic essay on the political economy of crime, the American sociologist Robert Merton adapted Durkheim's concept of anomie to help explain criminal behaviour.[37] This he saw as a reflection of the unequal distribution of the legitimate means that were available to people to achieve the dominant American cultural goal of material success. Merton argued that, when the scope for material success was blocked in recession because of restricted opportunities in the labour market, the social groups that felt blocked and insecure would seek to achieve material success through 'innovation', in the shape of crime against property. Alternatively they engaged in 'retreatism', in the form of drug use or vagrancy. Merton's worry was that a heavy emphasis in the US on material rewards as the main symbol of success, without concern for the moral basis of economic activity, led to individual insecurity, social instability and crime. This was the inevitable outcome of a culture in which money had 'been consecrated as a value in itself, over and above its expenditure for articles of consumption or its use for the enhancement of power'.

Merton's ideas are illuminating in the context of the New Right's legitimation of unrestrained individualism. They may also cast light, at the top end of the criminal market, on the behaviour of people such as Nick Leeson, the rogue trader who brought down Barings (of whom more later). At the other end of the criminal spectrum the emphasis on the structure of the opportunities in the labour market is clearly relevant to the plight of young unskilled males. It is not necessary to be a dedicated follower of Merton or a committed adherent of the narrower economic school of rational choice theory to recognize that economic incentives must play some part in the level of criminality.

Professor Richard Freeman of Harvard University is among those who have argued that labour-market inequality in the US has been associated with higher rates of urban crime because the risk of going to prison does not outweigh the cost of staying virtuous on the declining real income available to undereducated American youth.[38] And, as in the UK, economic deprivation also excludes unskilled male youths from the civilizing influence of marriage by turning them into unattractive marriage partners. In these circumstances, the criminal fraternity, or even prison, may offer welcome inclusion to the unskilled outcast, as well as a chance of economic betterment. The present political obsession in Britain and the US with sending people to prison is likely to strengthen this sense of criminal community, since prison is one of the few parts of the educational system that works consistently well. Its record in professionalizing inexperienced offenders is widely acknowledged, if not admired.

Britain, admittedly, has not suffered a fall in real incomes on the massive and perhaps unprecedented scale seen in parts of the US labour market. The British welfare state is more generous. It is also important to recognize, when discussing increasing labour-market inequality, that low-paid workers in any given year on which the statistics are based have diverse career and earnings prospects. The 'unequal' workers at the bottom may be different from year to year. That said, there is some evidence that the British labour market is characterized by a disturbing lack of upward mobility from one generation to another.[39] Most suggestive is the fact that, while the incomes of the poorest 10 per cent have fallen by 18 per cent since 1979 after housing costs, the consumption of this group has managed to rise by 14 per cent.[40] The borderline between the black economy of tax evasion and the rougher criminal economy is a fluid one. Our sense of safety and security may thus be threatened for the foreseeable future unless something is done to give young males – who constitute the social group most given to criminality – a better set of economic incentives.

The rewards and penalties offered by the labour market will be considered in due course. But the problems of unemployment, inequality and insecurity have a much broader range of causes, some of which stem from the workings of the capital markets. An important question for the proponents of stakeholding is whether its revisionist version of capitalism can coexist with an Anglo-Saxon financial system whose values can be profoundly hostile to the stakeholder ethos.

3

City Limits

A stakeholder society is built on trust. And there is an unhealthy shortage of trust in the relationship between the British and their business community. Nowhere is this more true than where the City of London is concerned. It is constantly suggested, especially on the left of the political spectrum, that industry has been ill served by British finance. The time horizons of dealers and executives in the Square Mile are allegedly too short and are said to impose constraints on long-term investment by industry. The great institutions of the City are also open to more direct attack. Lloyd's of London, the insurance market, has been beset by incompetence and fraud. The London Stock Exchange appears to have lost its sense of strategic direction and has unceremoniously fired chief executives with an alacrity that would have done credit to a Hollywood studio mogul. Even the Bank of England has been attacked over its role in supervising such institutions as the fraudulent Bank of Credit and Commerce International.

These impressions have been heightened by the collapse of Barings, once the most powerful bank in the world, as a result of dealings by rogue trader Nick Leeson. Others, such as S G Warburg, the top British merchant bank of the 1980s, committed strategic blunders which left them vulnerable to takeovers by foreign banking giants. Yet despite these ups and downs, many City executives continue to enjoy popstar salaries. When compared with continental Europe, and especially Germany, where banking is more soberly harnessed to the task of supporting domestic industry, the British financier conveys the impression of being unattractively self-serving. A recurring theme of left-of-centre declinist thinkers is that the City, in its loose non-geographical sense of the collectivity of the country's banks and other financial institutions, has somehow failed the nation; and that financial short-termism, which is unfavourably contrasted with the long-termist stakeholder systems of Germany and Japan, bears serious responsibility for Britain's poor post-war economic performance.

In the 1990s this argument has taken a new twist. Mainstream economists have always believed that one of the chief reasons – perhaps the most important reason – for Britain's sluggish economic growth in the post-war period was poor productivity. Yet one of the most impressive achievements of the Thatcher years was the enormous catch-up in productivity in relation to Britain's main competitors. This gives rise to a puzzle. If productivity is on the mend and Britain's industrial relations are no longer a battlefield, why did investment and employment fail to pick up more strongly in the mid-1990s? The absence of a stronger investment recovery has been cited by critics, most notably Will Hutton in *The State We're In*, as yet another indication that the City acts as a constraint on a crucial determinant of economic growth.[1] The central economic argument of Hutton's book is that 'the weakness of the British economy, particularly the level and character of investment, originates in the financial system'. He sees a need for a complete overhaul of the system to produce 'a less degenerate capitalism'.

A capitalist and a gentleman

There is no doubt that the anti-City critique contains a hard kernel of historical truth, which calls for a brief digression to put the debate in context. As Hutton rightly points out, one of the more curious features of British economic history is how small a role the City played in supporting the Industrial Revolution, which was mainly financed locally by rich individuals and provincial banks. London-based bankers, dubbed 'gentlemanly capitalists' by some economic historians, were busy financing international trade and overseas investment.[2] The Labour Party's longstanding mistrust of the City is also rooted in accurate folk memory of the inter-war years. After the First World War, the City lobbied fiercely and successfully for a return to the gold standard.

The decision to heed the financiers' plea, taken in 1925 by Churchill when chancellor of the exchequer, was made without due regard for British industry, which was thenceforth burdened with an uncompetitive exchange rate. The stability of sterling and the desire to reestablish the City's central role in international finance were seen by the government of the day as more important priorities. Within the gold standard system the interests of creditors were regarded as paramount.

The extent of this policy bias in favour of creditors sounds strange today. But it was, among other things, an enduring legacy of the reform of the British public finances that followed the Glorious Revolution of 1688. It was also the envy of foreigners throughout the eighteenth and nineteenth centuries. Voltaire, for example, marvelled in his *Lettres Anglaises* at the way the power of the City could instantly be put to the service of the state – or indeed of foreign powers – to finance wars. These essays of Voltaire were, incidentally, an extended tribute to the gentlemanly capitalism that is now regarded as part of the British disease. To Enlightenment philosophers in pre-revolutionary France, the readiness with which the younger brothers of English peers took to trade looked enviable when compared with *le préjugé nobiliaire* – the social rigidity and more entrenched aristocratic disdain for commerce that marked their own culture.

The right to convert sterling into gold at a fixed rate of exchange provided the British system with a firm monetary anchor. But financial stability often came at the price of unstable output and employment. Where France and Germany resorted to inflation to reduce the burden of wartime debt after the First World War, Britain relied on budget surpluses and sound money regardless of mounting unemployment. The workforce took the strain as industry, suffering from high real interest rates and an exchange rate that made exports uncompetitive, reduced wages and shed workers. Symptomatic of such pressures was the General Strike in 1926, which followed the return to the gold standard.

Too bad about the creditor

Yet, to return to the present day, the notion that financial markets have been managed in a remotely comparable fashion since the Second World War would be absurd. The creditor was, in effect, dethroned when Britain went off the gold standard in 1931 and has had a very rough ride since. In the immediate post-war period the Labour government imposed a policy of cheap money designed to help industrial borrowers at the expense of depositors and investors. Successive governments subsequently defaulted on their domestic obligations through inflation, which ate into the capital of the old and vulnerable as well as the rich. They also ratted on their foreign obligations, whether formally within the Bretton Woods semi-fixed exchange-rate system or informally in the floating system that followed its collapse in the early 1970s. Occasionally, as with Harold Wilson between 1964 and 1967 or John Major in his experiment with the European exchange-rate mechanism, politicians proclaimed their commitment to sound money. But the commitment always proved skin deep when the accompanying interest-rate or exchange-rate objectives led to serious losses of output and employment.

The high rate of inflation that prevailed in Britain for much of the post-war period was, in effect, a symptom of what a stakeholder theorist would have called a shortage of trust. For inflation is a way of reconciling the conflicting economic demands of different groups within society when the democratic process, unaided by social partnership, proves incapable of doing the job.[3] Indeed, interest group politics is a distinguishing characteristic of individualistic non-stakeholder societies; and the overriding dynamic of interest group conflict is that might is all too often right.

The irony is that the inflationary resolution of this clash of conflicting economic interests in post-war Britain delivered only a Pyrrhic victory to the numerically most powerful group, the workers. Wage-push inflation promised them much more than it delivered, while damaging society as a whole. The outright winners in the post-war financial sweepstake were, in fact, the debtors. In practical terms, those who fought in the war and subsequently borrowed to buy a home enjoyed a huge peace dividend, as house prices went up and the value of their mortgage debt was inflated away. Their children, the post-war baby boomers, then ensured that there was buoyant demand for the homes that their parents were selling, as those parents sought to climb the housing ladder. The other big winners were people who invested in equities – the ordinary shares of industrial and commercial companies – which provided a hedge against inflation and a stake in Britain's growing prosperity.

The biggest losers were those whose savings were devoted to supporting the war effort and financing the subsequent growth of peacetime public spending. Holders of government debt, in the shape of gilt-edged stock such as War Loan, saw their wealth ruthlessly appropriated by a predatory state. For long periods the return on their investment was negative, after allowing for inflation. This gave a new and rough-edged meaning to Keynes's celebrated remark on the euthanasia of the rentier. Looked at from the government's perspective, inflation worked as a convenient hidden tax: as the real cost of its borrowings fell, revenues increased because inflated incomes and profits enlarged the tax base. The other big losers were those, especially the young, who bought homes in the second half of the 1980s when the great post-war housing boom finally ran out of steam. For when baby boomers grow up, there are inevitably fewer first-time buyers to permit younger home owners to move on to the second rung of the housing ladder. The housing ladder then falls down.

Cheap capital and eurosclerosis

In short, the distribution of wealth in post-war Britain has been very differently spread when compared with the 1920s and the creditor has had a pretty modest look-in. So the instincts of the declinist left look atavistic on this score. What, then, of Will Hutton's argument that British industry is disadvantaged because its competitors in the stakeholder economies of Germany and Japan enjoy access to much cheaper capital? Here, too, the declinists are on weak ground. Since the debate becomes too easily bogged down in incomprehensible statistics, this *canard* is best tackled in terms of broad principle.

The cost of capital is the minimum return required from new investment projects to satisfy investors in the company. And on one aspect of the argument Hutton is probably right: for part of the post-war period German and Japanese companies, which were predominantly financed by debt, did enjoy an advantage, in that their financial systems were rigged to give industry low-interest bank loans and debt capital at the expense of depositors and investors. Equity shareholders also accepted low dividend returns, because cross-shareholdings were used to cement stakeholder relationships rather than generate immediate income.

In a closed financial world surrounded by exchange controls, and in high-saving societies where everyone was prepared to forgo immediate consumption and investment income in the longer-term interest of the nation, these subsidies from creditors and investors to industry were part of the social compact – a consensual bargain between stakeholders. It is also true that the Germans and Japanese continued to ration bank credit for far longer than their English-speaking competitors. The earlier liberalization of banking systems in Britain and the US meant that more credit was available to industry, commerce and private individuals, but at a higher cost. Inflation also had the perverse effect of putting British companies' cash flow under strain even when interest rates were negative in real terms.

Yet to argue that cheap capital was an advantage to Japan and Germany by the 1980s is to overlook what actually happened in those countries. In the second half of that decade money and capital in Japan were indeed absurdly cheap, as the Bank of Japan reduced interest rates in an attempt to curb the inexorable appreciation of the yen. This unbalanced the whole economy, as companies overinvested in relatively unprofitable plant and machinery and the stock market experienced one of the greatest bubbles in financial history. The outcome was the biggest stock-market crash since 1929, the near-collapse of the banking system and a recession which put an end to the one-party rule of the Liberal Democrats.

In short, the Japanese paid a very high price for delaying the liberalization of banking, in that the allocation of financial resources in the economy became exceptionally inefficient. Because financial markets were rigged, bankers were unfamiliar with market discipline and lent money to all the wrong companies. After years of bureaucratic guidance in a highly regulated system, they had excellent conditioning in the herd instinct – hardly needed in Japan – but none in assessing creditworthiness. They lent billions to property companies that went bust in the downturn.

Japan's low cost of capital, far from affording a competitive advantage, was in fact a symptom of serious structural imbalance in the economy arising from the country's excessive propensity to save. The continuing urge to pile up a mountain of savings when they are no longer needed for high domestic investment has contributed to a structural trade surplus: the Japanese lend their excess savings to the rest of the world to help buy Japanese exports. The failure to resolve this problem leads to the constant threat of a protectionist response from the US.[4]

In Germany, too, a low cost of capital has been a symptom of excessive saving. But while Japan was going through the manic bubble period, Germany in the 1980s was experiencing eurosclerosis. To talk of cheap capital providing competitive advantage is academic when the growth in British gross domestic product between 1984 and 1989 was 4 per cent, while the comparable rate for Germany was only 2.6 per cent. German bankers have been less inefficient than the Japanese, although they have become much more fallible in the 1990s than in the past. But the lifting of exchange controls and the resulting globalization of financial markets means that for the Germans, too, reliance on subsidies is more likely to lead to damaging distortions in the economy.

In a world where exchange controls have been abolished, the German and Japanese cross-subsidies from depositors and investors to industry are unlikely in future to be sustainable. At the risk of some slight oversimplification, if a country tries artificially to reduce the financial returns available to depositors and investors, its exchange rate will collapse in the long run as domestic and international capital pours out in pursuit of higher returns elsewhere. Because governments and central banks will act to forestall the inflationary consequences of a collapsing exchange rate, they will, in normal circumstances, raise interest rates, thereby bringing their industries' cost of money back into line with the international norm. If, on the other hand, industry is paying too much for its money, the exchange rate will appreciate as foreign capital is attracted into the country, thereby forcing the authorities to reduce interest rates.

In practice exchange rates are capable of defying this logic for quite long periods. Even so, if we consider what has happened to the Germans and Japanese in the 1990s, it is immediately apparent that their problem has not been one of cheap money and collapsing exchange rates. In the first half of the decade their industries were severely squeezed by the structural appreciation of their currencies, which reflected the snail-like pace with which their central banks brought down interest rates after the twin shocks of the bubble economy and the unification boom. The world's investors rushed into D-marks and yen, to take advantage of high real rates of interest and the prospect of further currency appreciation.

If industry in Britain and the US has suffered a financial penalty, this is now almost certainly less acute than in the past. Today the cost of capital will tend to equalize between countries after allowing for risk, which means, among other things, that German and Japanese companies now have to meet a global profit criterion. If they fail to do so, their stock markets will in the end fall, thereby raising the cost of equity capital. Because of this they have already been forced to adopt more flexible labour-market policies, including the Anglo-Saxon practice of downsizing – although the way they go about it is much more respectful of the workers.

It is always possible, of course, that the markets will make a bad assessment of risk. And Britain's poor historic record on inflation means that it cannot in any case escape a financial penalty on this score. But with much less of its gross national product in capital-intensive manufacturing, and much more in services, compared with Germany and Japan, the penalty is partly mitigated. Indeed, the British strength in many of the less capital-intensive, knowledge-based service industries of the future such as computer software is no accident. It reflects the flexible response of a market economy in dealing with the problem of an above-average cost of capital. But this is a legacy of history. At the time of writing, the alignment of interest rates and exchange rates hardly suggests that Britain is carrying an unsustainable weight in the global capital markets handicap.

Hungry for dividends

Where the City is more vulnerable to attack is in relation to the changing nature of the financial relationship between investors and the companies whose shares they buy. For there has been an important shift in the balance of power between the owners of ordinary shares, or equities, and the other stakeholders in the company. More than 60 per cent of all the equity share capital quoted on the London Stock Exchange is now owned by anonymous institutional investors such as insurance companies, pension funds, unit trusts and investment trusts.[5] They are hungry for dividends. And dividend payments tend to absorb much more of corporate profits in the UK than elsewhere, leading to accusations that institutional investors are acting as a constraint on industry's ability to invest in capital projects such as new plant and machinery.

Concern about dividends is not exclusive to Labour supporters. In 1994 Tory minister Stephen Dorrell, then financial secretary to the Treasury, embarked on a review of savings and the flow of funds within the economy. In revealing the objectives of the review, he fired a salvo across the bows of the institutions. 'Since institutional shareholders play such a crucial role in our capital,' he said, 'we are entitled to ask how well they function. Are they effective at identifying good investment opportunities and avoiding bad ones? Do they provide capital on terms which enable businesses to respond efficiently to market opportunities? In particular, do they place too much emphasis on dividend yield?'[6]

That 'in particular' stuck uncomfortably in institutional gullets. For dividends in the UK, at an average of just over 30 per cent of after-tax profits of non-financial companies in 1994, were much higher than in Japan or Germany, although they were lower than in the United States. So there was a clear divide between the English-speaking economies and the stakeholder economies. As Mr Dorrell spoke, dividend cover – the amount by which net profits exceeded, or 'covered', the dividend payment – was at an all-time low. This was a new and interesting development, in that UK dividend cover in the early 1980s had been on a par with that in Germany.

Moreover, British companies' dividends appeared not to go down much in recession, lending credibility to the suspicion that dividends were taking priority over investment and employment. Figures from the Department of Trade and Industry show that in the recession of the early 1990s, 60 per cent of large companies either maintained or increased their dividends, while only 12 per cent paid no dividend and 28 per cent cut the payout significantly.[7] It is increasingly common for British companies to raise dividends even when profits go down.

One striking feature of this change is that it flies in the face of conventional descriptions of how the Anglo-Saxon model of capitalism is supposed to work. According to liberal economic theory, companies are the result of a private contractual arrangement in which the central relationship is between shareholders, the principals, and the managers, who are the agents. The traditional justification for the primacy of the shareholders in the system is that they put up the capital and take the residual risk in the business. That is to say, their rights of ownership entitle them to the residual gains or losses on the venture after all the other contractual payments to suppliers, creditors, bondholders, managers, employees and others have been made. The right to decide on the dividend lies with the managers. Such private control of property, in which the directors' only duty is to maximize shareholders' returns, is assumed to lead to the most efficient use of society's resources.

This view may have made sense in the early phases of industrialization in the nineteenth century when, in Ernest Gellner's description, the individual capitalist was face to face with nature, and those who returned with greater booty wrested from nature could claim legitimacy in virtue of their very visible contribution to the greater good. Yet today no one is face to face with nature and the capital in most large businesses is at fifth (or fiftieth) hand. Innovation, as Gellner remarked, is carried out on the shoulders of countless others; it is entirely dependent on a shared scientific and technological culture to which many have contributed and it is quite impossible to disaggregate. The stakeholder concept derives much of its strength precisely from its ability to address this problem of legitimacy more effectively than any model of modern capitalism that gives primacy to the shareholder. Within the stakeholder economy the manager is seen as a trustee of the inheritance of the past, whose obligation is to preserve and enhance that inherited wealth in the long-term interest of the company, which aims for survival in perpetuity.

The Anglo-Saxon model, in contrast, seeks to maximize returns to the shareholder, rather than maximizing the wealth of the company. And the novel feature of what is happening in the English-speaking economies, as we have seen, is that the income on today's equity shares in the great mass of quoted companies appears to have become increasingly fixed instead of residual, especially when compared with Germany or even the United States. It looks remarkably as though institutional investors are having it both ways, enjoying a low-risk, fixed return as well as the benefit of future profits growth. Whereas the labour market has become more flexible, the capital market appears to have become less flexible. Does this also imply that there is, indeed, more pressure on Anglo-Saxon management in economic downturns to cut discretionary spending on investment, research and development and jobs?

Fending off the financiers

Consider the question through the eyes of the industrialist. Since 1979 the British motor components business has had to deal with the shocks of long-term decline in the British-owned motor industry and successive recessions of greater duration and depth than those in other leading industrialized countries. Between 1989 and 1992, for example, UK vehicle sales collapsed by 33 per cent. The best in the industry responded to these shocks by introducing Japanese-style methods such as lean production, involving close cooperation with suppliers to secure just-in-time inventory control. They have also taken aboard quality-management techniques and the Japanese philosophy of *kaizen*, or continuous improvement. In these techniques of the stakeholder economy they have been helped by the arrival of leading Japanese car producers such as Toyota, Nissan and Honda.

By the time the British economy started to turn down in 1989 the larger motor component suppliers had taken out insurance against trouble by further internationalizing their businesses. GKN, which is a world leader in the manufacture of constant velocity joints, the most important component in front-wheel-drive vehicles, started the 1980s with around two-thirds of its business in the UK and one-third overseas. By the recession of the early 1990s the proportions were the other way around. The result was that GKN was able through the recession to maintain spending on investment, training and research and development out of its overseas profits, even though domestic profits were under strain.

Yet its management clearly felt that there was pressure from institutional investors. In evidence to the trade and industry select committee, it said that shares in traditional manufacturers such as GKN were held for income rather than capital growth. It continued: 'The consequence is that UK companies distribute a relatively high proportion of earnings as dividends, putting pressure on the company to earn high rates of return and reducing the internal funds available for reinvestment (in times of recession, surplus funds can be eliminated completely). Consequently, UK companies are relatively risk averse and tend to seek growth primarily through acquisition. There is also pressure, particularly during a recession, to reduce discretionary costs such as R & D in order to protect the dividend; a reduced dividend can have serious consequences in terms of lower share price and possible predatory takeover.'[8]

This view is widely shared by industrialists. And it is certainly true that while dividends rose in the last recession, research and development fell in real terms by 10 per cent between 1989 and 1991. Nor is there any doubt that institutional investors can and do put both explicit and implicit pressure on companies to keep dividends up. Just as Anglo-Saxon politics are hostage to the clash of interest groups, the division of corporate spoils in the non-stakeholder economy is an intensely political process in which the interests of management and institutional investors often conflict.

Stand and deliver, says M & G

Perhaps the most vociferous institution on this score is the M & G unit trust group. In a memorandum to the same select committee it argued that a high dividend was necessary in the UK because of the country's low historic growth rate. That was why the dividend yield on the UK stock market was much higher than elsewhere: investors needed to be compensated for lower prospective growth and greater uncertainty in a mature economy that performed poorly in relation to its main competitors. M & G's view on dividend policy was that it should be consistent and that the payout should not be cut because of temporary fluctuations in profit; only if the future operations of the company were threatened by a maintained dividend would a cut be justified.

Others, such as the National Association of Pension Funds, argue in similar vein that companies should try to hold dividends at a sustainable level through the economic cycle, so that they fall as a percentage of profit during a boom but rise during a recession. They feel that dividend payments should be used to send signals about the prospects and stress that they are not, like Shylock, trying to extract a pound of flesh: by reinvesting dividends in the market they claim to recycle capital to those parts of the economy which hold out the best profit opportunities. A higher payout ratio, runs the argument, should thus lead to a more efficient allocation of resources. Fund managers also point out that they have supported long-term investment where there was a case for doing so, as in the pharmaceuticals industry or with North Sea oil – although the list always seems to begin and end with these two examples.

It is true that some of the critics of short-termism misunderstand the way in which the investment institutions operate. Paul Marsh of the London Business School has expertly demolished the more naïve of the arguments in his book *Short Termism on Trial.*[9] Yet the debate over dividends exposes the institutions in a curious light. In particular, the M & G line comes uncomfortably close to a counsel of despair, with its implicit assumption that Britain is still in an era of low relative growth. It seems that the British people's myopia over the turnround in the country's relative economic fortunes extends even to economically sophisticated folk in the City, who have failed to notice the convergence that has been taking place in growth rates in the developed world. The risk is that, if all investors in the stock market believe that Britain is still in an inexorable downward spiral, the prophecy will become self-fulfilling, since perceptions of risk and return affect the cost of capital that the stock market imposes on industry. Interestingly, M & G's investment performance, much admired in the dark days of the 1970s, has been lacklustre in the 1990s.

As for the institutions' insistence on having a stable dividend income across the economic cycle, common sense appears to have gone out of the window. In effect, powerful investment institutions, enjoying huge long-term inflows of cash from the nation's savers, are asking financially stretched industrialists in cyclical industries to provide them with banking facilities in the depths of recession. This is absurd, especially when industrialists themselves are saying that this leads to reductions in the kind of spending that secures the long-term future of the business.

Nor is it realistic to expect companies constantly to raise fresh funds in the capital markets to compensate for the financial pressure imposed by high dividends. The transaction costs of issuing new capital are high, when compared with using the company's internal capital. Other City fund managers such as PDFM (formerly Phillips & Drew Fund Managers) argue against M & G that directors are likely to be better judges, especially of more sophisticated high-technology forms of investment, than are institutional investors, who suffer from more limited information and are thus more likely to have an 'accountant' mentality.[10] Academics have argued that the information disadvantage suffered by investors *vis à vis* management could mean that investors in any case withhold capital, or make it available on less favourable terms than the company would normally obtain internally from its retained profits.[11]

All conspirators now

Yet to say on this basis that the City has failed the nation is to embrace too modest a conspiracy theory. The real problem is systemic and it extends far beyond the City. Starting at the least sinister end of the spectrum, it is significant that British actuaries who calculate the amount of money needed to meet a pension fund's future obligations usually make their assessment by reference not to stock-market values but to dividend and interest income. If overall income goes down, the trustees may have to ask the company to pay increased contributions, on the basis of the actuaries' advice, into the pension fund pot. Note, however, that a majority of the trustees of company pension funds are directors of the company that runs the pension scheme. They themselves are anxious to secure the best possible return to protect the company's profits from increased pension contribution costs. So if pension funds are applying pressure for higher dividends, industry is colluding in the crime.

Nor should the influence of taxation on dividend policy be overlooked. A recurring theme of this book will be that the performance of the economy and of individual companies is far more influenced by personal motivation, in the shape of the incentives and penalties that apply to individual managers, than economists sometimes allow. The level of dividends is no exception to this rule. Decisions on dividend payments are mostly taken by people who are top-rate taxpayers owning shares in the company. Between 1982 and 1992 the cuts in the top rate of income tax and the reductions in the rate of corporation tax had the effect of increasing the value of a dividend to a higher-rate taxpayer more than threefold: a pre-tax profit of £1000 went from being worth £170 after tax, if distributed in full, to £530. That huge change in the incentive to distribute was further reinforced by the growth of performance-related bonuses, stock-option schemes and the rest, where the overall shareholder's return is frequently the yardstick for measuring performance. Given the importance of dividends in the total return, the temptation to err on the side of a more generous dividend payment is obvious.

In the meantime, the pension funds that now dominate the capital markets are also greatly encouraged by the tax system to demand higher dividends. These funds pay no tax on the dividends they receive. But as the legal owners of the companies in which they invest, they do in effect bear corporation tax on company profits. If profits are retained in the company, the pension fund bears tax at the full corporation tax rate, which stood at 33 per cent in 1996. But if profits are distributed to the shareholders, the rate falls to 16.25 per cent.[12] To the extent that the increase in company dividends leads companies to finance more of their activities out of borrowings on which the interest is tax allowable, the yield of corporation tax is reduced. It seems remarkable that the Treasury has been willing to tolerate this aspect of the system, since it means that corporation tax has become an increasingly voluntary impost.

The present system of corporation tax was designed in the 1970s when institutions owned much less of British industry. Any attempt to improve the climate for business investment would need to address this tax bias in favour of high dividends. This is more likely to come from Labour (bold claim!) than from the Conservatives, if only with a view to raising more money. Stephen Dorrell's enquiry into savings was, in the event, put on the back burner, following intensive lobbying by the institutions. The pension funds had already suffered a reduction in their dividend income because of technical changes to corporation tax made by Norman Lamont in his period as chancellor. And a leading industrialist, James Hanson, publicly attacked the government for what he perceived to be a seemingly anti-capitalist stance on savings and investment. Lamont's successor Kenneth Clarke decided that it was not the moment to put another cat among the pension fund pigeons.

The biggest culprit of underinvestment, nevertheless, is not the City but government. When compared with the US, Germany or France, Britain has suffered unusually extreme swings in output and inflation. One unfortunate consequence is that the small to medium-sized business sector, which is the chief source of new jobs in today's economy, is disproportionately cut back through insolvencies in each new downturn. The absence of the more supportive style of banking that exists in Germany has been very costly for the UK.

Short-termists in industry

That said, much of the problem lies with the industrialists' own response to the government's dismal economic management. The penalties they claim to incur as a result of pressure for high dividends, especially in cyclical industries such as motor components, are probably real enough. But they pale into insignificance when compared with the damage which companies inflict on themselves by allowing their assessments of new investment projects to be overcoloured by the freakish inflationary experience of the 1970s.

One widely used method of assessing new investment is the 'payback' period, in which the chief criterion is the length of time it takes for the company to see all its money back. Even in normal times this is a crude, potentially misleading and usually short-termist method of appraising new investment. When inflation is fluctuating and high, the resulting uncertainty makes it desirable to achieve a more rapid payback. It follows that when inflation returns to low and stable levels, payback periods should be extended. Surveys by the Bank of England have shown that industrialists were extraordinarily slow to extend their payback periods in the new disinflationary climate of the 1990s.

Another more sophisticated method of appraisal involves calculations of the cost of capital which, as we saw earlier, is the minimum return required from new investment projects to satisfy the demands of investors in the company. A Bank of England survey of more than 200 firms in 1994 found that these appeared to incorporate assumptions about inflation that were absurdly pessimistic: their average required rate of return on new investment was a remarkably high 20 per cent, when inflation on the retail price index was less than 2 per cent.[13] Given that 20 per cent was just the average, many were clearly using phenomenally demanding target rates of return. There is evidence, too, that the real returns expected by institutional investors are substantially less than those assumed by industrialists in these cost-of-capital sums. Tim Jenkinson, Stock Exchange fellow in economics at Keble College, Oxford, has suggested that industrialists may have been assuming a cost of capital four or five percentage points higher than the return to which most institutions actually aspired on their investments.[14]

That the level of investment should be affected by a methodological aberration of this kind might seem a stunningly poor reflection on the competence of Britain's managers and finance directors. Yet they are no more at fault than Britain's overindebted home owners, in that they are victims of another form of money illusion. The lesson drawn from inflation by so many households was that the safest way to become rich was to break all the rules of prudent finance by borrowing to excess. For industry the comparable, though opposite, moral was that survival depended on extreme prudence in investing and financing and that it was always right to err on the side of underinvestment. The depressed view of profit opportunities in the British economy that results from overcautious ways of computing capital costs is really the business equivalent of the feelbad factor experienced by the wider British public in the mid-1990s. Both were responding to exceptionally misleading price signals. The cost has been high, both in terms of personal discontents and investment opportunities forgone.

Takeovers and the winner's curse

To call this a conspiracy would, of course, be going too far. As so often, muddle and policy error provide a more convincing explanation. But what of GKN's allegation that companies are too prone to prefer takeovers to direct investment in productive assets? And does the discipline of hostile takeovers blackmail industrialists into paying higher dividends and into an excessive focus on short-term profitability? This is where the City's critics come closer to the kill and employees should start to feel uneasy. The volume and hostility of takeover activity in the English-speaking economies undeniably exceed anything seen in continental Europe and Japan. Andy Cosh, Alan Hughes and Ajit Singh of Cambridge University have estimated that in the decade 1972 to 1982, one in three of the largest 730 companies quoted on the UK stock market changed hands, while between 1982 and 1986 137 of the largest 1000 non-financial companies died through takeover.[15] These are, they point out, extremely high rates of vulnerability for large companies in an advanced economy. Since then the pace has accelerated, in terms of the values involved. In the takeover frenzy of the late 1980s, spending on acquisitions and mergers topped £27 billion at the peak. In 1995 it reached a record £32 billion. This compared with total capital investment in plant and machinery that year of £41 billion.

These huge outlays reflect a big change in British business culture. For most of the twentieth century professional managers have enjoyed a high degree of autonomy in running companies. Their role has been close to one of trusteeship, in which they balance the interests of the various stakeholders in the firm. The growth in the number of takeovers and their steady march up the scale of the corporate hierarchy means that trusteeship sporadically gives way to something closer to the principal–agent model of corporate capitalism. By operating as a market in corporate control as well as a forum for raising capital and trading shares, the stock market allows alternative teams of managers to bid for the right to manage the assets of quoted companies.

Whereas in Germany and Japan it is the bankers who tend to exert ultimate discipline over management, that role in Britain is exercised by shareholders. Their chief sanction, when management is underperforming, is either to sell their shares in the market or to accept an offer for their shares in a takeover bid. Since institutional investors are the majority buyers and owners of shares in British industry and commerce, they cannot, as a group, sell out in the marketplace. They depend on corporate predators to prowl the market for underperforming companies and to offer them a choice between incumbent management and a new broom. The predators traditionally pitch their bid at more than the current market value of the company to provide an incentive to shareholders to accept the offer. This bid premium is said to represent the value of the efficiency gains that the new management expects to extract from the target company.

That, at least, is the theory. Yet in a study of 80 contested bids between 1985 and 1986 two leading academics, Colin Mayer of Oxford University and Julian Franks of the London Business School, found that the performance of the target companies in the six years before the bid was no different from that of other companies in agreed bids or not involved in bids at all.[16] They question the common assumption that markets for corporate control correct managerial failure. Most of the research into the profitability of companies before and after mergers and acquisitions suggests that profitability tends to deteriorate afterwards. The most optimistic conclusion was that of a study in 1980 of all mergers in the European Community. It found that 'no consistent pattern of either improved or deteriorated profitability can therefore be claimed across the seven countries. Mergers would appear to result in a slight improvement here, a slight worsening there.'[17]

This casts the succession of British takeover booms in a rather extraordinary light. The only consistent beneficiaries of the process seem to be the shareholders in the acquired company, the City professionals who extract huge fees from the deals, and the individual managers of the acquisitive companies who can use the increased scale of their responsibilities to justify fatter pay packages. Shareholders in the bidding company are more often than not the victims of a 'winner's curse'. Even in those cases where the takeover mechanism operates in accordance with the theory, it is a remarkably expensive way to get rid of management. In Granada's bid for the Forte hotel and catering group in 1996, the fees topped £150 million. In effect, the biggest shareholder in Forte, Mercury Asset Management, with 15 per cent of the Granada capital and 13 per cent of Forte, paid £22.5 million of its clients' money (15 per cent of £150 million) to get rid of the chairman and chief executive, Rocco Forte.

The Moses school of management

The winner's curse arises partly because the management of the bidding company inevitably has inadequate knowledge of the affairs of the target company. For their part, the institutional fund managers can have only a limited knowledge of the skills of the managers on both sides of the battle. Because it is difficult for them to have a detailed understanding of each and every company in which they invest, too many of them subscribe unconsciously to what might be called the Moses school of management: the idea that there is a special caste of heroic figures with an astonishing talent for hitting winning strategies to lead companies out of the wilderness. This emphasis on the individual, as opposed to the team, is further encouraged in takeovers by highly paid public relations experts, whose fees now put them at the upper end of the City food chain. They find it easier to win headlines and press coverage if they promote a single individual as the hero of the hour. Teamwork makes dull copy.

        The capacity of bidders to overpay also reflects the fatal attraction that deal making holds for businesspeople in the English-speaking economies. Takeover bids offer them far more excitement than does running the company. In commenting on the tendency of takeovers to reduce the wealth of the shareholders in the bidding company, Warren Buffett, the astute American investor who runs the exceptionally successful Berkshire Hathaway investment company in the US, has explained this behavioural temptation in characteristically down-to-earth fashion:

> Often the chief executive officer asks a strategic planning staff, consultants or investment bankers whether an acquisition or two might make sense. That's like asking your interior decorator whether you need a $50,000 rug. The acquisition problem is often compounded by a biological bias: many

chief executive officers attain their positions in part because they possess an abundance of animal spirits and ego. If an executive is heavily endowed with these qualities, they won't disappear when he reaches the top. When such a chief executive officer is encouraged by his advisers to make deals, he responds much as would a teenage boy who is encouraged by his father to have a normal sex life. It's not a push that he needs.[18]

For more risk-averse managers, takeovers are equally tempting, if for a rather different reason. Having lived through a period in which economic policy has produced extreme swings in output, employment and inflation, they feel safer investing in a company with existing assets, products and customers, which can be relied on to generate immediate cash flow from day one, than putting money into new plant and machinery where the returns are more uncertain. The looseness of accounting standards for takeovers and mergers in the past has further encouraged the takeover merry-go-round. It has been relatively easy, after a bid, for managers to declare much increased profits in the short term, even if the underlying cash flow of the business is weak.

Grand Met plays gin rummy

The bias towards takeovers in the British system results in a mercantile corporate culture not unlike that of the oriental bazaar. Managers increasingly see their role as being to trade in existing companies, rather than to invest in new plant or products. It is the mirror image of the hire-and-fire mentality, applied to the corporation as opposed to the worker. Perhaps the supreme example of this was the food and drinks concern Grand Metropolitan, while Lord Sheppard was in charge, which turned its portfolio of businesses upside down in short order. This left many shareholders confused as to the nature and operating performance of the underlying businesses and the employees stunned by the resulting adjustments and redundancies. It is an approach to business that Warren Buffett scathingly describes as the 'gin rummy' school of management: pick up a few businesses here, discard a few there, shuffle the pack. It need hardly be said that this is the antithesis of what stakeholding, with its emphasis on long-term relationships, is all about. It is also a substantial contributor to the insecurity discussed in earlier chapters.

An objective observer might conclude that the whole process of takeovers and mergers is crazy, serving the interests of no one but ego-tripping managers and fee-hungry people in the City. It is certainly bizarre that the employment prospects of so many should be subject to such a hit-and-miss process. Yet in the absence of arrangements where investors and bankers have close and committed relationships with company management, as in Germany or Japan, takeovers remain the only sanction of real potency within the system.

John Kay, who is particularly critical of this deal-making culture, has pointed out that merger booms vary in quality. In the first big one, in the 1920s, mergers helped bring about larger plants capable of achieving economies of scale in the new techniques of mass production. The durability of some of the products of those mergers, such as ICI and Unilever, bears witness to their strategic success. In the 1960s and 1970s, in contrast, there was a greater emphasis on conglomeration, whereby disparate businesses were brought together under a common management; also on building national champions to confront increased international competition.[19] These mergers produced mainly poor results. Few now have good words to say about the diversification carried out by the likes of tobacco giant BAT, or the attempt to build a volume car maker around British Leyland. Their deals help explain why the statistics on takeover activity paint such a dismal picture.

The present round of takeovers is something else again. In the 1980s, activity was partly geared towards predators undoing the conglomerate fervour of the 1960s and 1970s. In the 1990s it has been concentrated in the banking, pharmaceutical and utilities sectors of the economy, where there are very obvious efficiency gains to be derived from reducing excess capacity. There are, of course, bids that hark back to the 1960s, like the assault by Granada, a television-to-motorway-café conglomerate, on Forte. But more bids appear to make economic sense today than they did 20 years ago and I suspect that the statistics will in due course reflect this.

The likes of Hanson, before its decision to break itself up, and its clutch of younger imitators, may not be the most attractive inhabitants of the corporate landscape. But in an Anglo-Saxon-style market economy they are part of the ecological balance. Their activity provides an efficient means of shrinking capacity in mature industries, or of rationalizing businesses whose value lies chiefly in physical assets and fairly unsophisticated labour. The snag is that takeovers are not confined to businesses such as these. Hanson in the early 1990s even started buying into ICI, only to back off after a fierce defensive campaign by the industrial giant, which revealed some of Hanson's own quirky management practices. And with the managers of most quoted companies living in the knowledge that they are, in effect, up for sale each day, the ability to invest in long-term relationships with employees and suppliers, and the willingness of employees and suppliers to make their investments in the firm, run into a serious constraint.

The discipline of takeover does indeed encourage high dividends to keep the institutional investors sweet. Yet it promotes a culture of cost cutting in relation to everything else, as managers constantly look over their shoulder for fear of a predatory attack. The same discipline applies in a rather different way to the predator. The systemic tendency to overpay in hostile takeovers means that the acquiring company may be tempted to cut more costs than is good for the long-term health of the business in order to generate respectable returns on an excessive outlay. In a flexible labour market that means treating workers as just-in-time people.

For those employed by banks, building societies or utilities, where takeovers have become the preferred means of rationalization, an economic upturn does not generate much sense of well-being even if their pay goes up. A climate of fear inevitably prevails when employment prospects are in the hands of anonymous institutional investors who impose life or death on incumbent management on the basis of imperfect information and flawed incentives. There is a risk that the blunt edge of the takeover process is progressively undermining the legitimacy of Anglo-Saxon market capitalism.

Just-in-time people for sale

The takeover scramble also sits oddly with a world where corporate competitive advantage derives increasingly from human capital and from relationships of trust with employees, suppliers and other stakeholders. Charles Handy argues, for example, that companies are communities, not pieces of property, and that the concept of buying and selling people via takeovers is as out of date as the concept of a husband owning a wife. For him, profits and shareholder value are not ends, but necessary means for achieving the wider purpose of the company, which is to deliver quality goods and services to ever-increasing numbers of satisfied customers.[20]

Companies like Marks & Spencer have long operated in a way that tallies with Handy's model, without having any problem keeping shareholders happy. ICI has always sought to provide an environment in which employees would feel sufficiently secure to invest in company-specific education and skills. Smaller firms live in a different world where the deal-making culture has oppressive consequences. Crabtree Group, a quoted company which manufactures printing equipment for the can-making industry, has as its main competitor a German company that has seen only one change in structure, from partnership to limited company, over the past 100 years. In contrast, Crabtree has had at least 20 such changes of ownership or restructurings. As the directors have put it, 'that is 20 changes of direction, 20 times the balance sheet has been raped and 20 short-term views'.[21] They are equally revealing, incidentally, on what it is like to steer a small and medium-sized business through the extreme swings in the British economic cycle. In 1989 they were able to raise £160 million of bank borrowings to buy an engineering group, when the company was making profits of £1.6 million. In the recession in 1992 when they had raised profits to £3 million, they could not even borrow £2 million from the bank.

Even those who do not share Handy's fundamentalist critique of takeovers would probably acknowledge that today physical plant and machinery are of decreasing importance even in manufacturing; and that the value in a growing number of companies is tied up in intangible assets such as patents, skills, innovatory ability and brand names, which are, in effect, designed to reassure people that shareholders' interests are not being put before those of customers. There is even more value in the relationships and implicit contracts between the various stakeholders in the business, which were described in Chapter 2 as social capital. Inflicting hostile takeovers on businesses in which these intangible values contribute significantly to competitive advantage is the equivalent of taking a hammer to mend integrated circuitry. And the notion that an exclusive commitment to maximizing shareholder value in these cases will lead to the most efficient use of society's resources seems less convincing than with the more old-fashioned kind of business where competitive advantage derives from physical capital and a low level of skills. This is why the stakeholder view of the firm looks attractive in today's conditions.

For those who accept the conceptual basis of stakeholder theory, however, there is a fundamental difficulty over accountability. Neither economists nor accountants have come up with an adequate system of measuring and reporting the intangible values on which stakeholder theory is built. It follows that any move to stakeholder-type corporate governance will have to borrow from the existing shareholder framework to ensure that incumbent management does not end up with more discretion and less accountability. This will be explored in later chapters. Yet the problem of establishing accountability to a wider group of constituencies does not undermine the point that there are some stakeholders, most notably employees who have made investments in skills and relationships that are specific to the firm, who are as much or more at risk than shareholders. And, unlike institutional investors, most cannot diversify employment risk in a portfolio. If people are downsized, it hurts a great deal more than it hurts Legal & General if one of its company investments goes into receivership. (While Charles Handy argues that more of us will be able to diversify our job portfolio in future, I suspect that the majority will still spend our time in more conventional forms of employment.)

Accountant to Caesar's wife

Moreover, the accountancy flaw also affects the proprietorial form of capitalism which has given rise to the takeover game. When managers lay off workers after a takeover, the cost to the business of any erosion of human capital remains unquantified. It is not offset, in the profit and loss account, against the increase in profit that results from firing people. This is just one of many ways in which management can boost short-term profits at the expense of the long-term competitiveness of the business; and the temptation to do so is reinforced, as we shall see in Chapter 8, by incentive schemes that employ very narrow, short-term performance criteria. What is clear is that, in both hostile and friendly takeovers, managers in more sophisticated industries are acting on the basis of yet more inadequate information.

There is an urgent need, at the very least, for more soft data in company accounts on intangibles such as skills and intellectual capital. For while managers constantly proclaim that people are the company's most valuable resource, their actions are heavily influenced by accountancy which treats people as costs, not assets. There is also a need for some reinforcement of the independence of the auditor, who is the watchdog and backstop of corporate capitalism. One of the least discussed aspects of changing business practice over the past quarter-century has been the commercialization of the accountancy profession, which now offers a much wider range of services than in the past. Many auditors derive more fees from consultancy services rendered to their audit clients than from the audit itself. While it is impossible to prove that they use the audit as a loss-leader for other services, which would compromise their independence, there is a widespread suspicion that this is what happens.

The accountancy profession has also connived in creative accounting, in which the financial reporting process is carefully managed, with the assistance of merchant bankers and lawyers, to ensure that the company is always one jump ahead of the regulators in putting the most favourable complexion on its affairs. Creative accounting was particularly prevalent in the overheated conditions of the late 1980s. Once one merchant bank scheme for profit smoothing had been accepted by an auditor, other auditors found it difficult to face down a client in the light of the precedent.[22] Much has since been done by the Accounting Standards Board under the no-nonsense guidance of David Tweedie to tighten up accounting practice. But doubts remain about the auditors. They habitually express shock at any suggestion that they abuse the potential conflict of interest inherent in running financial service conglomerates. Yet their appointment and fees, although formally a matter for decision by shareholders, are in practice in the gift of the managers they monitor. If they are not compliant the managers have no need to sack them, which would bring adverse publicity. They merely wait a year and put the audit out to 'competitive' tender. The existing auditor is then dropped. Given the importance of the auditors' role in the system they should not just be above suspicion; like Caesar's wife, they should be seen to be so. That would call for some more formal separation of the audit from their other functions.

Declinism on trial

The question remains: how can intangible values be preserved from needlessly destructive and arbitrary takeovers? There are no perfect solutions. Yet if the huge volume of mergers and acquisitions has more to do with managers' egos and City fees than economic efficiency, there is an obvious case for trying to make the process more selective. One way that I have advocated in the past would be to ensure that all hostile takeovers above a given size are automatically referred to the Monopolies and Mergers Commission, which is responsible for assessing the competition policy and other public interest aspects of takeovers.[23] This is now part of Labour policy. There are those – not all of them vested interests in the City – who worry that such a move would entail a serious loss of discipline over management. Yet the constant monitoring provided by the movement of share prices and stock-market analysis offers continuing transparency. And I shall argue in Chapters 7 and 8 that there are ways of democratizing and energizing the big investment institutions which would compensate for the removal of the productivity-chasing role of the hostile takeover merchants.

Concern about the loss of discipline also ignores one of the more striking features of corporate life in Britain, which is the amount of innovation and improvement that has taken place outside the format of the quoted company. Consider some examples. Float glass, perhaps the most impressive technical advance in British manufacturing since 1945, was developed when Pilkington Brothers was an unquoted company. Its chairman told me, shortly after the firm's flotation in the 1970s, that the process could not have been developed had he been obliged to answer to a wider group of shareholders. Reuters transformed itself from a news-gathering organization into a phenomenally successful manufacturer of high-tech dealing systems for global markets while owned by a clutch of Fleet Street newspapers. When it was floated, its capital structure continued to protect it from hostile takeover. The Trustee Savings Bank pioneered the successful cross-selling of financial services without any outside shareholders and performed much better before flotation than after. The innovative car parts maker Unipart, which has developed an in-house university for continuous learning, is widely admired for its personnel management and training. It remains an unquoted company.

Nor should the achievements of public ownership be discounted. The remarkable transformation of British Steel took place while it was still in the public sector. Indeed, the private capital markets could never have shouldered the huge burden of its losses as it went through the rehabilitation process. The BBC, a nationalized industry which we all take for granted, has maintained an extraordinarily high degree of creativity without outside owners. (It also remains the chief bastion of journalistic independence in a media world dominated by right-wing proprietors.)

And some of the biggest companies that remain immune from hostile takeover have demonstrated a remarkable capacity for corporate renewal. The Anglo-Dutch multinationals Shell and Unilever, for example, have a collegiate culture which militates against high-profile individualism in the boardroom. How well the culture will stand up in the new world of share-incentive schemes remains to be seen. But I suspect that Shell and Unilever will still be around when most of today's predators are no more than a distant memory. The lesson is that innovation and renewal seem to thrive without capital-market discipline. Many would argue that they thrive precisely because they are free from a discipline that is excessively short term and financial.

It is possible, in any case, to exaggerate the importance of corporate governance and finance in discussing competitiveness. The cure for the declinist condition that attributes Britain's economic problems to the financial system is to look not at Germany, with which it is so fashionable to compare the UK, but at Italy, which arguably has a better claim than Germany over the past quarter-century to be considered the miracle economy of Europe. Italian business has neither the advantage of German-style banking, which provides committed support and monitoring, or Anglo-Saxon capital-market discipline, which is supposed to enhance efficiency. Its banking system is ramshackle: bank lending consists chiefly of a form of short-term credit not unlike the British overdraft, which gives banks the right to pull the rug from under companies at short notice; and these less-than-committed Italian banks are notoriously overdependent on the security of the borrowing company's assets rather than an assessment of the earning power of the company. Yet Italy's mainly family-owned businesses are among the most vigorous exporters in the world.

Those who seek to pin responsibility for Britain's poor economic performance on the City also have to confront an important question. If the British system militates so fiercely against investment, and so much of the corporate sector has changed hands in an arbitrary and inefficient way, why has Britain enjoyed much the same rate of economic growth over the past 15 years as the US, Germany, France and Italy?

To answer that question we need to look more closely at British manufacturing industry.

Part Two

Culture and Anarchy

4

The Competitiveness Conundrum

*T*he sorry state of British manufacturing is a great national obsession – a depressed perspective that is, in fact, another aspect of the 'declinist' phenomenon discussed in earlier chapters. In recent years it has often taken the form of an unfavourable comparison with Germany and Japan, whose stakeholder values are deemed to give them special advantages in manufacturing. Yet the obsession goes back a very long way. In 1903 Joseph Chamberlain, a passionate advocate of tariff reform, put the case for protecting manufacturing industry in terms that are instantly recognizable today:

> Your once great trade in sugar refining is gone; all right, try jam. Your iron trade is going; never mind, you can make mouse traps. The cotton trade is threatened; well, what does it matter to you? Suppose you try dolls' eyes…believe me…although the industries of this country are very various, you cannot go on for ever. You cannot go on watching with indifference the disappearance of your principal industries, and always hoping that you will be able to replace them by secondary and inferior industries.[1]

The spirit of Chamberlain, for whom all structural adjustment in the economy was for the worse, lives on. The same anti-service bias was apparent, for example, in the evidence of Arnold Weinstock, chief executive of Britain's General Electric Company, to the House of Lords committee on overseas trade in 1985. He declared:

> What will the service industries be servicing when there is no hardware, when no wealth is actually being produced? We will be servicing, presumably, the production of wealth by others. We will supply the Changing of the Guard, we will supply the Beefeaters around the Tower of London. We will become a curiosity. I do not think that is what Britain is about. I think that is rubbish.

Such concern about manufacturing is an exact replica of the nineteenth-century worry about agriculture. Between 1816 and 1914 agriculture's share of gross national product fell from 20 per cent to less than 7 per cent.[2] Many late Victorians and Edwardians were convinced that this was sapping the nation's strength and would leave it vulnerable to its enemies in the event of war. The opposite proved to be the case; and the shift of workers out of agriculture – which by the second half of the nineteenth century was mainly into services – helped facilitate economic development. Despite the agricultural Jeremiahs, British gross domestic product grew at about 2 per cent a year between the start of the Great Depression in 1873 and 1913. And Britain did, of course, emerge a victor at the end of the Great War.

The anti-service bias is the antithesis of gentlemanly capitalism, in that it rates Simon Rattle's music revenues from the United States as qualitatively inferior to those derived from British Aerospace's arms sales to the Middle East. Despite its apparent philistinism it also has a surprisingly respectable academic pedigree. Just as the agricultural declinists were heirs of the physiocrats, the eighteenth-century French school of economists that believed land to be the source of all wealth, the manufacturing preservationists are the remaindermen of the intellectual estate of Adam Smith. In *The Wealth of Nations* the great classical economist expressed a bias against services, arguing that while the labour of a manufacturer added value, the labour of a menial servant did not. Such services, he said 'generally perish in the very instant of their performance, and seldom leave any trade or value behind them for which an equal quantity of service could afterwards be procured'.[3]

In fairness to Smith, he could not have been expected, from his eighteenth-century vantage point, to foresee the great productivity increases that would be generated today in activities such as communications and financial services; nor, indeed, the robustness of a modern economy in the face of the disappearance of so much manufacturing activity. For despite the fall in manufacturing employment from 31 per cent of the workforce in 1975 to 25 per cent in 1983 to 18 per cent today, the economy continues to grow at the same old underlying peacetime growth rate of 2 per cent a year – the vicissitudes of government policy and the fulminations of Chamberlain and Weinstock notwithstanding. The point could be made even more strongly of the United States, which remains the world's richest country, with an exceptionally high absolute level of productivity, despite manufacturing employment having fallen to a mere 15 per cent.

Chemistry-set capitalism

Manufacturing, it is true, exerts a disproportionate influence on the economy because it accounts for nearly two-thirds of all Britain's exports, even though its contribution to gross domestic product is down to a fifth. That said, only a handful of further concessions need to be made to those who feel that a nation's strength can be measured by the amount of swarf on its boots. One is that manufacturing was subjected to needlessly brutal shock treatment in the early chemistry-set capitalism phase of the Thatcher experiment, which resulted in a far greater loss of output and employment than was necessary to cope with the changes imposed by the influx of North Sea oil. Indeed, for much of the 1980s the Treasury seems to have had a purist antipathy for manufacturing that carried an echo of its blinkered vision in the 1920s. Given the importance of manufacturing in trade, this policy bias towards over-rapid deindustrialization led, temporarily at least, to a weak balance of payments position. It could also be argued that in a very open economy, and in an increasingly liberal trade environment, there is a risk of overspecialization. The country may end up keeping too many eggs in too few sectoral baskets – the high-tech version of the banana republic problem.

That said, the distinction between manufacturing and services in the information age is becoming increasingly fuzzy. More and more services are in any case becoming tradeable across national boundaries. And as Hamish McRae of *The Independent* has often observed, a high service content in trade can be a sign of economic sophistication. Britain's balance of payments surplus of

$1.3 billion on royalties and licence fees, for example, is an important strength, especially when compared with a German deficit of $2.4 billion.[4] The Germans, whose education and training are so greatly admired in Britain, seem to have difficulty turning intellectual capital into a tradeable commodity. It is high time, then, that the left in Britain adopted a more inclusive view of the service sector.

There is only one truly fundamental point on which it is necessary to give way to the declinists, and that has nothing to do with economics. It concerns the loss in the twentieth century of Britain's position as the world's pre-eminent military power. This is a real, not a relative loss; and an erosion of national self-respect was inevitable in the face of a shift in power relations on this momentous scale. Yet even here, the great literature of national decay seems to impose an odd perspective. For a country with such a small share of the world's population and global resources to have held the international stage for so long was an extraordinary historical phenomenon which seems unlikely ever to be repeated. Barry Supple, the economic historian from whom I have borrowed the earlier quotation from Joseph Chamberlain, has aptly remarked that Britain's transformation from imperial colossus to diminished power 'turned out to be a relatively (and surprisingly) sluggish process'. 'It is,' he adds, 'perhaps the slow pace, rather than the rapidity, of Britain's decline on the world scene that is the more interesting historical phenomenon.[5]

Nor was the retreat from imperial grandeur economically harmful. Except in the free-booting early days when the enterprise was largely in the hands of private-sector buccaneers, the economic benefits of empire were probably less than is generally assumed. And by the time Britain was well into the period of imperial overstretch in the twentieth century, the white man's burden was almost certainly detracting from the economic welfare of ordinary people, as well as requiring them to sacrifice their lives in far-flung parts of the globe. An impressive undertaking it may have been; but at the end of it all it is interesting that a small inward-looking country like Switzerland, which chose to trade with other countries rather than rule them, has emerged richer in terms of income per head than the country that ran the greatest empire the world has ever seen.[6]

The efficient route to stagnation

To return to our theme, it should be clear from all this that many people have an exaggerated view of the importance of manufacturing in the economy. But that leaves an important question unanswered. Is what is left of British manufacturing as bad as the half-empty-cup school of political economy would have us believe? Certainly there is a problem. From the beginning of 1979 to the end of 1995, output per person in manufacturing rose by a very impressive 78 per cent; and as we saw in Chapter 2, the productivity gap against Britain's main competitors has narrowed substantially. Yet an even more impressive statistic is that manufacturing output between 1973 and 1992 increased by no more than 1.3 per cent, implying that the enormous increase in efficiency in British manufacturing has generated hardly any extra output. Small wonder that manufacturing employment has plunged. Over the same two decades, meanwhile, the rise in manufactured output in Japan was 68.9 per cent, in Italy 68.6 per cent, in the US 55.2 per cent, in West Germany 32.1 per cent and in France 16.5 per cent.[7]

Does this depressing statistical litany mean that Britain has a fundamental problem of competitiveness in world markets? The economic purist would immediately respond that competitiveness is a characteristic of firms, not of nations. Yet this seems a poor description of the world in which we live. Most people would accept that Japanese success in manufacturing derives as much from national characteristics as from the competitiveness of individual manufacturers of cars or cameras. The uniquely high degree of trust that prevails in the Japanese firm and in the wider *keiretsu* groupings in which large Japanese firms operate is very helpful in running large-scale manufacturing operations. That consensualism is harnessed to a wider sense of national purpose.

This chapter will nonetheless concede that in much of British manufacturing competitiveness is a reflection of the capability of firms, not of specifically national advantages. Indeed, that is part of its problem – witness how Britain's business culture can simultaneously accommodate the protracted decline of British Leyland and the astonishing transformation of British Steel into the world's lowest-cost steel producer beside the South Koreans. Such erratic contrasts in performance, which could be rationalized as wayward British individualism raised to the corporate level, might even be regarded as a symptom of a national cultural handicap. They are certainly not what people have come to expect from the more collective cultures of Japan and Germany.

Yet I will also argue that the differences between Britain and these two countries can be exaggerated. There are highly successful areas of manufacturing where Britain does enjoy clear national advantages and where the high degree of trust more normally associated with stakeholder economies

contributes to British corporate success. These contrasting aspects of manufacturing can be seen by looking in turn at two leading British firms, GEC and
Glaxo. The performance of GEC in particular will help in unravelling the
puzzling coincidence of soaring productivity, stagnant output and the convergence of Britain's growth rate with that of its main competitors.

Industrial welfare dependency

GEC is, by British standards, a manufacturing colossus. It owns great chunks
of the UK power generation, telecommunications and electronics businesses,
along with a stake in such well-known consumer electrical brands as Hotpoint
and Creda. In its present form the company is essentially the creation of Arnold
Weinstock, who held the post of chief executive for more than three decades
before agreeing in 1996 to move upstairs to become honorary president.

Weinstock was a classic outsider. The son of Jewish immigrants from
Poland, he studied statistics at the London School of Economics before joining his father-in-law, Michael Sobell, in a business that made television sets.
When this was absorbed into GEC in 1961, Weinstock became a director and
by 1963 he was appointed chief executive. Weinstock's great achievement was
to amalgamate the giants of British electrical engineering, GEC, AEI and
English Electric, at a time when management in the industry was poor, financial discipline weak and strategic direction lacking. He was the first great
downsizer, long before the term was coined. In this he was supported by the
Industrial Reorganisation Corporation, the body set up by the 1964–70
Labour government to galvanize industry into improved competitiveness.
When it came to handing over the reins nearly 30 years after the hostile
takeover of AEI, Weinstock left a company in which financial discipline was
unquestionably strong, turnover was more than £10 billion and profits were
close to £900 million. Yet the quality of the management was hotly debated,
while critics alleged that the record on innovation and investment was poor.[8]

Like a mirror of the British economy, in which a greater share of
national income goes to military spending than in all the country's main competitors apart from the United States, GEC in the 1970s and 1980s was heavily reliant on the public sector for contracts. The main customer was the
Ministry of Defence, followed by such lumbering dinosaurs of state enterprise
as British Telecom, the Central Electricity Generating Board and British Rail.
This led to several apparent contradictions. While Weinstock was an

outspoken advocate of free enterprise, especially when Margaret Thatcher first came to power, he shared every businessperson's instinctive desire to minimize competition in the interests of profit. Far from being a paragon of competitiveness, GEC in the 1980s suffered from the industrial equivalent of welfare dependency, exhibiting in its defence subsidiaries all the inefficiencies traditionally associated with military-industrial complexes.

On the one hand Weinstock shocked both his fellow industrialists and the trade unions with the ruthlessness of his plant closures and lay-offs in the 1960s and 1970s. Yet he was surprisingly indulgent in dealing with the inefficiencies of the defence businesses in GEC-Marconi in the 1980s. These were a byword in industry for internal strife, with managers of the different subsidiaries sometimes being in a state bordering on civil war. A decentralized management approach bred a baronial culture in which the group chief executive, Weinstock, tolerated a situation in which two of the company's top executives were simply not on speaking terms. In Francis Fukuyama's language, this was a low-trust corporate culture in which the only real antidote to destructive individualism came in the shape of top-down financial control rather than internal behavioural restraints.

Weinstock's obsessive hatred of waste and his famously sharp eye for unnecessary expenditure meant that he was prepared to send a frisson through the City establishment by refusing to pay fees to Baring Brothers for its unsuccessful defence of AEI, where the profit forecast made at the time of the bid proved wildly optimistic. Yet he also presided over the construction of the notorious Nimrod early warning system, which saw cost overruns of more than £900 million. Nor was Nimrod an isolated case. Similar problems have arisen with the remote-controlled Phoenix spy plane, for which GEC is the prime contractor. By mid-1995 it was six years behind schedule and wildly over budget. With £227 million already spent on the plane, it was still prone to break up on landing.

This bizarre combination of penny pinching and financial laxity on the grand scale extended even into the GEC boardroom, where the chairman and executive directors were expected to pay for their own newspapers and BUPA healthcare contributions and to accept unusually close monitoring of their expenses. Yet when Weinstock himself finally vacated the chief executive's seat, the remuneration committee of the GEC board conceded a pay and incentive package to his successor, George Simpson, that incorporated a £1/2 million 'golden hello' to compensate him for the loss of incentives at his previous company Lucas Industries. As well as £600,000 of basic pay he was offered incentives and 'phantom' share options where the performance criteria were so short term and undemanding that even the normally quiescent investment institutions felt obliged to register concern. This was despite earlier protestations by Weinstock and GEC to the trade and industry select committee that the prevailing fashion for performance-related rewards tended 'to emphasise short-term results and put under pressure our capacity for long-term thinking and investment'.[9]

Financial engineering

A fundamental criticism levelled at the GEC style of management is that it emphasizes finance at the expense of marketing and technological innovation. A small group of managers at the headquarters in London's Stanhope Gate watch over a highly decentralized empire, in which managing directors of all the subsidiaries are required to send back a monthly financial report containing a series of financial ratios. Weinstock, with a short code on his telephone to all the managing directors, used to pounce on them if there was anything untoward in the numbers. This ritual would culminate in an annual budget meeting with Weinstock and his head office acolytes. The experience was generally acknowledged to be nerve-wracking for the managers, who were frequently subjected to a fearsome interrogation.

One effect of this process, some insiders admit, was to focus the managers' attention on next month or next year, rather than on the medium and long term. Once again reflecting the wider picture in the British economy, GEC spent less on research and development and filed many fewer patents than most of its big international competitors. The individual businesses within the group tended to know very little about each other, because their lines of communication were almost exclusively to the centre at Stanhope Gate. The scope for cooperative exploitation of GEC's scientific and technological knowledge base was thus limited.

In a revealing series of articles on GEC for the *Financial Times* in 1992, Charles Leadbeater demonstrated that, despite the rigours of its financial controls, GEC had sometimes been slow to grasp the extent of its problems. In the most telling case Peter Gershon, then managing director of the telecommunications subsidiary GPT, told Leadbeater that while GPT had been highly profitable, it had been overmanned and woefully slow to create new sources of income away from its main customer, the privatized British Telecom. In the defence businesses, outstanding technological potential frequently lay unexploited. The acquisitions of the 1980s, such as the American office equipment group A B Dick and part of the British electronics group Plessey, proved less profitable than had been hoped. Even an industrialist as expert in the takeover game as Arnold Weinstock could fall victim to the winner's curse.

All in all, GEC failed to turn into the internationally competitive concern that was expected to emerge from the amalgamation of the three big original businesses. By the end of the 1980s, under the pressure of a potential hostile takeover bid by a consortium headed by John Cuckney, best known for his rescues of the Crown Agents and the Westland helicopter group, GEC put much of its power engineering and telecommunications activities into joint ventures respectively with Alsthom of France and Siemens of Germany. General Electric of the US, with which GEC had previously had no direct connection, became a 50 per cent partner in its consumer durable businesses.

The synergy in these joint ventures seemed to consist chiefly of GEC providing cost discipline, while the partners provided innovative technology and marketing strength. Meantime new market opportunities in areas such as mobile phones went begging. Symbolic of GEC's apparent sclerosis was its mountain of £1.5 billion in unspent cash and investments. Earnings per share, the stock-market analysts' preferred measure of corporate performance, were only fractionally higher in 1995 than in 1990, having dipped in between. The stock market's verdict on the company was by then thoroughly downbeat. The shares consistently underperformed the market in the ten years before Arnold Weinstock felt obliged to take his leave.

Managing in a cold climate

Weinstock was a highly unusual manager. Nobody could accuse him of the worst of British corporate failings: GEC never became a byword for poor industrial relations as did British Leyland, despite the big redundancies. Indeed, there were some respects in which the management of this huge industrial machine more closely resembled that of a Jewish family business than the standard British engineering company with its pronounced class division between management and workers. But GEC under Weinstock's control did share some other less constructive British characteristics: the concentration of power at the top, the lack of cooperative teamwork between

individualistic managers in the divisions, the important role of fear in motivating people, the absence of a board capable of operating as a check and balance over the chief executive. That does not sound like the definition of a
viable corporate culture at the top level of the international business league.

Yet it is easy to be overcritical. In the defence area, the cost overruns on
Nimrod and other projects owed much to the insistence of the Ministry of
Defence on making constant changes to its requirements. The figures must
also be seen in the context of the tacit agreement that existed between defence
contractors and the Ministry of Defence to pitch their bids unrealistically low
in order to sneak past the unremitting gaze of Cerberus in the Treasury. This
budgetary low flying ensured future cost escalation. More generally, expectations of GEC were pitched unduly high, in that many of its critics wanted it
to be a national champion in areas such as computers, semiconductors and
consumer electronics. The experience of trying to build national champions in
the rest of Europe has, in fact, been poor. The strategic investment by the
German giant Siemens in computers and semiconductors since the 1970s has
been hugely costly and not noticeably successful. Groupe Bull, the vehicle for
French attempts to build a presence in the global computer industry, has been
a disaster *tout court*. In consumer electronics Thomson of France has failed to
make a mark against the powerful US and Japanese competition, while the
Dutch group Philips, whose capacity for technological innovation is second to
none, found itself in dire financial trouble at the start of the decade as it tried
to meet the full blast of Japan's industrial might.

Weinstock told the *Financial Times* in 1992 that people were always
wanting him to make things that caused other companies to incur huge losses.
And with hindsight, there is much to be said for GEC not having been a
national champion in these areas. It is possible that the ever-cautious
Weinstock may have been more judicious in this than his critics. Geoffrey
Owen, a leading business academic and former editor of the *Financial Times*,
has suggested that the story of British electronics over the past 20 years could
be seen as a case of domestically owned companies redeploying their resources
on the basis of a realistic appraisal of their own strengths and weaknesses.
They chose to confront increasingly intense international competition only in
those products where it was feasible to operate profitably from a British base.[10]

Many of Weinstock's detractors also presupposed that capital investment, together with spending on research and development, was intrinsically
'virtuous'. This is a misleading assumption. Japan owes the dismal performance of its economy in the first half of the 1990s partly to excessive invest-

ment in the 1980s that yielded uneconomic returns. Here we have come close to the answer to the question of why Britain's rate of economic growth has been converging with the other main developed countries, despite apparent underinvestment. It is that in low-saving, low-investing countries such as Britain and the US the productivity of capital is much higher, which is just what one might expect where the system has been imposing much tougher pressure for high returns. The message is that continental Europe and Japan invest heavily but extract inadequate returns from their investments; the Anglo-Saxons underinvest, but squeeze the maximum out of what they do.[11]

Seen in that light, the amalgamations that Weinstock engineered with Alsthom of France and Siemens of Germany appear in a less negative perspective. If the result is that British financial discipline is extended to these joint ventures without impairing the innovative capacity of the Germans and French, it will be all to the good. Indeed, it could be argued that expertise in financial control is one of the few clearly national competitive advantages that the British enjoy in manufacturing. What is sometimes seen as an excessive reliance on accountancy in the British business culture has led to a more cost-conscious pursuit of productivity than in Germany or France. James Prior, GEC chairman, points out that it was a considerable advantage, in striking these alliances, to be able to bring Weinstock's formidable ability to control cash to the joint venturers' party. He argues that GEC's foreign joint ventures reflected both vision and realism on Weinstock's part in confronting the loss of domestic customers.

There have been other more tangible advantages in GEC's joint ventures. Since the Germans and French continue to protect some of the domestic markets that ought to offer opportunities to GEC, partnership provides market access. In the end, joint ventures with overseas partners were a logical, if belated, response to the predicament of a company that simultaneously confronted a much tougher environment for defence spending, the privatization of its biggest customers, deregulation in markets such as telecoms and electricity and an end to new investment in domestic nuclear power plants.[12] Those who attack GEC for its failures to innovate also forget that Weinstock was having to conduct a difficult balancing act in maintaining relationships with existing customers at the same time as establishing new ones. A big investment in mobile telephony might have risked alienating British Telecom.

The history of GEC provides a big clue to the extraordinary combination of dynamic productivity and dismal growth in manufacturing output that has characterized the British economy over the past two decades. Bad macroeconomic management has fostered an extremely defensive managerial culture in industry. Weinstock was the prime exponent of that culture; and his temperament was a very suitable one for managing a capital-intensive manufacturing business in a period of poor policy, difficult labour relations and exceptionally high inflation. When inflation is accelerating very rapidly, the rising cost of replacing stocks, and old plant and machinery, imposes heavy financial strains on such companies. A short-term financial focus is helpful, perhaps even essential, for survival in such an environment.

To have weathered successive recessions from the mid-1970s to the early 1990s and emerged with £1.5 billion in the bank was in reality a monumental achievement, given that Weinstock had to cope not only with ill-judged macroeconomic policy, but with much better judged microeconomic policy. The liberalization of telecommunications and electricity generation was intended precisely to make companies such as GEC more efficient. Weinstock may have been slow to recognize that industrial welfare dependency was ceasing to be a lucrative game. And there are other grounds for criticizing him, notably in relation to corporate governance and the management of his own succession, which will be considered later. But on business strategy history will, I suspect, be kinder to him than some currently allow.

After Arnold

The disciplines appropriate in a world of underperforming industrial management and high inflation are not necessarily suitable for today's much more competitive environment, in which disinflation rather than inflation is the overwhelming feature of the financial background. There is a growing body of opinion among management academics that business in the English-speaking economies has developed a cost-cutting culture at the expense of innovation and the generation of revenue. That looks an apt description of GEC, as indeed it does of many other decentralized industrial groups such as Hanson, which was similarly fearful of international competition.

These financially oriented companies rationalized and downsized at a time when it served a valuable purpose. In the 1960s and 1970s British manufacturing was in need of a shake-up. But just as the need for a continuing high level of aggressive takeover activity now looks questionable, GEC's style of financial management appears a less obvious virtue in dealing with the challenges of the twenty-first century. A national competitive advantage in finance may similarly be less helpful than in the past.

The question for GEC in the post-Weinstock era is whether it can acquire a *modus operandi* which is more sympathetic to teamwork and technological creativity. The alternative may be genteel decline. Another worry must be that Weinstock's own judgement on share-incentive schemes, which GEC expounded to the Commons trade and industry committee in 1994, will prove correct in his own backyard. The potentially distorting effect of short-term share incentives for the new chief executive and his colleagues could easily distract them from the long-term development of this extremely complex business. Adopting the gin rummy style of management and hacking away at the corporate structure would present an all-too-easy escape from uncomfortable economic reality. This is a theme which will be explored further in Chapter 8.

The British drug culture

Some UK companies have managed to strike a happier balance between financial discipline and revenue generation and have demonstrated more impressive capacity for growth in a cold climate. Foremost among them are the drugs companies, such as Glaxo, Beecham, Wellcome and Zeneca, the former pharmaceuticals business of ICI. Although now confronting more difficult market conditions, Glaxo could reasonably claim to have been the British wonder company of the past 15 years. Its rise is worth exploring, because it illustrates how flexibly companies and people can respond to the threats and opportunities of the global marketplace, and how competitiveness in the UK can arise from specifically national advantages and from stakeholder-type values.

To a considerable degree, Glaxo owes its position as the world's leading drugs company to Paul Girolami, the son of Italian immigrants. A chartered accountant by training, he was, like Weinstock, always more at ease with a large pile of cash in his balance sheet. While he did not rationalize a whole industry, the results of his overhaul of a well-known but unexciting company – its name was originally associated in the public mind with a brand of baby food – were spectacular.

Glaxo at the end of the 1970s was involved in wholesaling, foods, generic pharmaceutical and veterinary products, surgical equipment and many other disparate products. It then took a radical decision under Girolami to concentrate its activities on a single area: prescription medicines. It adopted a policy of organic growth, with no resort to takeovers. And it decided that its focus should be completely international.

Girolami was admittedly fortunate in that British pharmaceutical companies have operated in a much more benign domestic climate than the one enjoyed by the businesses in the modern GEC. In the early post-war period they were helped by the fact that economies of scale in pharmaceutical research were sufficiently small for medium-sized companies to be able to develop exciting new drugs despite living in a highly competitive market. Other advantages included a strong British science base in chemistry and biology, a receptive market for drugs in the national health system, sympathetic regulation and a patent system that guaranteed high profits for successful innovation.

While these factors were no doubt helpful, they cannot account for the full extent of Glaxo's huge international success under Girolami and his team of managers and scientists. Between 1980 and Girolami's retirement in 1994, expenditure on research and development rose from £32 million to £858 million. Eleven major new drugs were launched in world markets during that period, of which Zantac, the anti-ulcer treatment, was the most astonishingly successful. Profits rose from £66 million to £1.8 billion during that period.[13] By 1995 Glaxo had overtaken the giants of the Swiss and US pharmaceuticals industry to become the world's largest drugs company. It is an interesting reflection on the British national psyche that while most men and women on the Clapham omnibus know about the decline and fall of British Leyland, few know of the rise and rise of Glaxo.

At the outset Girolami staked Glaxo's future on Zantac. If the drug had produced unexpected side effects after millions had been spent on its development, that would have been the end of Glaxo as an independent drugs company and of Girolami's career at its helm. Much of its success derived from brilliant marketing, a supposedly un-British skill. Where a company like EMI foundered, in the 1970s, in trying to sell its superb brain and body scanners in the US and elsewhere, Glaxo succeeded beyond all expectation with its new drugs. It established a global marketing network almost from scratch. And it managed, with its most successful product, Zantac, to outsell the competition despite Zantac's not being a notably superior product to the chief alternative from SmithKline Beecham. Equally important, Girolami's research and development director at the time, David Jack, found ways of speeding up the tortuous development process. He took the risk, for example, of initiating long-term testing for the toxicity of Zantac before the results of the short-term tests were known.

Middle-class intangible values

The internal culture of Glaxo could not have been more different from that of GEC. The structure was not hierarchical but horizontal, which makes for easier dissemination and sharing of knowledge in a science-based business. Although Girolami's background may have been in accounting, there were no rigid planning and budgeting techniques. It was a teamwork system founded, according to Girolami, on qualities of competence, integrity and loyalty, rather than on bureaucratic control. The aim was to accommodate and make the most of the creative talents of the scientists, since the value in Glaxo lay not in its manufacturing processes but in the knowledge in the scientists' heads.

This is another way of saying that Glaxo was a company with a high degree of social capital, the wealth that derives from the readiness of individuals to subordinate their immediate interests to a wider group on the basis of shared values. The value in the business derived very largely from the quality of the relationships within the firm. Perhaps it comes relatively easily to a scientific community, since rivalry in science has always coexisted with a commitment to the sharing of knowledge. And the community ethos was cemented at Glaxo by the widespread participation of employees in share-incentive schemes. That is not to say that everyone in the company was invariably happy. When companies expand at break-neck speed that is rarely achieved, least of all when very creative people are involved. Yet no one can deny that the balance which Glaxo established between creative individualism and corporate cooperation produced results.

While Glaxo remains the biggest single supplier of prescription medicines to the National Health Service, its future is largely independent of the NHS. With only 9 per cent of its revenues coming from the UK in 1994 this immensely successful drugs company had achieved its own kind of immunity from the British macroeconomic disease. GEC was, incidentally, dependent for 45 per cent of its revenues on the UK at that time, while more than half its profits were still of domestic origin. As for labour relations, the great bugbear of large British companies in the 1960s and 1970s, this was no problem for what was, in effect, a middle-class company. The trust values of stakeholding are much more easily achieved when one of the biggest barriers to the sense of community has been removed. And Glaxo triumphantly demonstrated that it was possible to take on the international opposition by investing in research and development of the most advanced kind, instead of buying up other companies in Britain's hyperactive takeover market. In pharmaceuticals, research rather than manufacture is the difficult thing; and research seems to come more easily to the British than does production.

Thatcher's orphan

Glaxo's was undeniably the outstanding industrial success story of the Thatcher period. Yet Paul Girolami and his team were not greatly lionized by the press for their achievements. Indeed, perceptions of Britain's business successes at the time were oddly distorted. The Sunday papers devoted far more space to the acquisitive and mostly ephemeral entrepreneurs who were known as 'Thatcher's children'. Among them were Maurice and Charles Saatchi, the brothers whose expansionary global ambitions outstripped their managerial and financial capabilities; Martin Sorrell, of whom much the same could be said; John Gunn of the conglomerate British & Commonwealth, which collapsed; and John Ashcroft, of the carpets-to-crockery group Coloroll, where a succession of quick-fire takeovers, huge borrowings and controversial accounting policies led to sudden death at the hands of the receiver. Glaxo did admittedly feature in a book by a British journalist in which it was compared with its bigger US rival Merck. Yet the author was highly critical of the management and forecast, wrongly, that Glaxo would never overtake its US rival to become the world's leading drug company.[14]

There is, however, one place where Glaxo and the other pharmaceutical companies are given high praise. In the City the British drugs industry is invariably quoted as an example of the financial community being prepared to take a long-term view and Glaxo is happy to acknowledge good relations with the financial community. The stock market certainly tolerated a high level of spending on research and development and always accorded Glaxo a high rating while Girolami was in charge. A more sobering reflection on the Glaxo story is that, despite profits increasing by a phenomenal 27 times between 1980 and 1994, the average number of UK employees went down by nearly 20 per cent over the same period, from just under 15,000 to only 12,000. This compares with 56,000 employed in the UK by GEC. Under a new boss, Richard Sykes, the company also started acquiring and rationalizing, in the face of tougher public spending constraints on health authorities around the world. More jobs went after the takeover of Wellcome in 1995.

One important lesson that emerges from the Glaxo story is that the values of stakeholding are far from alien to the British business culture. They are characteristic of some of the very best British companies such as Glaxo or Marks & Spencer. It is only because the values are intangible and are not captured by an unreconstructed accountancy profession that the point is generally unappreciated. Another lesson is that in today's very open global marketplace economies and firms are exceptionally adaptable. Entrepreneurial effort can take forms that play to the innate structural and cultural strengths (or overcome the respective weaknesses) of the countries concerned in a manner that would not be possible in a more closed trading environment. Among those structural strengths is the quality of the higher education system, which has been particularly important for Glaxo. Should that quality decline, the research in British drug companies will be done by increasingly well-educated foreign graduates overseas.

A big question for companies such as Glaxo is how easily they can preserve their social capital, having grown to a size where trust can very easily become the victim of the bureaucratic imperative. Perhaps even more difficult is preserving the high-trust ethos while going through the rigours of the Anglo-Saxon takeover process. Since the takeover of Wellcome, Glaxo has inevitably been a less happy concern. This serves as a reminder that an important feature of the stakeholder economy is that social capital is difficult to accumulate and easy to erode. Nothing illustrates this better than the recent history of the City of London, to which we now turn.

5

'*If you want loyalty, get a dog...*'

*W*hile the British economy was steadily improving its performance in the decade and a half after 1979, London was cementing its position as the global leader in international finance. Few would have predicted the extent to which high finance contributed to growth and employment. The City's recent record is worth analysing because it tells us a great deal about how an economy can generate new jobs despite such fundamental disadvantages as a low level of fixed investment or a bias towards short-termism. It also holds a number of lessons about the value of trust in commercial relations and the high costs that arise when trust erodes.

An inherent feature of international financial activity is that it seems to gravitate naturally to a single leading centre. Over five centuries, leadership has passed successively from Venice to Antwerp, Genoa, Amsterdam, London and New York, with other cities acting as regional satellites to the pre-eminent centre of the day.[1] But unlike the others, London has not seen its role wane as might have been expected as a result of relative economic decline and the diminished role of sterling since 1914.

Helped by the liberating influence of information technology, finance has also become divorced from its geographical roots. The docks and depositories that made London the warehouse of the world in the nineteenth century have been closed or turned into flats. But finance still thrives beside and beyond the Thames in dealing rooms stuffed with electronic screens. The peculiarity of this trade in banking and securities is that it is no longer possible to identify the precise location of the market. It is, so to speak, the ghost in the global telecommunications machine. And while the dealers still occupy a physical location, they are among the few who genuinely inhabit what Marshall McLuhan dubbed the global village, maintaining close relations with fellow dealers in financial centres across the world.

A second, and more surprising, liberating force for British finance has been the influence of the Bank of England. In its desire to see London reestablish its international role, the Bank conducted from the late 1950s a carefully controlled experiment in liberalization, of which the most important feature was an open-door policy towards foreign banks in the Square Mile. While the economy was circumscribed by exchange controls, these banks were permitted to do whatever international business they wished, provided that they left the domestic markets to British banks and steered clear of sterling-related activity.

Under the Bank of England's regime, formal regulation was light while informal behavioural norms were reinforced by a system of nods and winks administered via the Bank's discount office. British taxation was accommodating to foreigners, as was the political climate. These things mattered, because regulation and taxes in New York, a financial centre backed by the world's strongest economy and leading reserve currency, were restrictive. The Bank of England had discovered the freeport principle. The result was that the centre of gravity in international finance shifted from New York, where it rightly belonged, to London, as US companies and financial institutions discovered that they could often raise and trade dollar capital more cheaply and flexibly in what came to be known as the Euromarkets. American bankers poured across the Atlantic to set up shop in the City. In a huge, successful continental economy where international trade and finance played a relatively minor part, American politicians scarcely noticed that their country was forfeiting its natural role in international finance. It was, in a curious way, fitting that a country with a strong populist distaste for banks should have exported so many of its bankers to Europe to do their business at a healthy distance from the American people.

The domestic side of the City, meantime, operated largely on a self-regulatory basis whereby the main markets such as the Stock Exchange and

Lloyd's of London were run as clubs, with little interference from Whitehall or anywhere else. Within the club ethos, misdemeanours were easily punished without resort to law. If, for example, an egregious case of insider dealing caused a loss to a jobbing firm – almost always the biggest victims of this practice – the jobbers could either find a way of squeezing the miscreant in the marketplace or seek informal redress within the club. Business could be diverted away from those who engaged in anti-social behaviour.

The banking system was hierarchical, with a complex system of licences and authorizations. While regulatory responsibility lay partly with the Department of Trade, the Bank of England supervised most banks of any size. It permitted advancement up the hierarchy on the basis of good behaviour, while employing an informal signalling system that used to be referred to as 'the governor's eyebrows'. The system was not meritocratic, but it was orderly. It embodied a high degree of social capital, in that people were happy to forgo opportunistic short-term behaviour in their own longer-term interest within the club. And the discipline of the hostile takeover was not permitted among the clearing banks and the long-established merchant banks.

Darwin comes to market

The big growth in the City's post-war business was on the international side. London was fortunate in that trade, which requires finance, grew at a much faster rate than the world economy in the post-war period. And the final ingredient which turned prosperity into an astonishing boom was the collapse of the Bretton Woods fixed exchange-rate system in the early 1970s. Until then, governments had undertaken the task of stabilizing currencies. They also chose to stabilize domestic banking and financial markets through tight regulatory controls – a legacy of the banking collapses of the 1930s. Once the fixed exchange-rate regime fell apart, the job of managing currencies was, in effect, privatized. At the same time, Edward Heath's government in Britain was among the first to start relaxing controls on domestic markets and sweeping away banking cartels. In the maelstrom that followed, all participants in the markets badly needed to take out private insurance against increased financial volatility, as currencies and interest rates fluctuated more abruptly.[2]

The academic fraternity, most notably the economics department of the University of Chicago, promptly obliged by providing new techniques and blueprints for financial products known as derivatives – swaps, options, forwards, futures and other esoteric financial instruments. When combined with computing power, these innovations provided the wherewithal to take much of the pain out of the new Darwinian financial environment. For example, they allowed industrialists to lock in today's exchange rates or interest rates to protect themselves from market movements that might otherwise destroy the competitiveness of their future exports or undermine their balance sheet by raising the cost of borrowings. At the hub of international finance, London was well placed to provide such new forms of insurance against the dramatic increase in market volatility. It was in the position of a drug company which sees its revenues soar in an epidemic.

When Margaret Thatcher took office in 1979, she gave the international financiers a further shot in the arm, when her chancellor Geoffrey Howe lifted exchange controls. From then on British fund managers were free to invest as much as they wished overseas. And as other countries followed suit in scrapping exchange controls, growing amounts of capital flowed around the global marketplace in search of the highest returns, much of it passing through London en route.

The financial revolution reached its peak with the Big Bang on the Stock Exchange in 1986. After heavy lobbying by the Bank of England, the government decided to short-circuit legal proceedings taken by the Office of Fair Trading over Stock Exchange restrictive practices. It struck a deal with the exchange whereby the stockbrokers and jobbers agreed to the deregulation of their marketplace. What had hitherto been a club was opened up to foreign firms; the fixed commissions on securities transactions were abolished; and the dealing system was completely overhauled. Trading quickly moved from the Stock Exchange floor to screens in dealing rooms. This was the last step in a chain of events that had transformed finance from a service offered chiefly to domestic customers into an internationally tradeable commodity. London had achieved a feat probably unique in history by retaining leadership in international finance without the benefit of a leading position in international trade or a dominant global currency. While New York and Tokyo were bigger financial centres, their respective shares of purely international business were less than London's. In a tripolar financial world, each was pre-eminent in its own time zone.

Just as the early stages of the Industrial Revolution were devoted mainly to making existing products more efficiently, the financial revolution offered little that was new in principle. Even derivative instruments had been known in one form or another to earlier generations: the ancient Greeks understood the principle behind financial options. But with an advanced technological spin, and a new demand for private insurance against financial instability, these markets turned into some of the most spectacular growth industries of the twentieth century.

The alchemy of high finance

The story of the City's post-war growth underlines a largely unremarked, if obvious, message that occurs repeatedly with British economic successes. More often than not, the achievement is rooted in industries or companies making themselves independent of the fortunes of a badly run domestic economy. This was starkly underlined in the City's case in the mid-1970s in the aftermath of the first oil crisis. Banks in the Square Mile played a central role in petrodollar recycling – the process whereby the oil producers' burgeoning revenues were transferred through the international banking system to other less-developed countries whose oil bills were soaring to the detriment of their balance of payments. But while the City boomed with the growth of petro-dollar business and foreign currency dealing, sterling was plunging, inflation as measured by the retail price index hit a post-war peak of 27 per cent and government borrowing was out of control. Such was the deterioration in the British economy that the Labour government was forced to subcontract its monetary and fiscal policy to the International Monetary Fund.

Much the same was true in the recession of the early 1980s. While industry wilted under the heat of a greatly overvalued exchange rate, the City thrived as the flow of cross-border capital movements accelerated. And just as the Americans had driven much of their financial business overseas through tight regulation, over-regulated banks in Japan – now the world's biggest cred-itor country – had started trekking overseas too. In the second half of the decade, London saw a boom in everything yen related, as Japanese companies discovered that they could raise capital more cheaply away from home.

This was, in fact, the perfect business activity for a country plagued by poor macroeconomic management. International finance is a service industry in which the capital that matters is human capital. Since the most important investments are in people, not plant and machinery, financiers are less both-ered than industrialists over payback periods and target rates of return in a period of inflationary and disinflationary extremes. To sell insurance against financial uncertainty in a country where politicians have shown a remarkable capacity for destabilizing the economy is to be in the position of the medieval alchemist who holds exclusive rights to a formula for turning base metal into gold.

Where macroeconomic management had failed, microeconomic management, partly thanks to the Bank of England, had been successful: Britain had hit on a tax and regulatory structure that was well designed to enhance the City's competitive position in the European time zone. It was a classic illustration of how comparative advantage in the modern world often stems less from geography and natural resource endowment than from the skills of the workforce and an enabling fiscal and regulatory environment.

Here, then, is a small but intriguing part of the explanation why Britain's growth rate has not lagged behind that of its main competitors since 1979, despite a seemingly low level of investment, and why its employment record looks better than that of continental Europe. Given half a chance by the politicians, economies are remarkably robust and adaptable. If one part of a reasonably flexible market economy is losing comparative advantage, resources will be redeployed to other, more promising parts of the economy. All the net new jobs in the British economy in the decade to 1990 were generated in services. Within that, the financial services sector, of which the City is an important part, made a contribution of more than a quarter of a million net new jobs. This was despite the dramatic decline in the fortunes of the Lloyd's insurance market following scandals that did irreparable damage to its reputation. And the figure understates the wider employment benefit from the City's international activities, which prompted heavy expenditure on new office blocks and substantial investment in computing and telecommunications infrastructure.

London's freeport game is rumbled

The question today is whether the City's success is really sustainable and whether it offers a model for the rest of the economy in terms of job creation. On the face of it the job-generating potential of the banks and securities houses in the 1990s appears to have slowed, while the competition in international financial services has increased. All across Europe governments have recognized the nature of Britain's financial freeport game and have responded by deregulating markets and staging their own Big Bangs. Such is the growth in the volume of international financial activity that the City's business has continued to grow. But its market share has been declining in most areas. And there have been ominous signs that a period of spectacular growth concealed fundamental weaknesses in the workings of the financial community.

One can be seen in the recent traumas of the London Stock Exchange. So disastrous were its attempts to introduce a new system for settling transactions in the mid-1990s that the Bank of England felt obliged to take over the whole project. Internal quarrels, particularly over the reform of the Stock Exchange's dealing system, have contributed to the enforced departure of two chief executives in quick succession. And the exchange's system for dealing in international stocks and shares, known as Seaq International, has seen a serious loss of business to continental European exchanges.

These tribulations owe much to the changing economics of running stock exchanges. In the days when the London Stock Exchange had a domestic monopoly, it was close to being a utility. It existed to enable mainly British investors to buy and sell securities and to permit companies to raise fresh capital. In today's deregulated global marketplace, stock exchanges are thrown into competition with each other and new exchanges are opening up in an attempt to win business from the established players. With technology taking securities activity away from dealing floors, it becomes harder to answer the question of what a stock exchange, traditionally the home of a physical marketplace, is really for.

In such a world, the need for more sophisticated management becomes imperative. The London Stock Exchange has conspicuously failed to rise to the challenge. One reason is that its ownership, which is dominated by the larger securities firms, is inappropriate to what is now a commercial business fighting for its own survival, even though it retains functions in which there is an important public interest. And the balance between the various stakeholders – securities firms, investors and companies – has been unevenly struck.

Because the big securities firms have invested heavily in the existing dealing system, they have been reluctant to move rapidly to a different system, even though many large investors, especially Americans who own not far short of 10 per cent of all the shares quoted on the stock market, would prefer this. And they know that most of the return on the exchange's investment in a new and expensive high-tech dealing system would accrue to institutional investors, not to the securities firms that put up the money. This means that any chief executive who wishes to sustain and enhance the exchange's competitive advantage is bound to quarrel with the owners of the business. The failure fully to complete the transition from a club to a properly accountable

commercial concern will lead to a progressive loss of market share. In its present form the London Stock Exchange is condemned to long-run genteel
decline.

Another sign of weakness in the City lies in the collapse of Barings,
Britain's oldest and most patrician merchant bank. At the time of its humili-
ating demise in 1995 at the hands of a 27-year-old rogue trader, Nick Leeson,
Barings was an insignificant force in international finance. If it was known at
all to the great British public, it was because a broker called Christopher
Heath, while a director of Barings, enjoyed the highest pay in the country
thanks to bonuses earned on his dealings in Far Eastern markets. Much nonsense was written about the irreparable damage to the reputation and credit of
the City that would result from the failure to mount a successful rescue for
Barings. Little devastation has since been apparent. The bank is now thriving
under its new Dutch owner, ING, which bought the business from the admin-
istrators. Yet Barings was important as both a symptom and a symbol of wider
weaknesses in the British system, starting with the failure of the management
to exert adequate control over its renegade trader in Singapore.

Management has not been the City's forte. Only recently have bankers
adopted the financial skills long used in manufacturing industry to establish
the cost and profitability of particular products and services. In merchant
banking the management style has traditionally been very informal, with
strategy taking second place to frenetic market activity and the demands of
corporate clients. In those cases where merchant banks have had a clear
strategy, they have often failed in the implementation. The botched attempt
by S G Warburg, Britain's most admired merchant bank, to merge with
Morgan Stanley of the US, and its subsequent ignominious takeover by Swiss
Bank Corporation, was a sad case in point. In Warburgs, as at Barings, many
of those at the top were experienced in corporate finance – raising capital and
advising on mergers and acquisitions – but less well versed in the securities
operations that they had purchased in preparation for the liberalization of the
stock market in 1986.

It is clear that the City's office blocks and dealing floors are peopled
with some of the most capable financial barrow boys, whiz kids and deal makers in the world, whatever we may think of their values. Yet the haphazard performance of its domestically owned merchant banks leaves the inescapable
impression that its officer class is deficient. This was no great disadvantage in
the pre-Big-Bang period when the domestic players in the City operated in a
club ethos. Even afterwards, the growth in financial services was so rapid that

the cracks were easily papered over. But today skilled management is at a premium in financial services, chiefly because the business of finance is being revolutionized by the globalization of markets, fast-changing technology, deregulation and the growth of trading in derivative instruments; but also because human capital in the newly meritocratic City is volatile and opportunistic to an unprecedented and dangerous degree. In place of trust has come the ethos of everyone for himself.

The economics of the zoo

The economist Albert Wojnilower, formerly of First Boston and now senior economic adviser to the Clipper Group in the US, has compared this deregulated global financial environment to a zoo. In the days before deregulation, everything in the zoo was well kept and orderly. Different species such as banks, securities dealers and insurance companies were neatly housed and fed in separate cages segregated by their respective functions and geographical scope. The bars between the cages prevented the various species from preying on each other. Within each cage, there was, as in a real zoo, competition over the pecking order and the best food; but vigilant keepers – the regulators and central bankers – made sure that this never led to injury or death. The British version was closer to Whipsnade than London Zoo, with more of the barriers being of a self-regulatory nature. But the broad principle was the same.[3]

A combination of technology and regulatory change then destroyed this orderly environment by smashing the barriers that separated the animals. Hitherto protected creatures were freed to become predator and prey in an unfamiliar jungle where there was not enough food – profit – to go round. In these circumstances, the ethical norms of the past too easily break down and the law of the jungle prevails.

The process had actually started in Britain in the 1970s, where the gap between the respective regulatory territories of the Department of Trade and the Bank of England had paved the way for the growth of 'fringe' banks run by entrepreneurs who were prepared to explore the limits of this regulatory no-man's-land in their pursuit of banking profits. Against a background of rising inflation they were particularly active in the property market, where under-regulated finance not only came to threaten the security of the banking system; it had a marked impact on the way we live. The fringe bankers acted as the catalyst for gentrification in the inner cities by financing a huge transfer of residential property from old and respectable landlords to the winklers who were expert in gaining vacant possession through various legal forms of harassment. Ill-conceived rent controls bore chief responsibility for the collapse of the normal relationship between landlord and tenant. But Tony Blair would probably not now be living in Islington if the fringe bankers had not been there to clear the way for the upwardly mobile middle class.

At Lloyd's, the insurance market, a shortage of capital encouraged leading members of the club to look to outsiders, both at home and overseas, to bring in new funds. This destroyed the trust ethos of the old club. The less reputable members then started to divert more lucrative business into separate syndicates for their own benefit, while pushing the more dangerous insurance risks on to those from outside. The introduction of foreign capital to the Stock Exchange had less obviously fraudulent consequences, but there too, ethical standards dropped under the much increased competitive pressure that resulted from deregulation. Much more capital was chasing too little business, especially after the 1987 stock-market crash. In the later stages of the Thatcher era, a 'greed is good' philosophy started to pervade the exchange as individualism triumphed over the more staid ethos of the old-style hierarchy.

Goodbye Barings

This was, in effect, a return to the financial environment of the nineteenth century. But there are important differences, one of which is that today's derivatives trading can make banks go bust much faster than when Barings last overextended itself by financing infrastructure in Argentina in the 1890s. At the end of December 1994, Leeson's losses stood at £24 million. By the end of February when the bank collapsed, the total losses had rocketed to £860 million. If there is management weakness in an organization, or weakness in the financial controls, derivatives trading will expose it ruthlessly. British financiers are thus in a similar position in the 1990s to that of British manufacturers in the 1880s who started to lose competitive advantage as new industries called for greater scientific education. Many are amateurs in a market that calls for increasing professionalism.[4]

That was certainly the case at Barings. The Bank of England's board of banking supervision found that the top executives had presided over a bank where there was 'a failure of controls of management and other internal controls of the most basic kind'. The biggest error was to allow Leeson to retain control over the back office where his dealing activities were recorded. He was thus in a position to falsify or conceal evidence of what he was doing. Communications within the bank were, at best, rudimentary. According to one former Barings executive, if you were not good at reading what was in the mind of the chairman Peter Baring and his fellow directors you were deemed to be poor merchant-banking material. The one thing that was not in the directors' minds was an understanding of the kind of derivatives trading that Leeson was conducting on the exchanges of Osaka and Singapore.

In a television interview before his extradition to Singapore, Leeson expressed little more than contempt for his superiors. Given the circumstances, this elicited sympathy in pubs across the land. There was even support for the dishonest dealer from the pulpit. Brian Quinn, then responsible for banking supervision at the Bank of England, was enraged to find himself listening to a Sunday sermon at his local church in which Leeson was held up as an object of sympathy. Part of the job of central bank supervisors is to deliver stern moral lectures to deviant bankers. Quinn brought this talent to bear on the hapless cleric after the service.

While some features of the Barings collapse were unique, it was nonetheless revealing about many of the changes that had taken place in the City. Under the impact of deregulation and new technology, relationships are eroding everywhere. At one level, large companies now cut out the banking middleman and go direct to the markets for funds. Even when they do raise money from the banking system, much of the borrowing is provided by syndicates of banks, which dilutes any sense of loyalty, especially on the bankers' side if the company gets into trouble. Meantime bank loans themselves have become a saleable commodity. The British home owner who raises money from a bank that appears to be offering an attractive mortgage rate may well find that in due course he or she is in debt to a completely different bank, because the first lender has sold its complete portfolio of mortgage loans. At the most basic level – cash – the automated teller machine has distanced the customer from bank employees.

This depersonalization of finance, and the erosion of relationships of trust, is even more apparent in the securities markets. Derivative instruments like futures and options incorporate only the most tenuous form of ownership right. In the main, those who deal in derivatives on a day-to-day basis for their bank as Nick Leeson did regard themselves as trading in risks, rather than in property rights. They have little or no interest in actual companies, even when options give them a potential claim on shares. There is also a lack of trust between the exchanges that preside over derivatives dealing. Many of those involved in investigating and picking up the pieces after the Barings fiasco believe that the competitive nature of the relationship between the Osaka Stock Exchange in Japan and the SIMEX exchange in Singapore prevented a sharing of information about Barings' exposures that would have led to earlier curbs on Leeson's activities.

The same erosion of trust has taken place within organizations. In the days of the club ethic, the City was admittedly not very efficient. Sophisticated marketing for many stockbrokers consisted of taking a client to the races or a nightclub. Hours were short and lunches long. But the clear class division between the people in charge and the lower orders meant that those who ran the City knew whom they could deal with on the basis of trust. My word is my bond, the old Stock Exchange motto, may not have been observed with absolute integrity all of the time, but it is certainly true that financial controls in banks and securities houses were buttressed by inside knowledge derived from personal acquaintanceship that went back to school. The ease with which Leeson rose within such a traditional merchant banks as Barings despite a checkered past that included a court appearance for non-payment of debt speaks volumes about the changing sociology of the City. He owed everything to the profits he declared; nothing to his family background.

The bonus before all else

Leeson's rise underlines another novel aspect of the new City sociology: the marked shift that has taken place in the balance of power between the corporation and the individual employee. The employee has been the clear gainer. This is because revenues in financial services can often readily be identified with the efforts of particular individuals. Moreover, the nature of the whole-sale financial markets, which involve transactions by big companies and institutions as opposed to individual investors and savers, is that banks can make huge profits by charging tiny fractions of a percent on the billions of capital that pass through the City. The same logic applies to individuals, who are increasingly rewarded with huge bonuses. At Barings, for example, Peter Baring, the chairman, and Peter Norris, who was responsible for the securities operations, were both expecting bonuses of £1 million when the bank went down. Deputy chairman Andrew Tuckey was scheduled to receive a bonus of £1.65 million. Leeson, meantime, stood to receive a bonus of £450,000 – all this on profits that did not in fact exist because they were being wiped out by Leeson's unauthorized trading in futures on the Japanese Nikkei index.

The incentive arrangements within banks today are sometimes such that a single deal will enrich the dealer for life. In that climate, the less principled dealers will cheerfully sacrifice the reputation of their bank in their own interest. Incentives can become doubly perverse if dealers run into losses. If they think that they will be out of a job if the losses are discovered, they may be tempted to increase their exposure in the markets, thereby jeopardizing the bank, in the hope of trading their way out of trouble. How far Leeson was influenced by such pressures in racking up his huge losses is unclear. But at Barings the incentives were perverse in the rather different sense that some of those at the top of the bank did surprisingly well out of the collapse.

One of the many iron laws of British public life dictates that failure must never go unrewarded. Ministers who have done their best to wreck the economy find their way into the House of Lords and on to the boards of large banks and industrial companies. Civil servants who have aided and abetted them move effortlessly up the Whitehall ladder. The Barings fiasco indicates that the iron law now extends to the City. For neither the chairman Peter Baring nor his deputy Andrew Tuckey were subjected to any penalty by the regulatory authorities, although sanctions were imposed on more junior executives. Tuckey, meanwhile, continued to earn large fees when the bank was taken over by ING and was rewarded with a considerable payoff and pension when he left in 1996.

This was all of a piece with the way Barings' executives conveyed the impression at the time of the collapse that they were more concerned for their bonuses than for the bondholders who had lent Barings their money. The preservation of bonuses was necessary, they argued, if the bank's most able employees were not to defect. In other words, people had to be bribed to ensure that creditors did not suffer even bigger losses.

Although morally reprehensible, this was probably an accurate assessment of the likely pattern of events. The same pleas would probably have been heard at any other merchant bank that went bust. That is the reality of the City labour market, in which implicit contracts based on loyalty and trust – social capital – have been replaced by legal contracts which are difficult and expensive to enforce. Talented traders, analysts and corporate financiers now move from one bank to another at the drop of a hat, when offered a bigger pay package or the lure of a bribe known as a 'golden hello'. This leads to a paradox. While most of the population is intensely worried about job insecurity, the more able people in the Square Mile revel in it. The only penalty these City anarchists incur for their high-speed job hopping is that their former employer may insist on a period of enforced 'gardening leave' in between jobs. In this world of bribes and distorted incentives, Leeson's lack of loyalty to his employer was typical, even if the extreme to which he took it was not. The ethos was aptly summed up in the celebrated remark of a footloose trader who is alleged to have told his employer, 'If you want loyalty, get a dog'.

The problem for employers is that the skills of the individual employees are not specific to the firm. The question is whether management can ever find ways of moulding such footloose talent into teams in individualistic, information-based industries and services like finance. The conventional wisdom here is that the interests of the individuals should be aligned as closely as possible with those of the owners, which implies that those individuals must be prepared to accept that their rewards go down as well as up when profits are poor. This ought to be easy for employers to achieve, since many of the employees in high finance cannot make money from their activities without the support of capital on a scale that only a sizeable firm can command. Yet there is a game-theory-style problem of getting from here to there.

Salomon Brothers, the big New York securities house in which Warren Buffett's Berkshire Hathaway is the biggest shareholder, responded to declining profits by trying in 1995 to put its pay structure on to a more rational basis. Key members of Salomon's notoriously individualistic team – or, more accurately, non-team – promptly defected to its competitors. Others were in open revolt. Top management was obliged to retreat from its elaborate revised pay and bonus scheme. All the other firms on Wall Street sympathized, because they suffered from similarly flawed pay structures – but not to the point where they were prepared to forgo the opportunity to poach Salomon's best people.

In the absence of cooperation between employers, the employees in quoted companies will continue to divide, rule and decamp. Goldman Sachs, another New York firm, has enjoyed a rather better record in retaining and motivating financial talent because it remains a private partnership, with only limited access to outside capital. But with high finance becoming ever more capital intensive, the younger partners would like the firm to go public. This has been pushed to a vote in which the preference of the elders for private partnership prevailed. But it is widely assumed that even Goldman will in due course bow to the inevitable and abandon its partnership structure.

All the same strictures apply in London. When Deutsche Bank decided to beef up its British-based merchant bank Morgan Grenfell, it poached a number of top people from Merrill Lynch in the US and S G Warburg in London. Then, when Merrill Lynch bought the UK firm of Smith New Court in 1995, it poached people from Morgan Grenfell. After the takeover of Warburg by Swiss Bank Corporation, everyone looked to Warburg as the best pool of available talent in the City.

Ironically, Barings was a bank in which the interests of the top managers appeared to be closely aligned with those of the employees. The bank was controlled by a charity, the Baring Foundation, whose trustees included the bank's top executives. In practice, this proved to be a weak form of ownership. The chief recipients of the bank's profits, within this admirably intentioned capital structure, were powerless beneficiaries of patronage such as the Royal Opera House or leading charities, rather than a group of people capable of acting as a check and balance over management.

In greed we trust

The rampant individualism in the City mirrors the retreat from the values of community in society at large. It bears an unpleasant resemblance to the Hobbesian war of all against all. This comparison can fruitfully be extended. In warfare, technology distances people from moral dilemmas: it is much easier for men to reconcile themselves to the killing of women and children from the comfort of a sky-high B52 bomber than it is on the ground at close quarters. With finance, the erosion of relationships can have much the same moral effect, if on a lesser scale. Distance – in the shape of impersonal exchange in markets as opposed to direct banking relationships – sharpens the profit motive while reducing the sense of responsibility to others. And the saga of Barings, in which individualism and greed so clearly ran riot, could well have been described as the belated apotheosis of the anti-social side of Thatcherism, were it not for the welfare safety net extended to the top executives who presided over the collapse.

Looking back at the Barings saga, there is something almost comic about the inept manner in which Britain's oldest merchant bank stumbled into the modern world of high-octane securities dealing. The bank was, after all, run rather like a private version of the national lottery. While Leeson gambled furiously at the bottom, the myopic managers at the top dispensed the Baring Foundation's largesse to worthy causes and chairman Peter Baring proclaimed that it was surprisingly easy to make money in securities trading. Yet apart from the fact that Barings' money ran out, it is worth highlighting another important difference in the comparison, which merits a brief digression.

While the exchequer enjoys a rake-off from the national lottery, the taxpayer is potentially at risk where banks like Barings speculate in the markets for their own account in what is euphemistically known as proprietary trading. Had it been a bigger bank that ran into trouble, the chancellor of the exchequer and the governor of the Bank of England might have felt obliged to stage a rescue to protect the British banking system from a run on its deposits. Given that the creditworthiness of the larger banks is underpinned by this implicit public guarantee, it seems strange that they should be free to punt in the markets to the extent that they do, especially since the banks' growing proprietary trading activities have little social function. In the main, they simply add more liquidity to markets that are already very liquid – liquidity being the capacity of investors to deal without causing significant movements in the price of the securities or currencies concerned.

It is probable that in this unrestrained environment a much bigger bank, whether in Britain or elsewhere, will in due course go bust. For another power shift that has taken place as a result of derivatives trading is at the expense of the central bank. Central bankers are often referred to as a priesthood: like the clergy, they are paid less than their flock for acting as the country's collective financial conscience. Part of their job is to ensure that the gambling instinct does not reach such a fever pitch that it poses a threat to financial stability and the public purse. Yet it is no longer possible for central bankers to keep abreast of the minute-by-minute changes in the risks run by banks in derivatives dealing without placing a costly army of permanent watchdogs on every dealing floor. So the most they can do is try to ensure that proper internal controls and risk-management systems are in place. Supervision has thus been privatized by default. In the circumstances, it is a mystery that central bankers and governments have not curbed the volume of this activity by changing the capital regime, whereby the amount of capital the banks deploy in their different activities is varied according to the degree of risk involved.

A guest house for foreign finance

So what does the future hold for the City? And what is the job-creating potential of the financial services sector into the twenty-first century? It should not be forgotten that much of the jobs growth in the financial services sector in the 1980s was in retail banking, which concerns consumer-related business such as mortgage lending. Capacity in the banking and building society sectors is still too heavily geared to a level of housing-market activity that will not be seen again in the foreseeable future. A further contraction in the number of building societies and jobs in retail banking is thus inevitable.

As for high finance in the City itself, it is possible to exaggerate the damage that results from managerial weakness in British-owned merchant banks. Names like Barings and Rothschild are full of historical resonance. But they have not been a particularly important part of the post-war City, in which the British clearing banks and the big foreign commercial and investment banks dominate. Other domestically owned firms are thriving in areas such as foreign exchange, where the clearing banks are powerful, or fund management. Nor are the world's other financial centres untroubled by managerial weakness. Japanese success in manufacturing is mirrored by equal and opposite incompetence in banking and finance: after a property lending binge in the 1980s, several of the country's larger banks were, on any realistic measure, insolvent by the mid-1990s. The French banking and insurance systems were crippled by losses in the property market at much the same time. Had Crédit Lyonnais been in the private sector, it would have collapsed and been rescued by the state. As for the Americans, New York in the past ten years has seen the demise of Drexel Burnham, the investment bank at the centre of the 1980s boom in 'junk' bonds, and the dismantling of Kidder Peabody, an old-established investment bank humbled by huge losses incurred by another rogue trader, Joseph Jett.

It seems likely, too, that the City will reap the benefit of continuing growth in demand for cross-border financial services, as more countries open up their economies, deregulate their markets and privatize their nationalized industries in line with the post-Cold-War economic consensus. In a growing market of this kind, there are huge advantages in being the established leader of the pack in any given time zone. Dealing and other transaction costs are lowest in the biggest financial centre because they are spread over a higher volume of business. The existence of a cluster of banks and securities firms will tend to reinforce the local base of skills. And the trading culture that underpins the City's success is regarded by many foreign banks as impossible to replicate in their home country. Just as the financially unsophisticated Spaniards in the fifteenth and sixteenth centuries relied on the Genoese to finance their huge international trade, the big German, Swiss and Dutch commercial banks have concluded that the only way to make inroads into the business of financing and advising on international mergers, acquisitions and privatizations is by buying British merchant banks to do the job for them. Hence Deutsche Bank's purchase of Morgan Grenfell, Swiss Bank Corporation's acquisition of S G Warburg, Dresdner Bank's absorption of Kleinwort Benson and, of course, ING's purchase of Barings.

Nor would European Monetary Union be a threat in quite the way some politicians appear to think. EMU would certainly lead to some loss of intra-European foreign-exchange business. Yet the City does relatively little of this business anyway: its strength is in non-European currencies like the dollar. If Britain were not part of the hard core of EMU the City would probably handle much less of the relevant continental European governments' bond and related foreign-exchange dealings. Yet issuing and trading government bonds is a mature and not particularly exciting area of international finance. For once, most of Europe is trying to reduce the level of government borrowing. No doubt the French and German governments will look for opportunities to penalize London if Britain does not go along with plans for a new European exchange-rate regime. That said, London has always derived profits in the European time zone from over-regulation in other financial centres. There must be a suspicion that the arrangements in any single European currency system will provide opportunities for more profits of that ilk.

It is nonetheless important to recognize that maintenance of the City's social capital is increasingly reliant on foreigners. So Britain's comparative advantage here partly consists in running the equivalent of a financial guest house, which provides a comfortable ambience and able servants to minister to foreign bankers and dealers. Is this sustainable? The Germans may have concluded that it is too difficult to replicate the skills of those servants; but the French, whose culture is less incompatible with the market approach to finance, are busy acquiring them. They tend anyway to be better educated than the British, with a higher level of numeracy. Provided with a plausible alternative, in an attractive capital city such as Paris, the foreign bankers may ultimately conclude that the time has come to sample *la douceur de vivre*. They would come to that conclusion rather more quickly if a Labour government toughened the regime for the taxation of foreigners.

The law is my bond

For much of recorded history, the standard way for international financial centres to fade from the scene has been through a change in geographical trading patterns or through war. Geography has been rendered irrelevant by technology. But a violent demise is not, if we substitute terrorism for war. It is just conceivable that the IRA might wreak destruction on a scale that would cause the footloose foreign bankers to disappear for the foreseeable future. Yet the incidence of terrorism in New York, where the World Trade Centre was bombed, or in Paris, where disaffected moslem youth is turning increasingly to violence, suggests that there is a dwindling number of safe havens for nervous international bankers.

An alternative way for a financial centre to lose its competitive edge is simply to price itself out of the market. It is here that the breakdown of trust and the resort to a more transactional culture become important. The increased levels of regulation that have followed the various scandals in the City impose costs on the firms that do business in the Square Mile. In the absence of the old trust ethos, the system is also more reliant on contractual rather than informal relationships. This leads to the creation of a new bureaucracy of compliance officers and to much higher legal and accountancy bills to match. As yet this has not posed a serious threat to the City's position, but it is conceivable that in future it might.

For the moment the likelihood is that the City will continue to grow in prosperity, while losing some of its market share and generating fewer jobs than in the 1980s. The unanswered question is: at what cost to the rest of the nation? Sir John Harvey-Jones, an outspoken champion of the manufacturing interest, has complained of the 'ludicrous salaries' paid to young people in the City:

> When I was chairman of ICI all the advisers that we used, advisers mark you, were all paid more than I was, be they auditors, be they the merchant banks, be they the City solicitors. Now I ask you, in realistic national terms, who is likely to have the biggest impact on the fate of the bloody country?[5]

In fairness to the youthful City dealers, it should not be forgotten that a majority of them are, like footballers, out of a job before middle age. As I argued in Chapter 4, there is more than a hint of Luddism in the belief that service industry employment is inherently less 'virtuous' than manufacturing employment and its contribution to the balance of payments less valid. Yet running the Clapham Junction of the international financial system – which is what London does – carries a risk that global upheavals will spill over into the domestic economy. The assets and liabilities of the British banking system are, after all, greater as a percentage of national income than those of any other country in the Group of Seven; and Britain's total external assets are larger, in absolute terms, than all but those of the United States.[6]

The risks were apparent at the end of the Lawson boom, when the Japanese banks that had poured into London in the 1980s pumped money into the commercial property market at the very peak of the cycle, giving it an extra speculative twist. It is here that there could be risks within the context of EMU, where the rate of interest deemed appropriate for Europe might be inappropriate not only to British domestic conditions but to the very unusual financial circumstances in London's international markets. This could lead to very volatile financial inflows and outflows whose backwash would be felt in the domestic economy. Too little research has been conducted into the costs, as opposed to the benefits, of having London operate as the pre-eminent international financial centre.

Yet values in the City do seem to be out of joint in a deeper sense. As de Tocqueville argued in *Democracy in America*, excessive individualism corrodes social values and can sap a country's vitality.[7] The City has admittedly been socialized somewhat since the excesses of the more ostentatious yuppies in the 1980s. There are fewer Porsches and more Range Rovers. But the follies revealed at Lloyd's and Barings, together with the lunacy of the overmobile City job market, have made a mark on the public consciousness, thereby eroding the legitimacy of the wealth-creation process.

Other countries have admittedly seen a loosening in the trust basis of financial relationships. Even Japan, the least individualistic of economies, has been afflicted by the rogue-trader phenomenon. The US operations of Daiwa Bank were recently closed down by the US Federal Reserve after Toshihide Iguchi incurred $1.1 billion of losses on unauthorized trading, while the chief copper trader of Sumitomo Corporation, Yasuo Hamanaka, saddled his company with a bill for $2.6 billion in a failed attempt to corner the world copper market. But these were salarymen who lost the money in appropriately low-key style. For sheer ego and ostentatious individualism, the British and Americans are in a league of their own.

Fears for the City, like those for the British economy, are exaggerated.

Those who worry about its prospects forget that if there is a decline in the competitiveness of financial services a flexible market economy will shift resources into other sectors. A more serious worry should be whether the City will infect the rest of us with its values. Few things better illustrate the new Hobbesian culture of legalistic individualism than the behaviour of some of the former employees of Barings. The most telling instance concerns Mary Walz, the sacked former head of Barings' global derivatives trading. Walz actually went to court in an attempt to retrieve a promised £500,000 bonus that was based on profits that did not exist. A society in which an employee of a collapsed bank can do that without apparent sense of shame or fear of ostracism is in danger of becoming very sick.

6

The Lure of the German Model

*T*he American thinker Francis Fukuyama has argued persuasively that the ability of firms to compete in international markets depends to a significant degree on their home country's endowment of social capital. In Japan, for example, workers instinctively subordinate their immediate interests to a wider group on the basis of shared, or consensual, values. A high level of trust between management and workers gives the country a remarkable edge in large-scale manufacturing in such industries as cars, semiconductors and consumer electronics. Indeed, part of the essence of the lean production techniques pioneered in Japan by Toyota lies in the requirement that the individual worker should bring the whole assembly line to a halt to solve problems of quality at source. This is the supreme example of stakeholding in the workplace. Among other things, lean production is an ingenious answer to the dehumanization of work that results from the division of labour.[1]

In contrast, the miracles of Chinese entrepreneurship in Hong Kong and Taiwan have produced hardly any giant corporations or international brand names. The low level of trust that persists in Chinese communities, where economic growth has been driven substantially by small companies, means that business rarely transcends the family. Those few occasions when it looks like doing so, as at the US computer company Wang, have often ended in disaster as an elderly patriarch has insisted that management succession stays in the family.

Similar observations could be made about social capital in Europe. Trust in German companies is high, even if decision-making responsibility is not devolved to assembly-line workers to quite the same degree as in Japan. Italians, in contrast, behave more like the Chinese. While the American sociologist Robert Putnam characterized Italian society as low trust in the south and high trust in the centre and north, the country remains a distrustful society by wider international standards. Although there are obvious exceptions to the general rule such as Fiat and Benetton, there appears to be a disinclination, partly cultural, to build large, internationally competitive private-sector companies. Business flourishes on the basis of familistic values: the real strength of the Italian economy lies in the small to medium-sized family-business sector. These family firms are intensely competitive in world markets, despite being based in an economy which is shackled to an almost unworkable state and burdened with near-disastrous public finances.

It is worth noting in passing that Italy is also a refutation of the idea that a high level of research is the key to comparative advantage. It invests less than half the amount in research and development in relation to its gross domestic product than do all the other members of the Group of Seven industrialized countries apart from Canada, but has grown as fast or faster than them over the past two decades.[2] This reflects an industrial culture which fosters plenty of low-tech but internationally successful industries such as textiles, shoes, ceramics and leather goods, where Italian design flair leaves low-cost Asian competition standing. But nor is Italy devoid of technological sophistication. It is the world's third largest producer of industrial robots, a third of them made by firms with less than 50 employees.

If Fukuyama is right, stakeholder economies such as Germany and Japan have a big advantage over economies with highly individualistic and class-bound cultures like Britain. Much of the British industrial culture can certainly be characterized as low trust, which is usually associated with a reluctance to train employees, inflexible working practices and minimal employee loyalty. It is a culture which makes it easier for firms to compete on price rather than quality and which relies more heavily on contractual relationships, which are costly, rather than mutual trust.

At first sight Britain's improved economic performance and the convergence of economic growth rates among the big European economies over the past 15 years might appear to sit rather oddly with the trust thesis. The paradox can, however, be explained by the fact that culture is just one of many factors that influence competitiveness, which range from the level of the exchange rate to the flexibility of markets. Most economies are in practice a mixture of high-trust and low-trust activity. And in a world of very open trade and investment flows, it may also be possible to compensate for a low-trust culture in other ways. Not only does liberal trade allow a country to play to specialist strengths in those areas of the economy where social capital does exist, as with Britain's pharmaceuticals industry. A cultural deficit – and indeed deficiencies in management capability, corporate governance, labour relations and much else besides – can be made good by importing someone else's surplus. In the city state of Singapore, for example, a very high proportion of gross domestic product is generated by large companies. They are not Chinese companies that have overcome their indigenous cultural disadvantage, but multinationals from countries such as the US or Japan. Singapore has made a considerable virtue of its dependence on outsiders.

In the 10 years to 1992 foreign direct investment by companies grew four times faster than world trade. At the start of the 1990s production by foreign-owned firms in other countries amounted to $4.4 trillion, compared with total world trade of $3.8 trillion.[3] Britain has been particularly good at attracting inward investment as a result of conscious government policy, becoming Europe's biggest single repository of inward investment. In effect, the country has contracted out the management of much of its physical and human capital to foreign companies whose corporate governance arrangements and managerial culture often lend themselves particularly well to sectors of British industry where domestic ownership and management have failed. The Germans have guest workers, the British have guest managers – although it should not be forgotten that Britain is a much bigger outward investor than Germany, France or Italy.

The Anglo-Saxon boss

A good illustration of how the subcontract economy works, and how stakeholder values can be imported, is to be found in the British forklift truck industry, where the two leading players have recently fallen into German ownership. In 1988 Lansing Bagnall, the private company owned by Emmanuel Kaye's group The Kaye Organisation, sold out to Germany's biggest forklift truck producer, Linde. With a turnover of £235 million and more than 5000 employees, Lansing Bagnall was the seventh largest forklift truck maker in the world at the time.[4] Six years later the assets of Lancer Boss were bought from the receiver by Hamburg-based Jungheinrich. By this time Linde and Jungheinrich were respectively the world's number one and number two, in a business where the remaining competition was almost exclusively American and Japanese. Boss Group, as it is now called, provides a particularly instructive case study.

Lancer Boss had been founded by Neville Bowman-Shaw and his brother Trevor. It was the kind of entrepreneurial British company in which much engineering creativity was combined with a very autocratic management style. Neville Bowman-Shaw practised the polar opposite of consensual German or Japanese-style management. At Lancer Boss instructions emanated from the top down; fear played an important part in motivating managers and workforce; and education and training were, by German standards, poor. In the 12 years before the company went into receivership, eight sales directors had left, while 400 salespeople had come and gone. This was the Anglo-Saxon flexible labour market with a vengeance.

Yet the problems of the British forklift truck industry owe much to another aspect of Tory policy: boom and bust macroeconomics. The big German companies first established a strong market position in the UK during the Barber boom of the early 1970s, when bubbling demand far outstripped the supply available from domestic British manufacturers. Foreign competitors enjoyed another helpful boost in the recession of the early 1980s, in which the overvaluation of sterling imposed a severe burden on manufacturers. In response to a collapse in output of 60 per cent, Lansing Bagnall slashed its workforce by a phenomenal 40 per cent. The problems of both Lansing and Lancer Boss were further exacerbated by the decline of the domestically owned motor industry, which used to provide a big market for materials handling companies.

Some argue that the British forklift truck industry never recovered from that recessionary blow. Yet the two leading UK companies still tried to expand through acquisition in a European market where the number of producers was contracting sharply as a result of rationalization. Lancer Boss had originally been a very successful producer of specialist, or 'niche', products, including side-lift trucks and big container-handling trucks. When the Bowman-Shaws decided to internationalize their operations, they also chose to abandon this strategy and to embark on an ambitious move into volume production. They did this partly by acquiring Germany's third largest producer, Steinbock, in 1983, while setting up direct distribution arrangements in other parts of continental Europe.

The risk in trying to make the jump into the highly competitive volume end of the forklift truck business is that the market is exceptionally volatile. It closely follows the swings in stock building and capital investment. For anyone based in a country like Britain, where economic policy has been marked by such savage gyrations from boom to bust, the risks were naturally even greater. It is much more difficult to maintain levels of investment and employment in the downturn than in a more stable environment such as that of Germany. The Bowman-Shaws compounded the problem by acquiring in Steinbock a company that was not only much bigger than Lancer Boss itself, but that already had serious problems.

They did well with Steinbock in the buoyant European economy of the second half of the 1980s. But unlike Emmanuel Kaye, who sold out at the peak of the cycle to Linde, the Bowman-Shaws persevered, only to be savaged in the bust that followed the Lawson boom of the 1980s. As an unquoted company, Lancer Boss lacked access to equity capital in the British stock market to help weather the storm. The extent to which it was overextended could be seen in the fact that less than a fifth of its £192 million turnover in 1992 was generated in the UK – a case of the foreign tail wagging the British bulldog. In that year it plunged from a net profit of more than £1 million to a net loss of nearly £4 million.[5]

With a hopelessly inadequate financial base, the attempt by the Bowman-Shaws to join the big league of international forklift truck manufacturers was doomed. And because the interests of the German bankers to Steinbock conflicted with those of the British banks behind the domestic business of Lancer Boss, it proved impossible to put together a rescue. More than £45 million of reserves accumulated over the years by the two brothers were wiped out at a stroke. Neville Bowman-Shaw remains bitter that the German banks withdrew their support, giving only six and a half hours' notice, after the British parent company had transferred substantial funds to Germany.

Trust me, I'm German

Jungheinrich's operations in Britain had been built up since 1967 by Robert Bischof, an articulate German manager who has not been afraid to express in the media critical views about British industry. When he took charge of Lancer Boss from the receiver in May 1994, his approach could not have been more different from that of the previous British management. At the outset he confronted a thoroughly demoralized workforce. Lancer Boss's main plant at Leighton Buzzard in Bedfordshire was in the kind of mess that he had previously only seen in east Germany and Russia, when he had temporarily worked for the Treuhand agency in helping to privatize east German industry: around 600 tons of scrap had to be cleared from the site when he arrived. Because the workers were not stakeholders in the business, they did not clear up unless told to do so; I was told that to clear up without instructions, under the old regime, would have been to risk the sack.

Bischof made a commitment that there would be no redundancies, while indicating that he expected employees to commit themselves to the company in return. The only way to improve the quality of the products, he argued, was to ensure that people felt that there was something in it for them and not just in the short term. Both white- and blue-collar workers were informed about the management's plans and objectives. Confidence building under the new German management has, he claims, released creativity and energy. Factory practice and training were greatly improved. And productivity, measured by output per head, soared under the new ownership.

Compared with the peak year of output under the Bowman-Shaws in 1990–91, Boss had recorded a 38 per cent productivity improvement within 18 months of the takeover; and this was before embarking on a £10 million investment programme. Production had doubled, quality was up and defects were down. The exceptional productivity improvement derived largely, according to Bischof, from the way the new management treated the workers. Looked at from another perspective, that productivity gain could be rationalized as the return on social capital.

Neville Bowman-Shaw is highly sceptical about these claimed improvements and points to the losses still being incurred by Boss. Yet the latest accounts show losses declining from £3.8 million to £1.9 million, despite a big increase in interest charges on the bank loans raised to finance the investment programme. This looks more like German long-termism than a company running into trouble again.

The forklift truck industry is precisely the kind of medium-tech business which is well suited to the German manufacturing culture, with its emphasis on sound apprenticeship training, constructive workplace solidarity and paternalistic management. While the British labour market is externally flexible in the sense that it is easy for management to hire and fire people, the German labour market is more flexible inside the corporation. Instead of thinking of themselves as a separate class of people, the managers usually have the same technical skills as the workers. And those well-trained workers are able to move more readily from one job to another as the needs of production dictate. Yet this flexibility is usually accompanied by much narrower wage differentials on the shopfloor and a much narrower disparity between the incomes of workers and management.

That productivity story, repeated time and again with inward investment into the UK, helps explain some of the big improvement in efficiency in UK industry since 1979. By 1992 foreign-owned companies employed 17.9 per cent of the labour in British manufacturing, produced value added per head 40 per cent higher than British-owned manufacturers and carried out 31.6 per cent of all capital investment. At a Japanese-owned car producer such as Nissan in Sunderland, British workers were achieving productivity and quality control as good or better than their opposite numbers in Japan; and the managerial techniques that brought this about were spreading through the rest of the UK industry. German industrialists and bankers have even established training centres in London, Slough and Milton Keynes to provide German-style apprenticeship skills that are so lacking in the UK.

It is impossible to quantify the direct contribution of culture to economic performance. But trust manifestly does affect competitiveness. And Francis Fukuyama is clearly right in asserting that a nation's sense of well-being is heavily conditioned by the level of trust within society and in the workplace. Indeed, it must be apparent from the story of Boss that the stakeholder approach addresses directly the problems of insecurity and anomie discussed in Chapter 2. Put more simply, the employees of the Boss Group are enjoying a much more civilized existence under German management than they did under the British. Given the history of the two countries over the past century, this is irony of a high order and rather uncomfortable too.

Admittedly, the Bowman-Shaws' approach to labour relations was a somewhat extreme version of old-fashioned class-based British management. Yet academic research into labour relations on greenfield sites in the 1980s suggests that one result of the Thatcherite labour-market reforms has been the development of a two-tier system. While most (although by no means all) foreign firms are pursuing modern human resource policies, British firms appear to have been exploiting the new, weakly unionized environment by introducing a much harsher approach to industrial relations. This entails less merit pay, greater use of payment by results, less use of consultation processes, less information and fewer employee benefits.[6]

The cost of macho management

This polarization in industrial relations is the behavioural equivalent of the big increase in disparities in incomes in the labour market itself. The impact on the morale of the workforce is not easy to measure precisely. But International Survey Research, an independent research organization which reports annually on the state of the European labour force, has found that British employees rate their managements less favourably than those of any other country in Europe. They are particularly critical of the training and information they receive from their employers. And in 1995 the firm reported that there had been the most precipitous decline in worker attitudes of any European country over the previous 10 years. Motivation and commitment were said to be lower even than in the confrontational industrial relations climate of the mid-1970s.[7]

No doubt the sharpness of the decline in sentiment in 1995 reflected the general outcry over directors' pay. The broader story is about the replacement, during the Thatcher years, of the militant trade unionist by the macho manager. The great achievement of such managers has been to break down restrictive practices and improve the efficiency of production and the quality of products. Yet International Survey Research's work suggests that another of the macho manager's achievements has been to help drive a wedge between corporate success and fulfilment at work and, at a higher level, to make national success in global markets difficult to reconcile with a sense of well-being among the electorate.

This raises an important question about the sustainability of recent productivity gains, which have been based extensively on borrowing from Japanese and German manufacturing techniques. The whole nature of Japanese lean production methods, or just-in-time manufacturing, and of Japanese quality circles is that they devolve responsibility to the workers, many of whom enjoy security of lifetime employment. Instead of being compartmentalized, production problems are collectively solved by teams of workers with a broad range of skills. New ideas for quality improvements are also spontaneously generated by these teams.

Some academics argue that the Japanese have developed a management technique that is perfectly adaptable to conditions outside Japan. Others claim that it is rooted in a culture of mutual trust and cannot be sustained for long where motivation is based on fear. Common sense would suggest that, even if these flexible systems do not break down where trust is absent, they will generate less innovation and less improved productivity than otherwise. Research carried out by the Institute of Work Psychology at Sheffield University has, for example, shown that engineering companies which emphasize worker participation, along with training and skill development, are more likely to improve long-run performance and facilitate innovation. This, it is claimed, is because workers suffer less stress where job responsibilities are widened. On a shopfloor where work practices are more flexible, workers are also prone to make the small improvements that make a more consistent contribution to technical progress than big scientific breakthroughs.

Macho management may have been a necessary catalyst for change in the 1980s. It is questionable whether it has much to offer in the 1990s, when the need is to build on past productivity improvements rather than to destroy a legacy of restrictive practices. As an antidote, and a way of dealing with the insecurity that plagues the British people, the German stakeholder approach, variously described as social market economics or Rhineland capitalism, might thus appear attractive.

The German way encourages self-respect and pride in the workforce, while reducing the antagonisms between labour and capital. Downsizing does not feature in the vocabulary of managers like the Boss Group's chairman Robert Bischof: under Jungheinrich's ownership the aim is to make the business grow and to engage the workforce in a cooperative effort to fulfil that aspiration over the long term. There are no stock exchange constraints on the passing of information to the stakeholders who are represented on the supervisory board and companies can usually rely on a supportive attitude on the part of its bankers. Managers conceive of their objective as being to promote the interests of the company as a whole rather than the short-term financial interests of shareholders alone. This objective is coloured by the demands of the German constitution, which stresses that property ownership imposes duties as well as rights and should serve the public weal. Could the stakeholder philosophy, operated with such success by the Germans in the post-war period, be more widely applied in the UK under a Labour government?

Stakeholding confronts its critics

Robert Bischof has put a powerful case for the stakeholder approach to successive leaders of the British Labour party, with whom he has had close relations. Ranged against him are those, including Samuel Brittan of the *Financial Times*, who have objected that the stakeholder company suffers from flawed accountability. In trying to account to such a wide group of different interests, which can include bankers, suppliers, employees and the community as well as shareholders, management is said to end up being accountable to no one because its objectives are confused. Proponents of the extreme form of this argument say that a business organization that seeks anything but long-term value for the owners is perpetrating a theft against the owners.[8]

Yet if the practical consequence of management adopting the socially conscious stakeholder concept is that it can generate nearly 40 per cent more productivity, as at the Boss Group, the accusation of theft will strike most people as somewhat academic. A German might counter that when shareholders pressurize British companies into paying dividends out of reserves while simultaneously sacking workers and cutting investment, they are stealing the company's social capital. The definition of theft varies according to the view of what a company is for. What is striking about Boss is that all, including the shareholders, workers, customers and the wider economy, appear to have been winners under the new dispensation.

More serious is Brittan's claim that accountability in the stakeholder company can be too widely drawn to be effective. Certainly there is scope for conflicts of interest. The banks that are frequently represented on German supervisory boards have a greater commercial interest in corporate growth than in profitability. It has been argued that the ill-judged expansion plans of Daimler-Benz, which culminated in losses of £2.5 billion in 1995, were an illustration of this weakness. Here, too, is part of the explanation for McKinsey's discovery that investment showed much lower productivity in Germany relative to the English-speaking economies, which was discussed in Chapter 3.

Supervisory boards peopled by top executives from Deutsche Bank and others, as well as trade union and employee representatives, have also proved ineffective at detecting and addressing management failure at companies like Metallgesellschaft, Kloeckner-Humboldt-Deutz and Schneider. And German long-termism can sometimes amount to an excessively permissive attitude to loss making. AEG, the electronics and industrial business in which Daimler-Benz took a controlling stake in the 1980s, had been in financial difficulties since the 1970s. Only in the mid-1990s did Daimler-Benz finally grasp the nettle and close down the loss-making plants. Such problems can be compounded by German accounting practice, which permits the creation of hidden reserves which management can use to disguise a declining profit trend. Those who engage in creative accounting often end up deceiving themselves about the health of the business.

Against all this could be set the recent experience of Jungheinrich. The forklift truck company's voting shares are still owned by members of the founding Wolf and Lange families, who play no part in the management but are represented on the supervisory board. It also has publicly quoted non-voting preference shares. At first sight that might not seem a recipe for tight accountability. Yet the evidence points in the other direction. Shortly before Jungheinrich bought Lancer Boss's assets, its chairman, Mr Eckart Kottkamp, persuaded the supervisory board that the company should diversify away from the volatile forklift truck market and buy into a large manufacturer of industrial cleaning equipment. The new acquisition was then caught in a price war with two large competitors. Organizational difficulties also started to emerge. In December 1995 Mr Kottkamp announced that he was leaving 'for personal reasons' after 13 years as a member of the management board. In reality he was pushed by the supervisory board for making a poor acquisition. The message seems to be that, while the system may have allowed weak accountability at some of Germany's biggest bank-dominated conglomerates, it exerts a genuine discipline where there remains a concentration of family ownership. Such concentrations are much more common in German quoted companies than in the UK.

Most members of German management and supervisory boards do not admit to any confusion about their objectives. Their legal powers are clearly defined and they know perfectly well what they mean when they say they seek to promote the long-term interests of the company. It could be argued that the objectives of the boards of British companies are much more confused, because non-executive directors who share the same legal duties as the executive directors are required by the recommendations of the Cadbury Committee, the Stock Exchange and institutional investors to act as advisers and supervisors as well as wealth creators.

Many Germans nonetheless acknowledge that the consensual approach to decision making in German companies can be slow and that there is far too much red tape in German business. They frequently argue, too, that foreign admirers of the German system attribute too benign a role to the unions, which have a genius for wrapping up management in knots with their superior understanding of the industrial relations rule book. In fact, most German managers in Britain delight in their ability to treat the workforce with due respect without having to cope with the bureaucracy that is required back at home. In Germany, meantime, an excess of socially conscious commitment to workers and the community has been cited as the cause of some *Mittelstand* companies – the small to medium-sized businesses that contribute so much to Germany's export strength – going bust. They have tried to keep people on the payroll too long in the face of mounting financial pressure; a civilized fault, but no less a fault for that.

The limits of cross-cultural fertilization

There are, of course, limits to the amount of stakeholding that Britain can import through inward investment. This might seem a pity, given its benign impact on the workplace and the fact that average productivity in the British-owned sector of manufacturing is still 29 per cent below that in the foreign-owned sector and investment per head is less than half that in foreign-owned companies. But inward investment is not uniformly supportive of a feelgood factor. Much German investment, for example, is driven by a push for market share, which causes other domestic businesses to close down. There is a risk, too, that in Britain's flexible labour market, the British subsidiary of a financially stretched foreign company will always be the first to be closed regardless of its productivity, because British workers can be fired more cheaply than those in continental Europe. So while the country has undeniably gained from inward investment in terms of economic efficiency, it would still be less painful for the workforce if more of its productivity gains could be home grown.

That said, the German approach to closures is less ruthless. Nor, despite the widespread British assumption to the contrary, is this necessarily a competitive disadvantage in dealing with low-cost competition from Asia. The speed with which German manufacturers are shifting their activities to Eastern Europe in their attempt to escape from high social costs in Germany is a salutary reminder that even for the stakeholder company corporate survival remains paramount. The difference lies in the fact that a large German firm which is seeking to downsize its operations at home is obliged to submit plans to a works council for the compensation, retraining and relocation of its workers. If this sounds more bureaucratic than British practice, the retraining aspect implies that when it comes to meeting the strain of structural adjustment flexibility does exist, but it lies within the company rather than in the external labour market. That is not to be despised. The heightened pace of creative destruction in the global economy is profoundly subversive of community. The stakeholding approach to managing change is a civilized way of offsetting the impact of these shocks.

The Germans are now addressing the problems that afflict their system by moving a little closer to the Anglo-Saxon model. At Germany's largest industrial company Daimler-Benz, for example, the response to catastrophic losses after years of ill-focused growth has been to put a new emphasis on shareholder value. In some companies the shift reflects the need to placate the foreign shareholders, who by 1993 owned 12 per cent of the capital of German quoted companies. Many large, capital-intensive German corporations recognize that they may in future need to go to the international capital markets to raise money. This entails a Faustian compact with the cultural values of American-style capitalism.

Germans, it should also be said, are no more immune to greed than the Americans or British and material incentives will further encourage them down that route. Daimler-Benz is a case in point. It decided in April 1996 to introduce a stock-option plan for its top executives, despite nine out of eleven members of the supervisory board voting against the plan for fear that it would lead to an excessive short-term preoccupation with profits. That rift could be a symbolic pointer to the direction in which the German social-market economy is going. Deutsche Bank, the biggest shareholder in Daimler-Benz and Germany's largest bank, is now following suit with its own stock-option scheme.

Yet this is more likely to lead to a shift in the balance of stakeholder interests than to the abandonment of the stakeholder approach. And the experience at the Boss Group suggests that Britain could profitably move to meet the Germans half way, not least because trust is becoming more important to competitiveness in a modern economy. The shortening of product lifecycles requires continuous innovation, which in turn calls for training, flexibility and loyalty in the workplace. At the same time the growth of the knowledge economy means that more and more work is of a kind that calls for self-supervision rather than external monitoring.

The will to emulate the Germans is, however, absent in the UK and most members of the British industrial establishment feel a visceral antipathy to the German-style supervisory board. This is not necessarily based on ideological opposition to stakeholding as such. For while most British managers pay lip service to the single-minded pursuit of shareholder value, they know that if they fail to take the interests of stakeholders into account they may end up damaging the shareholders' longer-term interests and, indeed, their own. To that extent, the polarization of the debate between stakeholder value and shareholder value is misleading: there are differences of emphasis between British and German managers on how they balance the different stakeholders' interests, but balance them they both seek to do, whether for better or worse. In most quoted British companies the interests of non-shareholder groups are far from being ignored or excluded; but responsibility to the shareholders remains the ultimate discipline.

There is nonetheless a preference among British industrialists for the traditional way of doing things, and more specifically for the exclusion of employees from the boardroom. This preference was transformed into extreme antagonism by the recommendations of the Bullock Committee during the period of the last Labour government in 1974–9. The enduring hostility is such that a two-tier board would be unlikely to work effectively if imposed by fiat. As for the wider subject of human resource management, there is an urgent need for more and better data on human capital which ensures that macho managers understand the costs that result from aggressive behaviour. And if Britain is to move to any kind of system that properly acknowledges the role of social capital – or for that matter all the other intangibles that go unrecorded in company accounts – pressure will have to come from investors and others for more useful non-financial indicators of corporate performance. This brings us to the role of Britain's anonymous institutional investors.

Part Three

Sticks, Carrots
and Stakes

7

Rotten Boroughs

*O*wnership plays a central role in the plumbing of the capitalist system; and public confidence in the system depends to a large degree on the responsible exercise of the rights attached to ownership. So far, so uncontroversial. Yet the whole nature of modern capitalism makes responsible ownership a singularly elusive concept. The first difficulty arises with the diagnosis of Adolf Berle and Gardiner Means, whose classic work *The Modern Corporation and Private Property* was published in the 1930s. Berle and Means suggested that the ownership of quoted companies had become so widely dispersed around hundreds and thousands of shareholders that it was impossible for owners to exercise effective control over managers. The resulting divorce between ownership and control meant that shareholders were the victims of what the eighteenth-century economist Adam Smith called an 'agency' problem, by which he meant that an agent can never be relied on to look after someone else's interests as well as his own.[1]

This principal–agent model still features heavily in economic textbooks. Yet it looks increasingly one-dimensional in a world where much of the value in the modern corporation lies, as we have seen, in human capital and in the network of relationships with stakeholders other than owners. Even for those who do still think of corporate accountability in terms of shareholders and agents, the Berle and Means analysis is no longer a wholly relevant description of the British system, thanks to a huge upheaval in the pattern of ownership. In 1939 shareholding was highly fragmented, with private individuals owning more than 80 per cent of all quoted equity shares. By 1963 the percentage had fallen to 54 per cent; and by 1994 it was down to 20 per cent. Over the same period the shareholdings of anonymous institutions soared to just over 60 per cent. The biggest of the institutions were the pension funds, with equities valued at £212 billion at the end of 1994, closely followed by the insurance companies, with £167 billion of equity investments, much of which was also earmarked for the provision of pensions.[2] This growth in pension fund ownership, which was chronicled in an earlier book by the author, leaves Britain in a very different position from the United States.[3] There the $2.8 trillion-worth of shareholdings owned by private households, equivalent to £1.8 trillion, was still slightly in excess of the value of institutional holdings at the end of 1994.[4]

Ownership, then, is no longer fragmented in Britain. The legal title to the residual profits of most of British industry and commerce is vested in the hands of a small number of private institutions that invest on behalf of the beneficial owners such as pensioners and policy holders. That is another way of saying that most employees, current or retired, acquire their direct stake in the growth of the economy through these forms of collective saving. A great deal of power is thereby conferred on a very small number of financial bureaucrats. It is generally reckoned that there are around 60 fund managers in the country who really call the shots, in terms of their buying and selling power in the stock market and the casting of votes at company meetings. These are the people who hold the fate of the British employee in their hands when companies make takeovers or seek endorsement for big strategic changes of direction. Together they control funds worth more than the combined national incomes of the Netherlands, Austria and Sweden.

The sheer concentration of the big institutions' investment funds suggests that they have the potential, in terms of the Berle and Means model, to close some of the gap that opened up earlier in the century between ownership and control. Or, in the vocabulary of stakeholding, the weight of the money they control gives the institutions an opportunity to assert their interests more forcefully *vis à vis* the other stakeholders in the longer-term interests of the companies in which they invest. This raises important questions for corporate governance, the rules under which management operates. And the implications are not confined to the narrow concerns of business. Jonathan Charkham, a former adviser to the governor of the Bank of England who sits on a number of company boards, emphasizes the relevance of corporate governance for society's wider values:

> The corporate governance system is as important to a nation as any other crucial part of its institutional framework, because on it depends a good portion of the nation's prosperity; it contributes to social cohesion in a way too little recognised. A proper framework for the exercise of power is an economic necessity, a political requirement and a moral imperative.[5]

In this chapter we will look at the the way in which the institutions use their power; and we will ask whether it is realistic to expect them to play a more active role in holding companies to account if the discipline of hostile takeover is softened, as advocated in Chapter 3. The nature of the stake conferred on the ultimate owners, the beneficiaries, by collective investment of this kind will be explored further in Chapter 10.

Semi-detached ownership

Constructive engagement does not come easily to the institutions. The training and mindset of many of their fund managers run counter to the whole idea of a close relationship with the companies in which they invest. For a start, many prefer to see their responsibilities exclusively in terms of buying and selling shares in the supposed interests of their beneficiaries, while keeping management at arm's length. Unlike the German banks which have substantial shareholdings in German industry, these investors are reluctant to become privy to inside information because they would then become 'insiders', which would inhibit their legal right to sell the shares in the market. This semi-detached relationship culminates, if the company runs into trouble, in what is known in the US as 'the Wall Street walk'. Such absentee owners are, in the words of the former deputy governor of the Bank of England Rupert Pennant-Rea, punters, not proprietors.[6]

One flaw in the logic of the punters' argument is that it presupposes that fund managers have visionary powers which enable them to identify in advance those companies that are about to run into trouble. There is a wealth of statistical evidence to suggest that very few of them do, in fact, consistently outguess the market. So most punters are deluding themselves about their ability to deliver on their arm's-length promises to pensioners and policy holders. Nor is it possible for the institutions to sell out in the aggregate because there are no obvious buyers. Individual investors are not increasing their share of the market significantly, while foreign investors who own just over 16 per cent of UK equities have been raising their stake, but not at a pace that would enable them to take the British institutions off the hook in the fore-seeable future. And because the fund managers, and the trustees who monitor them, are increasingly conscious of the difficulty of outperforming the market, they devote more and more of their cash simply to tracking the market indices. They are thus locked into a continuing relationship with the management of the companies represented in the index. This amounts to a powerful case for engagement, if the institutions are willing and able to bring anything con-structive to the party.

The relationship between fund managers and companies is nonetheless a peculiar one, because the so-called owners exercise none of the convention-ally understood rights of ownership involving possession and control of phys-ical assets. They merely have a right to income, and to capital on a winding up, together with whatever influence their voting power gives them over man-agement. Such influence is limited, except in the very unusual circumstances of an issue to raise fresh capital or a takeover, where the fund managers may have the opportunity, as in the case of Granada and Forte discussed earlier, to make a choice between rival managers who are competing for the right to run the business. Under the rules of the Stock Exchange, companies also have to submit plans for unusually large acquisitions, disposals or other big strategic moves to a meeting of shareholders. Most of the time, though, institutional investors delegate the right to manage to the board of directors. They play lit-tle or no part in the nomination of directors, whose appointment they are usu-ally invited to endorse after the choice has been made by the existing board, more often than not on an old pals basis. Although legally responsible for the appointment and remuneration of the auditors, they are, once again, un-involved in the actual process.

If institutions wish to muscle in on important decisions, or to replace an underperforming management, they may have to seek the cooperation of others in order to pose a credible threat that a majority of the votes would be cast in favour of throwing out incumbent management. This is the institutions' ultimate sanction, in the absence of a takeover; and it rarely has to be used since the threat alone, when backed by collective institutional support, is usually sufficient to do the trick. Even then, professional fund managers run the risk that they may end up owning a complex and troubled company with an empty boardroom.

So while the property in a company consists of a whole bundle of rights which are spread around the various stakeholders in the business, with the shareholders nominally pre-eminent among them, the reality is that the board of directors retains most of the powers of control that are usually associated with ownership, up to the point of a hostile takeover. The question is how far the institutional bureaucracy can and does use its voting power to ensure that those directors are held to account for their stewardship of the business in the way that the principal–agent model implies.

Flabby corporate governance

Jonathan Charkham argues that accountability is like a telephone conversation: it cannot take place unless both parties listen. Too many institutions, he says, prefer to leave the phone off the hook. Acutely aware of such criticism from Charkham and others, the institutions' trade associations such as the Association of British Insurers and the National Association of Pension Funds emphasize that their members are nowadays constantly involved in meetings with the managements of the companies in which they invest. These bodies run monitoring services which are designed to pick up contentious corporate governance issues. And they engage in collaborative intervention, under the aegis of an umbrella body called the Institutional Shareholders' Committee, to correct managerial failure and address other governance matters. When it comes to putting pressure on companies, they prefer, unlike many American institutions, to do it behind closed doors, arguing that this is less damaging to the interests of company and shareholders. Their usual method of applying pressure is through the non-executive directors on the board.

There is a marked lack of transparency in these arrangements. The public which entrusts its money to the giants of the insurance and pension fund world has little means of knowing how responsibly or otherwise the institutions are deploying its savings. Indeed, there is arguably a bigger divorce between legal ownership and beneficial ownership of companies than between legal ownership and control. And the institutions' own description of their relationship with industry is somewhat disingenuous. Many industrialists are scathing about the nature of the conversations they have with the institutions, which are often represented by relatively junior employees at meetings with management. A common complaint is that the talk is often very narrowly directed at issues such as the level of the dividend and the immediate profit prospects rather than more fundamental questions to do with the competitive strengths and weaknesses of the firm.

Fund managers can be remarkably timid in dealing with poorly performing companies. When the institutions were cited in a poll in the *Investors Chronicle* in October 1995 as being deeply disillusioned with the top management of the shipping, property and construction conglomerate P & O, the chairman, Lord Sterling, was dumbfounded because no one had put the criticisms to the company. Subsequently he received calls from fund managers who wanted to reassure him that they were not among those who had expressed negative sentiments to the pollsters. This urge to declare that 'it wasn't me guv' was a curious response from the institutions concerned, given that P & O's performance over the previous ten years had been one of the worst among Britain's biggest companies.

At Forte, meantime, the institutions did jointly express dissatisfaction to Rocco Forte about the poor returns that he was extracting from the company's assets. But when the returns subsequently failed to improve they did little. Nor was there sufficient pressure to improve the quality of the board, which was badly in need of more independent non-executive directors, or to bring pressure on Rocco to split his joint role as chairman and chief executive as recommended by the Cadbury Committee, which was set up to improve governance in response to a number of corporate scandals at the end of the 1980s. The biggest shareholder, the City fund management group Mercury Asset Management, is notoriously reluctant to vote against incumbent management except as a last resort. It rarely uses its votes to send signals other than of warm endorsement to a board. This flabby approach to corporate governance helps ensure that the hostile takeover is too often the discipline of first and last resort. Having sat on their hands, Mercury and the other institutions finally changed the management at Forte, as we saw in Chapter 3, in a very expensive way for their beneficiaries by relying on the emergence of a hostile takeover. The experience of Forte suggests that the institutions' demand to be allowed to do everything behind closed doors may, in many cases, be a self-serving plea for a quiet life.

The Pru cracks the whip, sometimes

That is not to say that nothing takes place behind closed doors. Collaborative action by institutional investors brought about changes at the top of the Fisons drugs group and the Spring Ram bathroom and kitchens concern. Institutional concern over the sharing of the roles of chairman and chief executive at Barclays led to the appointment of a new chief executive from outside, Martin Taylor, who had been running Courtaulds Textiles. There is a constant dialogue between the trade associations and companies over narrow financial matters such as the detail of share-incentive schemes. And some institutions, most notably Britain's biggest collective investor the Prudential, have a long and honourable history of confronting wayward or unsuccessful management. The Pru led one of the first shareholder revolts at Birmingham Small Arms in the 1950s, where Sir Bernard Docker was doing serious damage to the company. In the 1960s it helped remove Sir Leslie Rowan from the engineering giant Vickers, while in the 1980s it was responsible for persuading Stephen Gibbs to stand down from the board of the building materials and motor components group Turner & Newall. More recently it is believed to have played a part in speeding up the retirement of Sir David Plastow at Inchcape, the international trading group. At any given moment, the Pru reckons to have a list of problem companies with which it conducts a more intense relationship than with the others.

The scale of the Prudential's activity has nonetheless been unusual when compared with other institutions. As one of its former chief investment managers once confided to the author, it was not unusual for the Pru to reach agreement with other institutions for collective action against bad management, only to find that the others melted away when the moment came for serious confrontation. Some top executives in the big insurance company believe that, while interventionist rhetoric has increased in recent years in response to criticism, there has been little change in the appetite of most institutions for the difficult task of gingering up the British boardroom. Waiting for a takeover is always an easier option. But by then many companies may be mere shadows of their former selves. The roll-call of poorly managed companies where the institutions failed to take timely action includes British Leyland, Distillers, Plessey and numerous others.

A warm endorsement for Weinstock

Nor is the Pru itself immune from criticism. At GEC, where it is the largest shareholder with around 7 per cent of the equity capital, it sat tight, as did most others, when the abilities of the chief executive, Arnold Weinstock, were manifestly waning. He did not relinquish the post of chief executive until he was 72, by which time GEC's performance had been lacklustre for several years. There was a historic irony here, in that the Prudential had intervened indirectly at GEC to address the weaknesses of a previous management in 1959. The move helped precipitate the departure of the then chairman, Leslie Gamage, who complained bitterly at being pushed around by a 'bloody moneylender'. His exit paved the way for the arrival of the young Weinstock.[7]

GEC was admittedly an exceptionally complex company and Weinstock – a formidable presence – invariably demonstrated great mastery of the details of its operations when dealing with the institutions. And because he had always maintained a mountain of cash in the balance sheet, he never had to go to the fund managers with a begging bowl, which would have given them an opportunity to impose conditions on his remaining tenure. It was the fact that GEC was badly in need of fresh loan capital in 1959 that gave the Pru its leverage in pressing for change on that earlier occasion.

Yet Allen Sykes, a former director of Consolidated Goldfields with a special interest in corporate governance, has pointed out that there is no need for the institutions to acquire management skills in order to second guess the managers. All they need is corporate governance expertise. And at GEC in the first half of the 1990s it did not require genius to see that the company suffered from a corporate governance problem. The 18-strong board, with 6 non-executives, was widely regarded as weak. Weinstock was a hugely powerful personality who stocked the GEC board with a number of his own friends. This led to accusations of cronyism. There were only four board meetings a year. According to one insider, these were remarkably short by the standards of other large companies; and during most of Weinstock's period of office no substantive papers were circulated in advance. The reality was that Weinstock ran the company like a family business, even though the family's percentage shareholding was tiny. He did not make much use of the board in reaching strategic decisions and preferred to deal with the outside directors on a bi-lateral basis. Had they not been friends of his in the first place, this would have amounted to a strategy of divide and rule.

The management of Weinstock's own succession bordered on the farci-cal. Weinstock himself was reluctant to stand down and he nursed the hope that his son Simon would ultimately succeed him. Yet everyone knew that nepotism in a company of GEC's size and importance would have caused consternation among GEC's managers and shareholders. In 1992 the com-pany announced that it was setting up a committee to search for a successor. But Weinstock himself sat on it, despite his known feelings about bequeathing his fiefdom to his son; and in the summer of 1994 the board decided to allow him to extend his reign from the age of 70 to 72. By this time a disaffected executive director, Richard Reynolds, the managing director of the GPT telecommunications subsidiary, was beginning to think that the time was coming to force the pace of change. The following year he wrote to the chairman James Prior, asking to be considered for the chief executive's job. According to one GEC board member, Prior did not regard the approach as serious and failed to inform the board because he believed the other directors would think that Reynolds, who was not the most highly regarded of GEC's executive directors, had taken leave of his senses.

For want of any movement, Reynolds then talked off the record to a *Sunday Telegraph* journalist, Patrick Weaver, about a looming boardroom coup. Unknown to him, a successor had already been chosen: George Simpson, the chief executive of Lucas Industries. But GEC could not make an announcement because Simpson had not reached a final conclusion about leaving Lucas, which he had only just joined. Weinstock then established that Reynolds had made the mistake of talking to the *Sunday Telegraph* from his phone at GEC's offices. So his less than ceremonious departure preceded that of Weinstock himself. A sad postscript was the premature death of Simon Weinstock from cancer after he had agreed to Simpson's appointment.

This seems an odd way to conduct the affairs of one of Britain's biggest companies, although it should be said in mitigation that succession is always a difficult management task and the overdominant chief executive syndrome is far from being a uniquely British phenomenon. The *président directeur-général* in France – the PDG – often enjoys absolute power in a tradition of centralized leadership that goes back to Louis XIV. In the US there have been notorious instances of chief executive officers hanging on to power despite longstanding poor performance. Perhaps the most egregious was that of paper and packaging giant Champion International, where Andrew C Sigler survived several attempted coups over 20 years of flagging profit figures in which he was supported by a board so packed with friends and allies that it was dubbed 'the Amen choir'.

Disciples of Brezhnev

The much greater concentration of ownership in the UK nonetheless means that the scope for improving corporate governance in the interests of enhanced competitiveness ought to be that much greater than elsewhere. The report of the Cadbury Committee, which was set up in response to a number of corporate collapses and scandals at the end of the 1980s, provides a blueprint for better boardroom practice.[8] Yet the heart of many institutions – if they could be said to have one – is simply not in it. This can be seen, first, by looking at their voting behaviour. A poll in 1995 by the National Association of Pension Funds showed that only 28 per cent of pension funds regularly exercised the voting rights on their shares. A mere 32 per cent reckoned to exercise their votes on contentious issues that fell outside the normal business of company meetings. And 21 per cent never exercised their votes at all.[9] In reality the performance is even worse than it looks. A survey by Pensions and Investment Research Consultants (PIRC), the independent corporate governance consultancy, found that 20 per cent of all votes cast by the institutions are exercised at the discretion of the chairman under proxy powers delegated to him by the fund managers.[10]

Frequently the votes are cast in Pavlovian fashion. In 1994 a shareholder resolution at Yorkshire Water's annual general meeting urged the directors not to commit illegal acts in relation, for example, to the environment. Some 700,000 institutional votes were cast against the resolution, implying that these institutions were in favour of illegal action by the directors.[11] What had probably happened was that the institutions concerned automatically voted against all shareholder resolutions on the basis of thoughtless knee-jerk support for the board. If ever a company called for something other than a knee-jerk response from shareholders, it was Yorkshire Water. The company's treatment of consumers in the drought of 1995, together with its directors' astonishingly inept public statements, became notorious throughout the land.

As for the early warning systems set up by the Association of British Insurers and the National Association of Pension Funds, they frequently fail to pick up some of the larger corporate governance controversies. The NAPF, for example, did not alert its membership when the advertising agency WPP proposed to give a wildly overgenerous remuneration package to Martin Sorrell, the man responsible for the collapse of WPP's finances in the early 1990s. Nor did it initially pick up controversial proposed changes to the memorandum and articles of association at both Hanson and British Aerospace, which would have resulted in a loss of shareholders' voting rights. As so often, it was left to PIRC to campaign on these issues and, in the case of British Aerospace, negotiate changes with management. The same was true on the issue of boardroom pay, which will be explored in the next chapter.

There is, then, a lack of democratic process, and of transparency, in the exercise of institutional power. In effect, there is a rotten borough at the very heart of modern capitalism. This raises important questions about the effectiveness and legitimacy of the system. Indeed, the economists John Kay and Aubrey Silberston have compared governance in British companies with the entrenched authoritarian political systems of Eastern Europe before the fall of the Berlin Wall:

> The governing elite is self-perpetuating, in the sense that it appoints its own members by reference to its own criteria. The process of succession is normally internal and orderly, but from time to time there are peaceful palace revolutions and occasionally externally induced *coups d'état*. The hostile bid for the corporation parallels the military takeover of a government. There is a nominal process of accountability through election of directors, but in practice it is defunct. There are no genuine alternative candidates and incumbents are re-elected with overwhelming majorities. The formal ritual of the corporation's annual general meeting parallels the meaningless elections which routinely returned Mr Brezhnev and Herr Honecker to power. The flow of information about the affairs of the organisation is managed by incumbents and, except in times of acute crisis, is uniformly favourable and optimistic in tone.[12]

Silberston and Kay argue that such authoritarian structures are corrupting because leaders hang on to power for too long, cults of personality develop and empty rhetoric replaces meaningful information. Just as socialist bureaucrats purported to exercise power on behalf of workers who were wholly uninvolved in the governmental process, managers in British and American companies defend their more self-serving actions by claiming that they are undertaken in the interests of the shareholders. Anyone who has ever looked at the annual report of a company will recognise the truth of this description. The directors' references to 'your company' are as vacuous as the cliché about employees being the company's greatest asset.

The underlying point is that, despite the growth of so-called pension fund power, accountability is weak. Institutional shareholder democracy, as the National Association of Pension Funds' own figures show, is at best a very tentative business. As far back as the early 1970s the Heath government and the Bank of England tried to galvanize the institutions into a more active role. Yet the institutions themselves have shown an instinctive reluctance to become productivity chasers and active voters. Most have ignored the recommendation of the Cadbury Committee on corporate governance to publicize their policy on voting.

Much of the problem arises from the existence of conflicts of interest. Professional fund managers in merchant banks in the City compete fiercely to manage company pension funds, a majority of whose trustees are usually directors of the company. As Mike Bishop, a director of the Gartmore fund management group, has put it, 'maybe some of our corporate pension fund clients are not that well managed and they are not going to be happy with us doing this sort of thing'.[13] There is, in addition, a problem that relates to the clients of the bank to which so many fund management groups are attached. In theory, fund managers operate independently of their banking colleagues, maintaining informal barriers between the respective operations, known in the City as Chinese walls. Yet privately some fund managers admit that it is difficult to act aggressively towards a company that is a client of the bank; and the fact that any company could be a potential client is a very powerful force for a non-interventionist stance. The fund managers' incentive schemes may also be related to the performance of the group as a whole, not the fund management business. Such personal incentives are a very powerful motivating (or demotivating) force in the workings of business.

At insurance companies, too, there is a natural reluctance to take issue with companies that have policies with the insurer. And then, of course, there are boardroom links. A fund manager will not lightly take a tilt at a company whose chief executive or chairman sits on his or her own board as a non-executive director. Nor should the costs of shareholder activism be forgotten. The clerical time involved in voting on all issues at annual general meetings is not negligible; and the direct cost of requisitioning an extraordinary general meeting can run to anything from £20,000 to £100,000 at a large company with a big share register.

Stakeholder alternatives

Kay and Silberston are sceptical whether the institutions can ever be persuaded to do a better interventionist job and argue that more shareholder involvement and the provision of fuller information would ultimately undermine management. They reject the principal–agent model of corporate capitalism, arguing instead for a model based on the concept of trusteeship, which is closer to an accurate description of the way in which directors of large companies behave. The objective of the trustee-directors would be to pursue the long-term interests of the business while balancing the interests not only of present stakeholders such as customers, employees and suppliers, but future stakeholders as well. Theirs is a view which accords with the German and Japanese approach in which the task of management is to foster the value of the corporation's assets, rather than the value of its shares. Those assets include the skills of the employees, the expectations of customers and suppliers and the company's reputation in the community.

Kay and Silberston's practical recommendations are for a governance framework in which the independent directors of the company lead a group of independent advisers in selecting a chief executive officer, in consultation with all relevant stakeholders, for a maximum period of two four-year terms. The role and functions of the chief executive and other senior officers of the company would be defined in a new Companies Act. The aim of the blueprint would be to give the chief executive the freedom to manage without undue interference, within a time horizon that is reasonably long term.

This is the nearest thing yet to a proper attempt to develop a full-blown UK version of corporate stakeholding. It is hard to quarrel with Kay and Silberston's diagnosis that the explanatory power of the principal–agent model of capitalism is weak in today's circumstances. What we have is a system where the prevailing norm of managerial trusteeship is sporadically punctuated by manic swings into the assertive form of shareholder control produced by excessive reliance on takeovers. The remedies proposed by the two economists are both radical and thought provoking. Yet their alternative model, which implicitly institutionalizes the view of the chief executive as superhero, poses a number of practical problems. One is the extreme hostility of British industrialists to consulting with worker-stakeholders, or indeed anyone else, over appointments to the board. Another is that many, perhaps most, of the people who run insurance companies and pension funds still believe instinctively in the principal–agent model of capitalism and would probably lobby hard to prevent what they would see as an erosion of their ownership rights. The fact that they do not all use them responsibly now does not mean that they would let them be taken away without a fight. The climate of opinion will have to move a long way before even a Labour government feels able to legislate for this version of the stakeholder idea.

If accountability to a wider stakeholder group is a political non-starter for the moment, there is little alternative but to rethink the nature of the relationship between the institutions and the board. Here it could be argued that Kay and Silberston are overpessimistic about the potential for incremental reform, especially if it is given a political push. The process set in train by the Cadbury committee on corporate governance has greatly improved standards of corporate behaviour. Equally important, there has been a considerable upsurge of interest in voting among pension scheme trustees since the boardroom pay row erupted at British Gas. An awareness finally dawned that the failure to exercise the rights of ownership responsibly not only tarnished the system but led to serious concern on the part of pension scheme members and policy holders, many of whom deluged the institutions with letters on this issue. City fund managers have since been forced into more active voting at the behest of the trustees.

The vacuum left by the trade associations of the insurance companies and pension funds is now more often than not being filled from elsewhere. PIRC, which provides guidance on voting to institutions with more than £120 billion of funds, has played an increasingly active role in advancing the Cadbury pressure for better constituted boards and has put shareholder resolutions in response to the more extreme examples of corporate excess, as at British Gas over boardroom pay. (Ironically, the British Gas pension fund is a PIRC client.) Other corporate governance consultancies have recently been springing up to offer competing services. It is beginning to look plausible that the institutions could play a more effective role in holding industrialists to account in a world where takeovers are no longer the first and last resort for changing management. But the process needs the encouragement of modest legislative change, which will be considered in the next chapter.

The voice of America

At the same time a new and immensely powerful force threatens to bounce both institutions and companies into better corporate governance willy nilly. This is the invasion of Europe by giant US pension funds – a striking new phenomenon that merits exploration in some detail, since the fund managers concerned already exert a far greater influence on Europe's larger companies than most people realize. The big US investment institutions are exporting huge amounts of capital in response to theoretical academic arguments about the value of portfolio diversification. Diversification reduces risk; and there is much statistical evidence which suggests that overseas diversification provides fund managers with a useful way of hedging portfolio bets. The academics have told them that they will either earn higher returns at the same degree of risk, or earn the same returns at a lower degree of risk. This, in simple English, is the investment equivalent of a free lunch. It is probably also academic nonsense, because the more fund managers invest overseas, the more the movement of national markets becomes correlated, so that the benefits of diversification evaporate. Future statistics will probably show that the free lunch has been very unsustaining. But the future has yet to arrive and the American lunchers are here in force. As well as gobbling up a growing percentage of the capital of Europe's larger corporations, they are actively exporting their corporate governance habits as well as their capital.

The US corporate governance movement is a much more lively affair than its UK counterpart. It began in the early 1980s in response to moves by companies to incorporate anti-takeover devices – poison pills – in their internal constitution and to raise boardroom pay to what were perceived to be excessive levels. It has been spurred on by the Securities and Exchange Commission, the chief securities watchdog, with rules to improve disclosure on executive pay and to make it easier for investors to submit shareholder resolutions. The Department of Labor, meantime, makes it compulsory for pension funds to exercise their votes.

Having started as a way of protecting shareholders' rights, the corporate governance movement has increasingly been concerned with companies' performance. This is particularly true at the big state pension funds, most notably the California Public Employees Retirement Fund, known as CalPERS. In the US there is none of the ambivalence or scope for evasion that stems from the British insistence on secrecy. The Council of Institutional Investors, which represents funds with $900 billion of investments, even publishes an annual hit list of poor corporate performers. CalPERS, which controls assets of about $100 billion, identifies every year what it calls 'the Failing Fifty' in its portfolio of 1500 US companies. From this hit list it chooses 10 companies as the focus for its annual gingering activity and publicizes the action it takes.

At first the corporate governance movement ran into an exceptionally hostile response from US industry. General Motors, despite being in serious trouble in the 1980s, refused to answer CalPERS' telephone calls. Now there is a much closer dialogue. And while it is impossible to quantify the impact, it is clear that increased activism did play a role in changing the fortunes of large underperforming companies in the US. Big changes made at such corporate giants as Sears Roebuck, Westinghouse and Eastman Kodak came in response to specific shareholder pressure. CalPERS is convinced that its high-profile activism delivers good shareholder returns. In the US markets people talk of 'the CalPERS effect', by which they mean that when the giant Californian fund decides to take up the cudgels, the stock price of the company concerned usually goes up. A study commissioned by the fund in 1994 looked at the share price performance of 53 companies that it had targeted between 1987 and 1994. It found that having trailed market indices by 75 per cent in the five years before being targeted, these companies had then outperformed the market by 54 per cent in the following five years. The Californians concluded that their activism was generating $150 million in additional returns per year. Subsequent studies have confirmed them in their belief that activism works.[14]

The American spanner in the British corporate works

The fact that the Department of Labor now requires US pension funds to vote on their foreign shareholdings has important implications for governance in the UK. Just how important these could become is underlined by the success of PIRC's campaign to protect shareholders' rights at the Anglo-American conglomerate Hanson. This was the first big example in Britain of what Americans call a 'proxy campaign', with the novel twist that institutional shareholders on both sides of the Atlantic cooperated to safeguard the value of their voting rights.

In essence Hanson was seeking to curtail shareholders' rights in relation to the appointment of directors; to move amendments to resolutions; to speak at annual meetings; and to call polls at meetings. The proposals were sent to shareholders only in a bland, summarized form. A detailed examination of the changes to the articles revealed that the potential erosion of shareholders' rights was significant. PIRC circularized institutions accounting for two-thirds of the Hanson capital with the facts and followed this up with telephone calls which revealed that most of the institutions had not appreciated the nature of Hanson's proposals. Only then did the British insurance and pension fund trade associations wake up. At the same time the United Mineworkers of America, a shareholder in Hanson which was in dispute with the management at Hanson's Peabody coal subsidiary, started to canvas support from US investors, who controlled 20 per cent or more of the capital. The

State of Wisconsin Investment Board and the State of Florida openly declared their opposition to the changes.

Had it been a purely British affair, Hanson might have won the day, even though it needed a 75 per cent majority on a special resolution to do so. But the unaccustomed combination of US compulsory voting and British voting inertia meant that the power of the American investment institutions was magnified out of all proportion to the scale of their shareholdings. Hanson, a very pro-American company that had always claimed to be wholly dedicated to the concept of shareholder value, was forced under pressure from mainly US shareholders to drop the proposed changes. It was, in its way, symbolic of the waning of the Hanson phenomenon, as the world moved on from the red-meat capitalism of 1980s to the more refined business cuisine of the 1990s. But it was also, in the words of Yve Newbould, Hanson's company secretary at the time, a case of the American tail wagging the British dog. She admits to having thought twice about the case for compulsory voting in the light of this experience.

Hanson's management was the first in Britain to discover that the inertia of the majority of its shareholders could actually militate against its objectives. As it happened the US institutions were doing their British counterparts a favour. But the message for the future was clear. As long as the British institutions failed to exercise their votes more actively, British companies were potentially beholden to a minority of active US shareholders whenever they sought to take any important initiative that had to be sanctioned at a company meeting. A *de facto* two-tier voting structure had come into operation.

Few people are aware of how Hanson's retreat was forced on it by American pressure, or of the extent to which sovereignty in British corporate affairs stands to be so casually thrown away. Concern has tended to focus instead on the overassertiveness of one or two individual US funds. In the best-known case a Chicago-based fund manager, David Herro of Harris Associates, used his influence to oust Maurice Saatchi from the Saatchi & Saatchi advertising group, which now goes under the name of Cordiant. Herro felt that Saatchi, who had earlier presided over a 98 per cent fall in the share price, was an expensive luxury on the company's board. Not surprisingly, given Maurice Saatchi's unique relationship with the Tory establishment, this unilateral initiative ran into criticism from predictable quarters. Lord King, president of British Airways, wrote to the *Daily Telegraph* saying: 'Are we to believe that a Chicago-based institution, owning less than 10 per cent of the company's stock, is able to dominate board policy in the United

Kingdom?'. Stanley Kalms, chairman of the Dixons retailing chain, followed suit, declaring that 'this is one of the worst examples of corporate governance I have ever seen'.

Certainly there were grounds for criticizing the undemocratic nature of this crude exercise of power. It would have been better if the issue had been put to an extraordinary general meeting. Yet there will undoubtedly be more such incidents, as US investors expand their overseas portfolios. After Herro's efforts, however, the initiatives may be more discreet. An executive at the New York City pension fund told me that when the fund was worried about Arnold Weinstock's succession at GEC, it approached the board secretly through an intermediary, in the shape of the US shareholder activist Bob Monks, in order not to attract public opprobrium. But voting, as opposed to indirect pressure, is a different matter. In fact CalPERS, which aims to invest 20 per cent of its money overseas, has been voting on its foreign shares at all shareholder meetings since 1990. And it does not go in for the pussy-footing preferred by so many British institutions. In the financial year 1993–4 the fund voted against 138 management proposals out of a total of 950 votes in 13 foreign countries.

Set the beneficiaries free

American activism may ultimately shame the British fund managers into a less supine stance. If the legal climate is to be made more difficult for takeovers, as it should be, this would be all to the good. But it needs to be recognized that if shareholder activism becomes a substitute for hostile takeovers, there can still be some harsh consequences. When, for example, the Council of Institutional Investors in the US put Scott Paper on its hit list, the chief executive officer was replaced by one of the most forthright advocates of downsizing, 'Chainsaw' Al Dunlap, who promptly fired 11,000 people while causing the company's stock market value to triple. Clearly redundancies can be necessary in the interests of competitiveness and survival. But there are dangers if shareholder activism is harnessed to a very narrow concept of shareholder value, as we have seen in Chapter 3.

Kay and Silberston, meantime, worry that a bigger role for shareholders will lead to a relationship similar to the disastrous one that existed between government and the nationalized industries before privatization. Yet the risk here seems remote. Fund managers have none of the incentives to interfere in day-to-day management experienced by politicians and bureaucrats in their dealings with state enterprise. Nor do quoted companies have the problem of being obliged to compete annually for funds for investment with the health service or the nation's schools. Most fund managers continue to believe that they cannot second guess management on managerial issues and prefer to limit their influence to corporate governance matters such as the composition of the board. And if a means could be found to galvanize the institutions into a more active stance on boardroom pay and other areas where the directors are involved in conflicts of interest, this would provide a more effective check and balance than reliance on non-executive directors.

There are no easy or perfect answers to the corporate governance problem. But there could be an alternative, if less radical, stakeholder approach to the one advanced by Kay and Silberston. Given that shareholder activism has been moving, albeit slowly, in a positive direction, it would make sense not to reduce the power of shareholders, as they suggest, but to enfranchise the other main stakeholder group that is substantially excluded from worthwhile involvement: the beneficiaries, who consist chiefly of employees in their capacity as policy holders and members of pension schemes across the country. Later chapters will explore how such a move towards democracy and transparency in corporate governance could advance both the political and economic objectives of stakeholding in ways that would enhance the legitimacy of the system.

In the meantime there is a powerful case for addressing the inertia problem by making voting compulsory. No doubt the response of some funds would simply be to use their votes to provide mindless support for the board. Yet compulsion in the US has, despite this snag, raised consciousness about corporate governance issues. The experience of Hanson is also a salutary lesson in the costs of institutional inertia over here. A further leaf that could usefully be taken from the US book would be a move by the Department of Trade and Industry to follow the US Securities and Exchange Commission in making it easier for shareholders to lodge resolutions. The timetable stipulated by the 1985 Companies Act does not permit such resolutions to be drafted before the publication of the report and accounts, which means that shareholders are denied the crucial source of information on which they would normally wish to base their action. Yet it will take more than this to address the biggest hole at the heart of Anglo-Saxon capitalism, which concerns the handling of boardroom pay. For if anything can be said to have raised questions about the legitimacy of modern corporate capitalism, it is the saga of the fat cats, which is the subject of the next chapter.

8

Survival of the Fattest

*W*hen the public uproar over boardroom pay was at its peak, the right-wing Centre for Policy Studies, founded by Keith Joseph in the 1970s, called a meeting at the Reform Club in Pall Mall to try to bring sense to the debate over the supposed excesses of fat-cat directors. Chairing the meeting was Brian Griffiths, the economist who had once been in charge of Margaret Thatcher's Number 10 policy unit. His chief contribution was to bewail the extent to which envy was driving the argument. Yet most participants at the meeting were clearly impressed by a brilliant presentation in which Andrew Alexander, the far from left-wing City editor of the *Daily Mail*, demonstrated the efficient and systematic means by which directors were transferring money from shareholders' pockets to their own. Some wanted to know why these industrialists were hell bent on losing the election for the Tories. Others were concerned about a failure of accountability at the heart of the capitalist system.

Griffiths had, in fact, got it wrong. The fat-cat episode was not just another example of the egalitarian 'levelling-down' syndrome that had prevailed through much of the post-war period. Nor was public criticism much motivated by that other great bugbear of British industry, class antagonism. Most of the directors of the privatized utilities at the centre of the row had been educated at several removes from Eton and Harrow. The point was rather that the system of incentives and penalties that operated in the utilities and in the wider commercial life of the country had become dangerously distorted. Not only was the great boardroom pay inflation indicative of dismal business leadership when the workforce was having to cope with massive changes and redundancies, it was destructive of the wider sense of national cohesion. The signal emanating from the top of British industry and commerce was that the bosses were in charge; and as far as they were concerned, stakeholding would begin and end in the boardroom. The fat-cat phenomenon was an enormously important contributor to the feelbad factor and was exceptionally destructive of morale in the workplace.

A gong-ho culture

That is not to say that incentives were undistorted before. If we start by considering the utilities, there was, in the pre-Thatcherite period, an implicit social contract in the public sector whereby employees enjoyed job security, while the directors accepted relatively low pay in the knowledge that their public-service commitment would probably be rewarded via the British honours system. This gong-ho culture was tolerant of overmanning and generally inefficient. But the employees, understandably enough, were happy with it. And when customers confronted power cuts or water shortages, they grumbled, but on the whole took it in good heart.

With privatization, all that changed. Formerly low-paid managers of utilities were encouraged to think of themselves as dynamic, entrepreneurial businesspeople. Now that Whitehall was no longer looking over their shoulders, they felt able to pay themselves a great deal more. To some extent this was justified. Under the new dispensation, they were obliged to address the severe problems of overmanning in their industries and to do so in a more transparent and demanding regulatory environment. At the same time the government's propaganda about privatization raised the public's expectations about the quality of service it could expect from the formerly nationalized utilities. In place of the old implicit contract came a commitment to market discipline and efficiency.

Unfortunately efficiency gains were slower to emerge than were spectacular gains in boardroom pay. And the public twigged that the boardroom, whether in the utilities or in the wider corporate sector, was completely exempt from market forces in the specific matter of remuneration, which was nothing more than a fix. In lieu of Adam Smith's invisible hand came the all-too-visible executive hand in the till. When employees at companies like British Gas were being laid off in droves, and the quality of service in many privatized utilities was being heavily criticized, it was simply too much for the public to bear. The processes of the British boardroom were rightly seen as lacking in legitimacy. This episode did immeasurable damage to the Tory political cause. The embarrassment for the government was all the more acute because British Gas had been the vehicle for the most ambitious of its attempts to promote popular capitalism via the privatization programme. Its share register contained countless private investors who had been wooed by an advertising campaign built around the legendary Sid. And now the Sids were threatening to revolt.

All four feet in the trough

The discontent was directed at British Gas with good reason, although it was somewhat invidious that its then chief executive Cedric Brown was singled out for so large a share of the public opprobrium. While his annual salary showed an increase that year of 75 per cent to £475,000, he claimed before the employment select committee of the House of Commons that the rise came down to 28 per cent after making allowance for various changes in bonus and incentive schemes. Some suspected that the chairman Richard Giordano – an American who for many years had been Britain's highest-paid executive while running the industrial gases group BOC – would have been cast in an unflattering light in the absence of a big increase in Brown's pay. Giordano, who sat on the remuneration committee, was being paid £450,000 a year for working a two-day week – a task he somehow managed to combined with the chairmanship of BOC Group, the deputy chairmanship of Grand Metropolitan and a further directorship of the world's biggest mining company, RTZ. If the chief executive had continued to earn less than £300,000 for doing a full-time job, the chairman might have looked unconscionably greedy. In the event the pig that put in an appearance courtesy of the GMB trade union at the rowdy annual meeting of British Gas in May 1995 was called Cedric, not Richard.

The case advanced by Giordano for Cedric Brown's pay rise was that it was needed to retain his services as 'the right man to lead this large, complex and currently very challenging company'. Much emphasis was placed on the international nature of British Gas's business and the need for commensurate rewards. Yet British Gas's profits in 1994 were substantially below their level five years earlier; the dividend was not covered by earnings; and only a marginal proportion of its turnover was derived from overseas activities. So the pay increases were not related to performance at all. They were an advance on future managerial performance of unknown quality. And the suggestion that international yardsticks should apply to the directors' pay was patently self-serving.

Moreover, having informed shareholders that Cedric Brown was the right man to lead the company, Giordano had concluded within a year that there was no place for him in a reorganized British Gas. As it turned out, four of the executives whose services the American had deemed so absolutely indispensable as to require large rises in 1995 had been allowed to depart by the following year. There had long been a concern among British Gas's institutional shareholders that Giordano had been slow to change and improve the quality of the top executives. Subsequent events demonstrated that the rises had been granted to the wrong people.

Throughout the row John Major's government maintained that it was the responsibility of the shareholders to hold management to account over boardroom pay. Yet the response of the giants of the insurance and pension fund business was characteristically weak. A handful of institutional clients of PIRC asked the independent corporate governance consultancy to approach British Gas with a view to seeking amendments to the directors' pay packages. When Richard Giordano failed to budge on the issue, PIRC put a shareholders' resolution at the annual meeting, making the not unreasonable request for British Gas to review its remuneration policy and raise it to the standards advocated by such bodies as the Institute of Directors and the National Association of Pension Funds. At the same time a group of private investors led by Professor Joseph Lamb, a scientist from Fife who was enraged by the size of the pay increases, joined in with another motion calling for British Gas to establish and take advice from a committee of outside shareholders.

The annual general meeting in London's docklands was packed and the atmosphere was hostile in the extreme. As Anne Simpson, joint chief executive of PIRC, put it, ordinary people had been given an unusual glimpse of the wiring of the system and they did not like what they saw. For his part, Joseph Lamb is fond of quoting J K Galbraith:

> The salary of the chief executive of the large corporation is not a market award for achievement. It is frequently in the nature of a warm personal gesture by the individual to himself.

At British Gas, of course, the warm gesture was rather more expansive in that it came from a remuneration committee staffed by like-minded individuals.

Many of the private shareholders who vented their anger by supporting PIRC and Lamb at the meeting were disillusioned and unhappy employees and customers. The grilling they gave the British Gas management sent a message to boardrooms across the land. It felt, says Simpson, a bit like the Peasants' Revolt. As revolts go, it was only partially successful. The turnout for the vote on the peasants' resolutions was 50 per cent – double the previous year's – and of this only 1 in 50 consisted of small shareholders. Some 16.9 per cent of the mainly institutional voters backed the substantive resolution on pay. There is no legal requirement to record active abstentions, of which there were many.

That was the highest level of support ever achieved by a shareholder resolution; far higher than achieved by activists in, for example, the anti-apartheid campaign against Barclays. Yet the fact remains that a majority of the institutional shareholders chose to support the board. This failure to act as a check and balance suggests, once again, that there is indeed a vacuum at the heart of the capitalist system. Why, when it was their money that was being handed over in greatly increased amounts to directors in whom they did not have much confidence, did they back the board in this way? And why were the legal owners of a majority of British Gas's share capital prepared to abrogate responsibility in this crucial area?

The blunt answer is, of course, that they were not the real owners, but the managers of other people's money. No real owner disposing of such large shareholdings would ever have behaved in this way. Bureaucratic owners nonetheless have to justify their actions, which they do by claiming that it is the task of shareholders to delegate the job of management to the managers. And unlike their American counterparts, many British institutions regard opposition to any item on the AGM agenda, even including the directors' pay, as a vote of no confidence in the board and an interference with the right to manage. Giordano played on this feeling to good effect in lobbying the institutional fund managers before the controversial annual general meeting.

While fund managers usually claim to want to see a relationship between pay and performance, there is a general reluctance to pass judgement on absolute levels of pay. This is often justified with the argument that the sums involved are trivial in relation to company profits and shareholders' returns. Alternatively, fund managers claim that too much of the corporate governance debate concerns issues of 'hygiene', such as directors' pay and perks, rather than corporate performance. If something needed doing about performance at British Gas, the argument runs, this could be addressed more effectively by bringing discreet pressure on Richard Giordano behind the scenes rather than having a bruising public confrontation.

Excuses, excuses

These arguments are flimsy. To take the view publicly that the sums involved in directors' pay are immaterial in relation to shareholders' returns comes dangerously close to inviting the directors to loot the company. The concept of materiality is in any case one which the institutions define very narrowly. As Richard Giordano himself admitted, the mishandling of directors' pay at British Gas damaged the company in the eyes both of its employees and customers. Many in the workforce felt betrayed; and what was left of the public service ethos at British Gas was seriously eroded – all of which had an adverse effect on future profits. That shows that the distinction between 'hygiene' issues and performance issues is entirely artificial. The whole episode was symptomatic of the way in which the British boardroom had become unduly remote from the concerns of employees and the public, and of how 'macho' management was destroying social capital.[1]

Boardroom pay surveys consistently reveal that top directors' pay has been rising at up to four times the rate of increase in average earnings. It is hard to believe that the growing disparity between the boardroom and shopfloor can have anything other than a damaging effect on the motivation of the workforce when it is sustained over such long periods, regardless of performance and the wider employment picture. A working environment where some are so blatantly more equal than others is bound to fuel a sense not necessarily of envy, but certainly of injustice and exclusion. Why put in extra performance for no additional reward, when the boss is taking extra reward for no additional performance?

As for the investment institutions' argument that voting against the board constitutes undue interference in the management, this is rather like a nuclear power denying itself the right to use conventional weapons. The issue is anyway not one of management but of corporate governance. 'Undue interference' here is in reality the legitimate and overdue exercise of the ownership right, or stakeholder responsibility, to address the abuse of a potential conflict of interest that stems from directors fixing the remuneration of their colleagues. These longstanding institutional attitudes pre-date the self-regulatory process of corporate governance set in train by the Cadbury committee. Yet the whole Cadbury approach depends on institutional shareholders using their votes to impose a more effective system of checks and balances on management. Resolutions do not have to be defeated for this approach to work. Opposition from a significant minority can amount to serious pressure on the board.

To those who argue that the conflict is best managed behind closed doors, rather than through a 'no' vote, it should be said that the whole idea of checks and balances working in secret to address conflicts of interest comes close to being a contradiction in terms. Few believe that the forceful Richard Giordano would have bowed to private institutional pressure over directors' pay. The institutions claim to have had some subsequent influence on the shape of a long-term incentive plan at British Gas and to have applied pressure for managerial change. Yet they knew perfectly well that a shake-up at the company would not have happened so quickly without a public row. And the visible impact of their wider efforts at secret diplomacy on directors' pay has, as we have seen, been consistent pay inflation in the boardroom.

So even in their own terms, the big investment institutions have failed to exercise proper oversight: the academic evidence suggests that boardroom pay increases are wholly uncorrelated with improvements in company profitability.[2] The evidence at British Gas is that the demoralization of the workforce that results from big boardroom pay increases at a time of financial stringency within the organization can contribute seriously to poor performance. Nor is the impact of the boardroom pay fiasco on the workforce confined to the utilities. The data from International Survey Research quoted in Chapter 6 suggest that it is spread across the whole of industry and commerce.

Cadbury opens Pandora's box

Why, it might be asked, were the institutions deaf to the pleas of a Conservative government that was desperate to be taken off the hook? As so often, it was a mixture of conspiracy and cock-up. The underlying behavioural explanation for blind institutional loyalty to company boards over pay is partly a question of the higher-level conflict of interest in the position of pension fund director-trustees and of insurance company directors. They, too, participate in the gravy train in their capacity as directors of companies, so it is not in their personal financial interest to put an end to boardroom pay inflation. That said, the inflationary ratchet in the boardroom is partly accidental – a perverse outcome of the work of the Cadbury committee itself.

Cadbury encouraged a more formal process of pay setting in the board-room by recommending the establishment of remuneration committees con-sisting mainly of non-executive directors. The task of these committees is to establish a kind of internal market in which the directors' pay is pitched at lev-els which realistically reflect what is required to recruit appropriate people, motivate them and retain their services. The trouble with this, as with the more general reliance on non-executives to act as watchdogs, is that non-executive directors have the same legal obligations as executive directors. Many are exec-utive directors somewhere else and feel a tribal loyalty to the people whose pay they are setting. They thus frequently award them sums that are above the average figures for directors' pay produced by pay consultants.

The pay consultants, members of an under-regulated semi-profession of mixed repute, are in any case anxious to please their clients by producing the numbers they want to see. The Tory former cabinet minister Norman Tebbit, well versed in the ways of remuneration committees, aptly summed it up when he told me he had never come across an executive pay consultant who suggested that anyone was overpaid. And Howard Davies, the deputy governor of the Bank of England, has publicly acknowledged that there has been mutual backscratching in the boardroom over directors' pay.[3] All in all, the remuneration committees have failed to grasp that if everyone is paid more than the current average, the boardroom falls hostage to an inflationary ratchet. The same directors who attack the absurdity of trade unionists declar-ing that they want all their members to be paid more than the average are themselves falling hostage to the same contradiction. The unforeseen risk in Cadbury's otherwise well-intentioned blueprint was that the average would soar. And soar it did.

The fat-cat saga exemplifies the extent to which opportunistic individ-ualism, so prevalent in the City, now infects the boardrooms of British indus-try. It also shows what happens when a system governed by mutual trust and collective restraint gives way to a more formal approach in a sensitive area of corporate behaviour. Before Cadbury many executive directors had no idea how much their colleagues were paid and felt embarrassed about making a big issue over their own remuneration package. From the moment it was turned into a more bureaucratic process, with a greater role for pay consultants and remuneration committees, everyone started to make comparisons. It was only natural that they should feel obliged to assert their own merit in relation to their colleagues in what quickly turned into an explicit bargaining process.

Such behaviour is the opposite of the stakeholder approach and it entails large costs both for the company and for society at large. No political party that wishes to create a real sense of social cohesion in Britain or in the workplace will do so without addressing the issue more directly than Labour has been prepared to do so far. The marked lack of interest displayed by the institutions in asserting control over the great boardroom pay inflation also makes a nonsense of John Major's repeated declarations that it is for the shareholders to curb what he clearly regards as thoroughly unattractive behaviour. And to the extent that there has been any attempt by businesspeople themselves to remedy the abuse, it has had mixed results.

Into the power vacuum left by the institutions stepped a committee under Marks & Spencer chairman Richard Greenbury, set up at the behest of the Confederation of British Industry with only a modest institutional presence. The Greenbury committee obviously represented a big vested interest. But the experienced leaders of industry and commerce who filled most of its seats did at least understand the demotivating effects on the workforce of the fat-cat fiasco. Greenbury's own company, Marks & Spencer, is run on lines close to the stakeholder philosophy. In his report he explicitly urged remuneration committees to be sensitive to pay and employment conditions elsewhere in the company, to ensure that decisions were seen to be consistent and fair.

It is interesting to note, in passing, that a leading luminary on the British Gas remuneration committee was Sir Stanley Kalms, chairman of the Dixons retailing group, who is one of Britain's most outspoken critics of stakeholding. Had the British Gas remuneration committee been more conscious of the intangible values inherent in stakeholder relationships with employees and customers, the whole fiasco might never have happened. In this instance it seems incontrovertible that British Gas would have done better with more Greenbury and less Kalms.

Greenbury's call for remuneration committees to show due sensitivity to what was going on in the rest of the company carried an echo of the only significant statement in company law that comes close to embodying stakeholder values – the injunction in the 1985 Companies Act that 'the matters to which the directors of a company are to have regard in the performance of their functions include the interests of the company's employees in general, as well as the interests of its members'. The trouble with the law here is that it is pretty well unenforceable and has thus been largely ignored. That was a problem that also arose with Greenbury's report, which attracted much criticism from industrialists.

Paws in the pension fund pot

Considering its composition, the committee came up with a surprisingly tough set of recommendations on boardroom pay determination, share options and incentive schemes. Greenbury also recognized that the extent of the inflation in boardroom pay was understated because of a loophole in the disclosure provisions of the Companies Act 1985. Under this legislation companies are not required to show the real value of the pension benefits that the directors grant to each other. The mechanics of pension fund arithmetic are such that if directors' pay is raised sharply before retirement, it can lead to huge increases in retirement benefits and an undisclosed burden on the pension fund which ultimately falls on the company. Actuaries Lane Clark Peacock cite the case of a typical executive director whose retirement pay at 60 is £300,000. The undisclosed capital cost to the pension fund of a pension fixed at two-thirds of final salary, or £200,000, would be £3.5 million. If the final salary is raised, the capital cost increases disproportionately. So as well as having a visible hand in the till, many directors have also had an invisible paw in the pension fund pot.

The Greenbury committee rightly identified a gap that was urgently in need of plugging. In recommending that the true cost of these backdoor pay increases should be revealed in the annual accounts it caused consternation among industrialists, who feared that public concern would be aroused all over again as the press reported multimillion-pound pension payments. For once the institutions started to take an interest, perhaps because they had finally realized that the multiplicity of warm gestures that top executives were making to themselves was causing the bill to add up. A fierce political battle took place between the insurance companies and pension funds on the one side, and leading industrialists on the other, over the method of disclosure. The actuarial profession was caught uncomfortably in the middle.

The outcome was a fudge, whereby the full cost was to remain unrevealed. The compromise reflected the conflicts of interest in the positions of all involved. To those, including the great majority of industrialists, who subscribe to the proprietorial model of capitalism, it might have been thought self-evident that the owners have an absolute right to know how much they are

paying the agents to manage their company. But the industrialists' commitment to the model is once again more apparent in the rhetoric of the annual
report to shareholders, with its references to 'your company', than in their
readiness to disclose in the report the pension consequences of their pay
increases. In reality many subscribe to a somewhat self-serving version of
stakeholding in which they, the trustees, are granted a high degree of managerial freedom with only limited accountability.

The institutions' record over pay and perks has not been wholly negative. Their biggest, and entirely justifiable, concern has been with rolling contracts in the boardroom. These ensure that if a director makes a hash of the
job, he or she cannot be removed without a huge payoff. The rolling contract
is the legal embodiment of the entrenched establishment belief that failure
must never go unrewarded: anyone on a three-year rolling contract can automatically expect to receive three times final salary when sacked for wrecking
the company. Alastair Ross Goobey, chief executive of the Hermes group
which manages the pension funds of British Telecom and the Post Office,
caused a minor sensation in boardrooms around the country when he told
them that he would use the funds' votes against rolling contracts of more than
two years. Greenbury completed the job by suggesting that in most circumstances contracts should be for one year or less. But on just about everything
else the institutions' performance in this area looks hopeless.

Incentive schemes: all carrot and no stick

Arguably the most damaging of the institutions' derelictions of duty over pay
and perks – and Greenbury's biggest failure – concerns share options and
incentive schemes. These have contributed more than anything else to the
growing sense of inequality and injustice both in and out of the workplace.
Since they cannot be discussed without referring to the odd technicality, some
readers may wish to skip a few paragraphs to where we come to their impact
on fixed capital investment. Meantime, for those made of sterner stuff the
story is as follows.

The logic of share-option schemes, which were granted special tax
reliefs by the Thatcher government in the mid-1980s, was that shareholders
would be happy to see their stake in the company diluted in favour of the
management on the basis that the managers would compensate for the dilution by performing much better. Yet the chief result has simply been to provide

them with an indiscriminate windfall gain at shareholders' expense, as the overall level of prices in the stock market has risen. Where share options have been granted just before a decline in the stock market and the price at which they could be exercised turned out to be well above the prevailing share price on the appointed date, companies have simply responded by starting a new scheme in which the options can be converted into shares at a much lower price.

In the case of the privatized utilities the windfall effect was multiplied because so many of them were underpriced at the time of flotation. The extreme case concerned the regional electricity companies, which were floated with excessively strong balance sheets – a point that emerged when Northern Electric promised to pay astonishingly large special dividends to shareholders as part of its defence against a hostile bid from Trafalgar House. By the end of January 1996 the rise in the prices of the shares of these companies ranged from 146 per cent to 346 per cent.[4] Much of the acrimony at British Gas arose precisely because the public recognized that share-option schemes in the privatized utilities were delivering windfall bonuses, often to people who had previously been running the same companies very inefficiently. The irony is that the windfalls were much less at British Gas than at many other utilities because share options were not introduced there until well after privatization.

That is not to say that share options have no incentive effect. As Christopher Fildes of the *Daily Telegraph* has pithily observed, one of the peculiarities of corporate life after privatization is that the grant of share options seems to bring about an instantaneous awareness that the business can suddenly be run with far fewer people. The problem is rather that the incentives often work perversely and in ways that are not in the long-term interests of both shareholders and employees. In a typical share-option scheme the director acquires a right to buy shares at a future date on the basis of a price fixed today. If the shares go up, the director will be able to acquire shares for nothing, by selling some of the entitlement in the stock market in order to finance the purchase of the rest. The crucial point is that the incentive is all carrot and no stick: there is no penalty for managerial failure. It amounts to a one-way bet in which directors can only lose the extra reward they might otherwise have had if things had gone well. Most companies use share options as a handout; most directors sell shares when they are exercised. They are thus more often a perk than a stake which enhances loyalty to the firm. And since a high proportion of share-option schemes exclude all but the most senior executives, they are the embodiment of the values of divisiveness and exclusion.

The class divide that governs the world of incentive schemes is further reinforced by the different rules that apply to employees' participation arrangements. Employees' tax reliefs are dependent on their contributing part of their pay to the scheme, whereas directors do not need to contribute anything. This reinforces the mentality that share options are simply part of directors' pay. In the case of the particular form of option scheme known as statutory employee share-option plans (ESOPs), the tax relief is conditional on the shares being made available to all employees. But in practice most companies that use ESOPs adopt a 'case law' format which allows them to restrict the benefits to directors and top executives. This involves forfeiting the tax advantages, but many boards have been happy to do this in order to run the ESOP as a slush fund for themselves.

The law permits them to use the company's cash or bank borrowings to speculate in its own shares for the benefit of the members of the scheme. This was a one-way bet for the directors. It was also a one-way bet, in the opposite direction, for the shareholders, since they had to pick up the bill if the value of the shares bought on borrowed money went down. Until the Urgent Issues Task Force of the professional accountancy bodies suddenly realized the extent of this abuse and decided to clamp down, it was not necessary to disclose the arrangements to all shareholders.

Greenbury's own goal

Richard Greenbury tried to remedy the worst aspects of share-option schemes by calling for a longer-term approach to incentives and for the grant of options to be subject to challenging performance criteria. In response, companies have adopted a variety of schemes. Among the most popular are so-called performance-based plans, where directors are allocated a notional number of shares and are awarded a proportion of them depending on performance against a target. In deferred payment plans the director buys or is given shares which are then matched by free shares provided by the company depending on performance. A variation on this theme is the equity partnership plan, in which the director's own funds are used to purchase shares in the scheme.

Despite its good intentions, the committee inadvertently sabotaged its own work. In calling for a more long-term approach it made the mistake of suggesting a minimum three-year period for the exercise of options and the implementation of any grant of shares. For most companies the standard definition of long term for the purpose of incentive schemes thenceforth became three years – a maximum as well as a minimum.

This highlights one of the chief difficulties of such schemes. To reward directors on the basis of a company's performance over less than a complete economic cycle will often produce absurd results; and since the 1970s the duration of the economic cycle has tended to be closer to a decade than Greenbury's three years.[5] For a large capital-intensive company – for example, an electricity generator – the success of the directors' investment plans may not be measurable over less than 10 or 20 years. If pay consultants have given any thought to these problems, it is not reflected in the schemes that they have presented to most companies.

Another flaw in the Greenbury report was its call for a change in taxation whereby people would incur an income tax liability when the option was exercised, instead of a liability to capital gains when the underlying shares were subsequently sold. This penalizes people lower down in the company whose profits on the sale of shares would normally fall below the threshold for capital gains tax. The consequence of the committee's recommendation could only be a broadening of the gap between top management and employees, since it made it harder for people to acquire a real ownership stake in their company. In this respect the report was curiously at odds with the stakeholder-type values of Greenbury's own company, Marks & Spencer.

As for the challenging performance criteria, they are turning out to be anything but challenging. The performance trigger for the exercise of options in many post-Greenbury incentive schemes calls for growth in earnings per share of 2 per cent above inflation. This is little more than the average rate of growth in the economy as a whole. That kind of performance would scarcely justify a director's basic pay. Yet the trade bodies of the investment institutions have cheerfully sanctioned these arrangements which deliver incentive payments and bonuses for sheer mediocrity.

The growth of such schemes is producing bizarre results. One of the more extreme cases was at HSBC, the parent company of Midland Bank and the Hongkong and Shanghai Banking Corporation. The directors proposed a restricted share-option plan for executive directors that gave them awards worth up to four times the participants' annual remuneration, equivalent to a maximum of £16 million, if they achieved real growth in earnings per share of 2 per cent. This was hugely generous by the standards of most other incentive schemes, even if the performance targets were measured over four years rather than three. And given that HSBC still earns a significant part of its profits in

Asia, where the more dynamic economies are capable of growth rates that sometimes run into double figures, the performance criteria looked astonishingly unchallenging. In response to criticism Sir William Purves, the chairman, took the novel step of urging shareholders to vote for the scheme on the basis that it was not the board's intention to pay anywhere near the maximum permitted amounts.

If a government announced its public spending plans while declaring that it had no intention of implementing them in full, its ministers would be laughed out of court. But corporate governance is different. And investors are very different from voters. Despite the obvious signs that someone at HSBC had bungled, the great majority of votes – 89 per cent in HSBC's sterling-denominated shares and 72 per cent in its Hong Kong dollar shares – were cast in favour of this 'incentive' plan at the annual general meeting. The implied protest vote respectively of 11 per cent and 28 per cent was, however, unusually high by the standards of the corporate world.

In practice it is hard – perhaps even impossible – to devise an incentive scheme based on total shareholder returns that delivers consistently sensible results. Michael Brett, a former editor of the *Investors Chronicle* who now advises PIRC, has demonstrated that such schemes tend to over-reward companies that show low growth with a volatile share-price performance relative to those that show higher overall growth with a steadier share-price performance.[6] These schemes also tend to be complex and for that reason they are popular with boardroom pay consultants, for whom complexity is a money spinner. As Warren Buffett, the sage investor from Omaha, has put it, 'consultants cannot easily send a large bill unless they have established that you have a large problem (and one, of course that requires an annual review)'.[7] Yet complexity means that the motivational link between incentive and human behaviour is weakened: some directors find it hard to explain to outsiders what it is about a given scheme that makes them behave differently.

Contrary to Greenbury's recommendation, many companies are introducing long-term incentive schemes not as a replacement for their existing share-option schemes, but as an addition. The institutions have once again failed to exercise effective oversight, often permitting a baroque outgrowth of different incentive arrangements in the same company. In some cases the total cost is far from trivial. Once again, the question is why the institutions fail to exert any kind of control. In fact, they do carry out some monitoring through their trade associations, the Association of British Insurers and the National Association of Pension Funds. But its chief focus concerns the threat of dilution – that is to say, the threat that managers will issue themselves with so many shares that the other shareholders' percentage stake in the company will be forcibly reduced.

A big boost for short-termism

The real answer is that the institutions themselves are, of course, part of the game. The directors of insurance companies and the director-trustees of pension funds are beneficiaries of their own largesse in adopting a permissive stance towards overgenerous schemes. A further complication is that the non-executives sometimes share in the same incentive schemes as the executive directors. This can mean that they are monitoring the terms of a share-option scheme in which they themselves participate. And since directors normally forfeit their options if they resign, the non-executives have a powerful disincentive to use their biggest sanction – a noisy public resignation – against poorly performing executives. The threat of resignation, which in itself is an important weapon, also becomes less potent.

In the end the Association of British Insurers has been goaded belatedly into action, helped (or prodded) by the outcry in the press over the absurdly unchallenging performance criteria in most incentive schemes. It finally came out in public for the first time against a scheme at United Utilities, the multi-utility based in the north west of England. Yet this was not notably worse than some schemes already in operation. The ABI was simply nibbling at the edges of the problem – a problem, moreover, which has important motivational effects.

Just as the Cadbury committee inadvertently unleashed an explosion in boardroom pay, a lack of institutional restraint may now mean that the Greenbury report becomes an unexpected and exceptionally powerful force for short-termism. This is because companies usually interpret the committee's call for challenging performance criteria in terms of two measuring rods – earnings per share or shareholder return – over which the directors wield direct influence. Earnings are notoriously capable of accounting manipulation, while dividend policy, a key component of shareholder return, is in the hands of the directors.[8] Within the standard post-Greenbury time frame of three years, such arrangements are a recipe for a fast-buck financial culture. Instead of encouraging the long-term prosperity of the business they are likely to exert a powerful motivating influence for more and less judicious takeovers, endless downsizing and low fixed investment. This is one more reason to believe that the insecurity phenomenon discussed in Chapter 2 will not go away.

In the privatized utilities, meantime, such incentives may contribute to a further tilt in the balance of advantage away from the consumer in favour of directors and shareholders. Nor will the British system of price-cap regulation provide much of a safeguard. As we will see in the next chapter, the directors of utilities are adept at pulling the wool over the regulators' eyes. Incentive schemes will give them a powerful additional reason to exploit their information advantage to keep prices higher and standards of service lower in the natural monopolies.

One problem with addressing the consequences of this ill-conceived incentive structure, with its bias against long-termism, is that so much of the policy establishment sees fixed investment in terms of the macroeconomic big picture, while tax reliefs on incentive schemes are in a wholly separate microeconomic pigeon hole to do with responding to pressure from lobby groups such as the CBI or the Institute of Directors. Few in the Treasury see the connection between the two; no one monitors the behavioural impact of such tax breaks. If politicians wish to address a perceived problem of underinvestment, the traditional means, exemplified in Labour policy, is to juggle with capital allowances within the corporation tax system.

It is strange, too, that the impact of financial incentives on managerial behaviour is not the subject of more detailed academic analysis. In the post-Cold-War world there is an enormous amount of research on the distorting impact of socialist planning on human motivation. Public choice theory provides sophisticated – some would add cynical – analysis of the motivation of politicians and bureaucrats in the capitalist world, with its view of them as 'personal utility maximizers'. Yet the motivation of individuals within the boardroom, which is a matter of great importance for the workings of the economy, remains underdiscussed, except by those such as consultants who have a vested interest.

It is only natural that any manager whose remuneration is related to company earnings will think twice about making an investment that will cause those earnings to fall in the short run despite increasing later. And when managers' rewards are related to the total return to the shareholders, they will naturally convince themselves that a higher level of dividend is desirable. These things are not susceptible of direct proof. But common sense suggests that the sudden proliferation of incentive schemes with a three-year time horizon will entrench short-termist thinking in industry and commerce to an unprecedented degree.

Political and economic fallout

The wider question concerns the motivation of the workforce and the perceptions of the public at large. How much inequality can they stomach without there being some adverse response? How long before the shrinkage of social capital and the loss of trust within the firm have an impact on competitiveness? The erosion of trade union power under the Thatcher government means that the damage, in terms of industrial disruption, is less today than it would have been in the past. But there are other costs, economic and psychological. If labour-market conditions tighten, it will become much harder to resist inflationary wage demands from a disgruntled workforce. At a broader level, there is a strong case for more academic work on the diseconomies of a business culture in which conduct is taken to the limits of legality, unrestrained by social mores.

The evidence discussed in earlier chapters suggests that extreme individualism, whether in the boardroom, on the dealing floor or in the street, is not the most efficient way to conduct economic relations, if only because mutual trust – the stakeholder ethos – is a less expensive way of reaching agreements than private contract. The story of British Gas in the present chapter makes the same point in a different way. With such a dismal example being set by the board, the employees would be less than human if they were not now restricting their service to the customer and their loyalty to the company to the minimum they could get away with. Many feel badly let down. And sure enough, this industry which used to be admired for the excellence of its technology and the safety of its supplies is showing signs of waning – some would say collapsing – service standards in the wake of the public row.

It is impossible to measure the damage that the boardroom pay saga has done to society at large, but it is hard to believe that the impact on values has been other than corrosive. It is instructive, for example, that water consumption in Yorkshire actually went up in response to an expensive advertising campaign to encourage restraint in the 1995 drought after the chief executive had misled the public about how often he took a bath. Foolish behaviour by a fat cat whose pay increase was deeply resented appears to have resulted in a clear loss of civic engagement among the people of Yorkshire.

So far, then, the attempt to establish an internal market for pay in the British boardroom has been a sorry affair. The outcome has been to destroy social cohesion, demotivate the workforce and embed even more firmly in the bloodstream of British management Keynes's notorious dictum that in the long run we are all dead. The political, economic and social ramifications of the problem are very serious. No political party that claims to believe in stakeholder values can allow this to persist without proposing tangible remedies. So what should be done?

Democracy and daylight

The conventional answer to corporate abuse, offered by proponents of the principal–agent model of corporate behaviour, is to try to align the interests of managers and owners more closely. But as we have seen, what happens in practice is that any attempt to do this is more likely to align the managers' interest with those of other managers in insurance companies and on boards of pension funds; it does not align them with the interests of the ultimate owners, the policy holders and pensioners.

What is needed, to start with, is a reinvigoration of the trust concept which is supposed to govern the institutions' operations by making those operations more transparent. This could be done by giving rights to the other important stakeholder group that is substantially excluded from worthwhile involvement: the beneficiaries. In practice, pension scheme members and policy holders are mainly employees making provision for retirement and other contingencies. If they had the right to see how the institutions had voted on any given issue, the institutions might well be forced into a more responsible exercise of voting power.

Some, including Labour front bench spokesman Alastair Darling, argue that beneficiaries would not be interested. While it is true that they would probably not pay much attention to the routine resolutions, there are still areas such as boardroom pay, big acquisitions and changes in the company's internal constitution where passions often run high. Had the institutions been compulsorily obliged to disclose how they voted over boardroom pay at British Gas, for example, it is a safe assumption that angry employees and customers would have been delighted to make use of the right to find out how the managers of their insurance policies and pension funds had behaved.

Insurance companies and professional fund managers operate in competitive markets. If they thought that the way in which they cast their votes might be disclosed in the press, they would think twice about offering unwavering support for the directors on boardroom pay for fear of losing both existing and new business. Many did, in fact, receive a big postbag over the British Gas pay issue. And employee trustees at some of the big pension funds were incensed to discover that fund managers had committed themselves to supporting the board without consulting them. A number have changed voting procedures to ensure that trustees now have a bigger say on the more important votes.

The advantage of letting daylight into the voting process is that it then makes it possible to deploy institutional muscle in other constructive ways. The suggestion by Jonathan Charkham and others that institutional shareholders might be more directly involved in setting boardroom pay would, for example, become a more realistic option. It would also make sense to address one surprising omission in Greenbury's recommendations: the absence of a compulsory requirement to put the remuneration committee's report to the vote. While some companies do this voluntarily, others – including many of the privatized utilities that would probably encounter hostile votes – do not. This could be simply remedied through the existing self-regulatory process, in which the Stock Exchange provides the disciplinary back-up.

For democracy and transparency to be effective it would be necessary for the more important votes to be exercised not by City fund managers, who would be reluctant to be seen to have voted against present or potential corporate clients, but by pension fund trustees. To provide an additional safeguard, disclosure provisions would probably have to stipulate that, where the votes were cast by professional fund managers and insurance companies, these institutions should also reveal the existence of potential conflicts in relation to their existing corporate clientele. No doubt many would complain about the cost of keeping a voting register and making it available to the beneficiaries. But it would probably be much smaller than the cost of the annual increase in boardroom pay; and by bringing much-needed legitimacy to the system it would produce a much wider offsetting gain.

On the more specific issue of incentive schemes, it is tempting to argue that the difficulty of arriving at any watertight form of performance measurement means that we would be better off without them. That point has been made to me by top executives at a leading Anglo-Dutch multinational, who believe that they are profoundly destructive of the teamwork ethos and of stakeholder values. But the same executives also argue that as long as other companies adopt such schemes, it would be impossible to recruit and retain good managers. It follows that if anything is to be done to change the system to make it less corrosive of the teamwork ethos, it will require alterations to the tax system.

That suggests, for example, that tax relief for incentive schemes should be restricted to those which are open to employees on broadly similar terms. Clearly there is a need for inequalities in pay if people are to be motivated and success rewarded; and there have to be different levels of participation in incentive schemes, since executive staff bear greater responsibility for corporate performance. But equal tax status for directors' and workers' share incentives is a powerful antidote to the message implicit in the whole fat-cat saga: it would send a symbolic signal to the effect that the capitalist game, far from being exclusive, was worth the candle for everyone.

Also necessary is some stipulation that tax relief will be available only where an incentive scheme is genuinely long term and entails an element of stick as well as carrot. The obvious way to do this is to restrict relief to those schemes where the participants commute part of their salary in exchange for a future stake in the company. The Prudential offers some elements of a potential model here, in a deferred payments scheme whereby senior managers can use their performance-related bonuses to buy shares in the company which are lodged with a trustee. Provided that the director leaves the shares with the trust for five years, the Pru puts in additional shares for the director. The important point is that top managers suffer if the shares go down, just as they profit if they go up.[9]

If these relatively modest legislative changes fail to curb the abuse of share-incentive schemes, then the only alternative would be to regard the whole problem as a rather peculiar form of market failure to be addressed through alterations to the capital gains tax regime. Long-termism could be imposed, for example, via a higher percentage rate on realized gains made in the first five years, tapering down to the normal capital gains tax rate in subsequent years. This would have the additional advantage of acting as a counterweight to the directors' personal incentive to make excessive dividend payments, since it would encourage them to participate in profits via long-term capital gains instead of immediate dividends.

Perverse incentives for the utilities

Particular difficulties arise, however, in the area where the fat-cat row began: the utilities. The decision to privatize the natural monopolies in the form of public limited companies has resulted in their adopting the same types of incentive schemes as other plcs. Yet when it comes to striking a balance between the different stakeholders, the customers of the utilities do not enjoy the protection that comes from the operations of a competitive product market. There is no countervailing power to restrain the directors' pursuit of shareholder value, other than that of the regulator, which has not offered consistently sound protection for consumers. Incentive schemes thus introduce a further behavioural bias in favour of directors and shareholders.

This further underlines the oddity of the Major government's argument that the determination of boardroom rewards should be left to the shareholders. It is absurd to reward the bosses of monopolistic utilities purely on the basis of the returns they deliver to a single stakeholder group, the shareholders, while other stakeholder interests are ignored. It is even more ridiculous to look to the shareholders to police the conflict of interest inherent in the directors' position. A typical result is that water company bosses enjoy large performance-related bonuses, while simultaneously giving poor service to the consumer and incurring a high level of prosecutions for pollution. Small wonder that the public's sense of civic responsibility is breaking down in the face of appeals for restraint in the use of this most basic commodity.

Should the performance criteria for the utilities' incentive schemes include criteria based on data from the regulators about levels of service? This would be logical – but for it to work, someone would have to play a policing role. In practice, the regulators are the only people who could pass an impartial judgement on whether the criteria were in the public interest. The auditors would then have to pronounce on compliance. Yet this seems cumbersome and the problems would be compounded by the soft nature of much data on the quality of service. The fact is that incentive schemes in the monopolistic utilities give rise to conflicts of interest on such a scale that it would be better to dispense with them, even at the cost of higher basic pay for the directors.

Consider, for example, the extreme case, which concerns the privatization of the nuclear industry. The remuneration committee of the newly privatized British Energy is proposing that a significant proportion of directors' pay should take the form of bonuses which will be related to challenging performance targets. The risk is that safety standards could be eroded because the costs of shutting down a nuclear reactor are so great that they could have a marked effect on people's bonuses.

As the Institution of Nuclear Engineers has pointed out, a cautious approach of shutting down plant before a problem develops into an accident is the safest course of action; but if it is subsequently and frequently found to have been unnecessary, caution becomes harder for individual managers to justify. There are, of course, watchdogs such as the Health and Safety Executive and its Nuclear Installations Inspectorate. But think of the comparison with Barings, which was supervised before its collapse by powerful watchdogs ranging from the Bank of England to the notoriously tough government authorities in Singapore. The lesson at Britain's oldest merchant bank was that when the people in charge are expecting big profit-related bonuses, their critical faculties are dulled – and that the regulators provide an inadequate line of defence.

In fairness, it should be said that British Energy is proposing to include safety targets in its performance yardsticks and its executives are acutely conscious of the unusual nature of the risks. It could also be argued that the biggest nuclear accident, at Chernobyl in the former Soviet Union, took place under public ownership. But the fact remains that we are testing the hypothesis that bonuses are safer in the nuclear industry than in banking through a process of trial and error. Whatever the past record, and however unlikely an accident now appears, this takes experimental method to the borders of lunacy. No sane person would object to the directors of British Energy being compensated with higher basic pay for any decision to abandon the scheme.

Where boardroom pay is concerned there are limits to what can be achieved through fiscal juggling, changing the corporate governance rules and playing with the regulatory structure. We need to recapture a culture of moral responsibility and collective restraint. This ought to be possible at least in the utilities, which are a natural home for managers who feel a strong sense of public service. Rebuilding that ethos will call for change in the intellectual as well as the political climate. In a civilized society the higher priority in responding to inequality should anyway be given to addressing the problems of the many at the bottom end of the income distribution rather than the few who exhibit greed at the top. It would be nice to think that Labour's lack of interest in penalizing the fat cats reflected such concern. But pre-electoral opportunism seems a more likely explanation. And shadow chancellor

Gordon Brown's proposed tax on utilities to finance education and training seems an odd response, since the cost can only fall on shareholders, many of whom bought their shares after the windfall gains were reaped, rather than on the people who did the damage.

On a matter that touches so obviously on controversial issues of fairness and inclusiveness, as well as economic efficiency, it remains a worrying feature of the way democracy now works that there has not been a more serious political debate. The fat cats are, after all, one of the biggest obstacles to the creation of the stakeholder economy which Tony Blair so enthusiastically outlined in Singapore.

9

Unpopular Capitalism

*T*he belief of the early Fabians in the absolute efficacy of state ownership has been matched only by the passionate dedication of late twentieth-century Tories to the idea that business is best conducted through the vehicle of the public limited company. The Tories' enthusiasm found its ultimate expression in the privatization programme, in which the vast lumber room of state enterprise, chock-a-block with the detritus of empire, socialist ideology and tired corporatist nostrums, was cleared out in the jumble sale to end all jumble sales. This enormous divestment of public assets was on a scale matched in British history only, perhaps, by the dissolution of the monasteries and the sale of the great aristocratic country estates after the Great Depression of the nineteenth century. Privatization was conducted in the name of greater economic efficiency, better public finances and wider share ownership. It was, in its way, the Conservative version of stakeholding.

Nigel Lawson, an enthusiastic advocate of popular capitalism, put the case in these terms, as the privatization programme was beginning to gather steam:

Those who, in the nineteenth century, argued the dangers of a mass democracy in which a majority of the voters would have no stake in the country at all, had reason to be fearful. But the remedy is not to restrict the franchise to those who own property: it is to extend the ownership of property to the largest possible majority of those who have the vote. The widespread ownership of private property is crucial to the survival of freedom and democracy. It gives the citizen a vital sense of identification with the society of which he is a part. It gives him a stake in the future.[1]

One difficulty in this view, as it applies to shareholding, relates to the questions raised by Berle and Means about fragmented ownership (see Chapter 7). Private share ownership may indeed deliver a stake in future prosperity, but it remains a very limited franchise, affording little say in the affairs of the companies that pay the dividends. Another is that the Tory version of popular capitalism reflects an exaggerated and somewhat one-dimensional view of ownership – a subtle and complex concept which has been unduly coarsened by the political debate of the past century and a half. Nowhere have the complexities been more clearly demonstrated than in the sale of the Trustee Savings Bank, a story that bears telling because it exposes the shallowness of much conventional thinking on the nature of ownership and control. It is also a classic case study in the destruction of social capital accumulated over generations.

The flotation of the TSB was not technically a privatization because the government was not, at the outset, the owner of this old-established high-street banking group. The Treasury's decision to float the TSB on the stock market in fact precipitated a protracted legal dispute to establish whether it was owned by itself, by its depositors or by the state. Indeed, Nigel Lawson talks of this decision in his memoirs as though there were something inherently absurd about a bank with no owners. This is odd, given that the concept of trusteeship, which is entirely distinct from the forms of control embodied in the Companies Acts, has a long and respectable pedigree in English law. It is doubly odd in the light of the superior profit performance of the TSB before its flotation when compared with the joint-stock clearing banks.

The narrow view displayed by Lawson and his colleagues towards anything other than standardized shareholding was to have unfortunate consequences for the TSB, whose chequered life as a public company came to an abrupt end when it disappeared into the maw of Lloyds Bank in yet another cost-cutting takeover. The TSB's fate sadly demonstrates how the erosion of Britain's hitherto pluralist tradition of ownership, embracing mutual organizations, trusts, cooperatives and other forms of tenure, has resulted in a real loss of social capital.

Real Victorian values

The original trustee savings banks were a good example of how a vital civil society spawns all kinds of intermediate groups to solve problems that the existing system fails to address. In Lawson's own words, the trustee savings movement 'consisted of a constellation of somewhat curious organizations, whose origins lay in the Scottish thrift banks established during the industrial revolution for labourers too poor to afford the £10 minimum deposit then required by the joint stock banks'. In reality, they were no more curious than the countless savings banks that are still to be found in most other countries of the developed world. And their original purpose was to address a welfare problem that is once again at the forefront of the political debate.

The first savings bank in the United Kingdom was founded by the Reverend Henry Duncan in Ruthwell, Dumfriesshire in 1810. He was motivated by the worry that the introduction of the English poor law into Scotland would destroy the independence of the Scottish people, erode incentives to work, loosen the bonds of the family and sap initiative. His legacy was a savings movement which, in the early 1980s, retained very distinctive features. Unlike the leading clearing banks, the trustee savings banks remained under autonomous regional control, with a strong bias towards Scotland, Northern Ireland and the north of England. They continued to cater for people in the lower income brackets, some of whom might not have been regarded as profitable clients by the clearing banks. And they still embodied those values of thrift and community which, despite the Thatcherite rhetoric about Victorian values, went largely out of the window in the Thatcher years. In effect, the trustee savings banks offered the nearest thing to an ownership stake to which the poor could aspire. Instead of a return in the form of dividends and capital growth, they received a modest interest payment together with the social insurance that came from the redistribution of any surplus towards the less well off in the community.

Why it should have been thought necessary to float the TSB in the first place is hard to fathom. Lawson had sensibly given the trustee savings banks the freedom, while he was financial secretary to the Treasury under Geoffrey Howe, to offer a wider range of banking services, thereby increasing competition in the banking market and providing a better service to customers. Their operations, which were confined to the consumer market, were very profitable. They were not in need of capital, nor likely to be so for the foreseeable future, if left to continue their business unmolested.

Despite the absence of any identifiable owners, the TSBs, which were integrated into a single bank in the early 1980s, were also innovative. They were well ahead of the clearing banks in finding ways of cross-selling insurance and pensions products to their existing clientele at the branches. So successful was this operation that it frightened even the most aggressive of the insurance companies in the 1980s, as the TSB shot up the league tables for sales of life assurance and pensions. As well as being profitable, this business delivered a useful social dividend, since the C2 and D social groups that the TSB looked after were underinsured and overdependent on a state pension system which the government was busily eroding.

No doubt the Thatcher government's preoccupation with the conventional version of popular capitalism lay behind the decision to float this unusual savings institution. There was an assumption that the discipline of the capital market would lead to improved accountability for the TSB and increased competition for the clearers. Launching the bank as a quoted company nonetheless proved harder than anyone had expected because depositors raised substantial objections. Leading them was Dr John Vincent, an articulate methodist clergyman from Sheffield, who argued that the bank had always been held 'upon trust' for the depositors. The original Sheffield savings bank, he pointed out, had included 24 ministers of religion in its governing body as a way of emphasizing the uncommercial intent of the institution. Surpluses of trustee savings banks across the land had been used, in the earlier days of the TSBs, to build schools and libraries in local communities, while profits in more affluent branches had frequently helped subsidize the poorer branches. Vincent's fear was that a commercialized TSB would cease to serve the poor. He suspected that it would open branches in the prosperous south and south east, while closing them in northern areas of unemployment and poverty.

A lengthy process of litigation ensued, in which the courts tried to resolve the question of who owned the bank. It culminated in a surprise ruling by five law lords, with Lord Templeman to the fore, that the bank was owned not by itself or by the depositors, but by the state. This appeared to mean that the taxpayer was entitled to the proceeds of the sale. However, the politics of turning the float into a genuine privatization were tricky, given the strength of feeling against the whole enterprise from those who feared that the TSB would lose its strong regional and social characteristics. While the Treasury might have welcomed the benefit for the public finances, the politicians would not have relished a political row in which the Treasury's serendipitous windfall could all too easily have been characterized as the rape of the TSB by a predatory state. The government's law officers came to the rescue with some helpful sophistry. 'The state', they argued, was entirely distinct from 'the government', so the proceeds of the float could be redirected away from the taxpayer to the TSB's own coffers.

Meantime the Scottish lobby succeeded in throwing a spanner in the works. When the flotation was put before the House of Lords in a poorly attended debate at a late hour, Lord Taylor of Gryfe moved an amendment for the Scottish TSB to be floated as a separate, independent Scottish bank. To the consternation of the government and the directors of the TSB, the amendment was carried. Lord Taylor was only persuaded to drop his amendment on the basis of assurances from ministers, and from the TSB, that the Scottish TSB's headquarters would be in Edinburgh and that the independence of its operations would be respected.

Spend, spend, spend

After these legal and political upsets the TSB finally came to the market in September 1986. It was inevitably and absurdly underpriced, for as Nigel Lawson himself has pointed out, if the bank was worth £1 billion and sold to the public for that amount it would be worth £2 billion after receiving the proceeds. If, to take account of this, the company was sold for £2 billion, it would become worth £3 billion after the sale and so on, *ad infinitum*. In City terms the flotation was therefore a success. The TSB acquired 3.5 million enthusiastic shareholders and £1.3 billion of new capital which it did not need. Some months later the Comptroller and Auditor General, Gordon Downey, warned ominously that Parliament might have taken a different view of the enabling legislation if it had been better informed about the TSB's capital requirements. 'This matter does not appear to have been as fully considered as the sums at stake would seem to justify,' he said. And sure enough the sudden influx of cash quickly burned a hole in the bank's pockets.

In 1987 the TSB spent £777 million on the acquisition of Hill Samuel, a merchant bank that had never quite made it into the big league. In the midst of the takeover process in October that year the stock market collapsed, leaving the bank with a purchase whose value had suddenly declined. The TSB's attempts to withdraw from the bid ran foul of the Bank of England, which was seriously concerned about the soundness of the banking system after Black Monday, on which stock markets around the world had crashed. The last thing the Bank of England wanted was for Hill Samuel to be deprived of the TSB's huge cushion of capital in an incipient banking crisis and it did not hesitate to apply what is euphemistically called moral suasion. Although it had no legal powers to prevent the TSB backing away, the management, led by John Read, the former chairman of EMI, could not bring itself to call the Bank of England's bluff.

Thus (expensively) enlarged, the TSB embarked on a strategy that involved supporting Hill Samuel in an ambitious expansion of its lending operations. Its advertising cheerfully declared that it was 'the bank that likes to say yes'. It had earlier bought the Target fund management and insurance group for £229 million. When Nicholas Goodison, the former chairman of the London Stock Exchange, took over as chairman in 1989 he scrapped the TSB regional board structure and got rid of 100 regional non-executive directors. What had once been regarded as regional strength was now seen as an undesirably fragmented structure. By the end of the decade 200 of the top 300 senior and middle managers inherited from the old TSB had been replaced. A single long-serving savings banker was left in the top management team. The assurances given to Lord Taylor proved utterly worthless.

None of these changes did the TSB or its shareholders much good. In 1991 the bank was obliged to announce losses of £150 million. Much of Hill Samuel's lending spree had involved saying yes to companies like the leisure and property concern Brent Walker, an early victim of the recession, so there were large provisions for bad debts. The Target group was sold at a substantial loss. In the event Hill Samuel ate up more than £1 billion of the group's capital, while Target absorbed another £300 million. The sorry outcome was that the capital raised in the TSB's flotation had been wiped out within five years.[2]

The paradox was that a TSB with owners was not only less successful than one without, it appeared to be subject to no real accountability: neither the chairman nor the chief executive resigned after this chapter of accidents. As for capital market discipline, its impact on the TSB's customers was unfortunate in that the resulting pressure to generate increased profits led to the TSB becoming deeply implicated in the scandal involving the mis-selling of personal pensions. In the end the government's desire to have the TSB increase competition in banking had a wholly perverse outcome. The takeover by Lloyds, with its attendant branch closures, inevitably reduced competition in the retail banking market.

Proud remnant

Compare and contrast the fate of the TSB with that of Britain's last independent savings bank, the Airdrie Savings Bank in Lanarkshire. Founded in 1835, this mutually owned organization is constituted under its own separate act of parliament. With seven branches it offers a wide range of banking services to personal customers and local businesses. The distinctive feature of the Airdrie Savings Bank is that it is firmly rooted in the local community; and the commitment goes well beyond that of any joint-stock bank. Its staff go into local schools to teach children the basics of banking and finance, for example, and they also take banking services to homes for the elderly. These activities are acknowledged as non-profit making. But they are undertaken as a matter of community commitment.

The Airdrie Savings Bank was invited shortly after its inception in the nineteenth century to join the burgeoning trustee savings bank movement, the incentive being that the government had agreed to guarantee the trustee savings banks' deposits. The bank, which valued its autonomy, said no. When the TSB was about to be floated in the 1980s the Airdrie bank was once again invited to join up. Again it opted for self-reliance. Today it survives and thrives in splendid isolation and even manages to win business from larger banks, while the whole trustee savings bank movement has disappeared. Lloyds, which bought the TSB, is the most committed of all the clearing banks to the concept of shareholder value and the most efficient exponent in banking of the cost-cutting takeover. Its culture is thus wholly antipathetic to the values of the old savings bank movement, which were close to those of the stakeholder ideal. Nothing could more clearly underline how much easier it is to destroy social capital than to create it – or how an obsessive preoccupation with putting enterprise into the strait-jacket of the public limited company can produce perverse results.

In spite of this experience, commitment to alternatives to the plc form of ownership is rapidly eroding. Mutuality in the building society movement, for example, is on the way out as the societies, led by Abbey National and Halifax, have opted to become plcs or fallen victim, like National & Provincial, to takeovers from outside the movement. Proponents of this push towards shareholder ownership argue that mutuality protects the boards of building societies from any real accountability to the ultimate owners, the depositors. Yet this supposed lack of discipline did not prevent the societies from holding on to their position as the dominant force in the market for the deposits of the great British public and for mortgage lending before demutualization gathered pace. This they achieved by offering a more user-friendly service than the clearing banks.

While building societies lack access to the stock market, this has scarcely been a disadvantage. It is striking that their competitors, the clearing banks, have been no more successful than the TSB in making use of the capital they have raised from their shareholders. In the inflationary 1970s the clearers incurred huge losses in property; in the 1980s they made expensive mistakes in Latin American lending; and by the early 1990s they had succumbed to an extraordinary case of collective memory loss whereby they threw away yet more money in another property *débâcle*. So much for accountability. For their part, the building societies, despite the deep recession in the housing market, continued to prosper.

In spite of all this, the building society movement will continue to shrink, not least because the old mutual ethos has not proved robust in the growth-hungry, profit-conscious environment of the Thatcher years. One symptom of this weakness was the way in which societies persisted for many years in offering the best mortgage deals not to the existing customers, the mutual owners, but to new customers who were not necessarily members of the society at all – a needless betrayal of the values of mutuality. Today the existing customers are finally receiving a better deal. But the individualist ethos in the rest of Britain's boardrooms has rubbed off on many of the larger building societies. Amid all the elaborate justifications they offer for floating on the stock market, building society managers fail to mention the most powerful incentive for abandoning mutuality: the lure of share-incentive schemes. For that reason alone it is safe to predict that the building society movement will increasingly go through its own equivalent of privatization, although without obvious improvement in performance.

Nationalization: the failed experiment in stakeholding

That is not to deny the merits of privatization, the supreme policy innovation of the Thatcher period, which Peter Riddell of *The Times* has called 'the Jewel in the Crown of the [Thatcher] government's legislation programme'.[3] In a world where electoral imperatives often reduce the economic debate to cynical discussion of how to bribe the voters with their own money, a policy that brings huge sums into the exchequer while on the whole delivering worthwhile benefits to shareholders and consumers borders on the inspirational. Helped by the collapse of the former Soviet empire, privatization has been adopted across the globe – a well-justified tribute to those who pioneered the policy. Even so, privatization, like the nationalization it seeks to negate, is not the all-embracing solution that so many of its advocates claim; and the imposition of the plc formula on everything that has been privatized in Britain has thrown up problems, especially in the large and intractable area of the economy occupied by the utilities. The evolution of these industries, such as telecommunications, electricity, gas and water, merits some exploration because they have come to play a surprisingly important role in the political debate.

Before 1945 nationalization was a relatively uncontroversial, all-party enthusiasm. Churchill, for example, was responsible in 1914 for taking more than half the capital of British Petroleum (then the Anglo-Persian Oil Company) into public ownership in order to secure the fuel supply of the Royal Navy. He even nationalized the Carlisle pubs. Most nationalizations before those of the Attlee government were undertaken by Conservative or Liberal administrations. The notable exception was the creation of London Transport in 1933 under the guiding hand of the ardent Labour advocate of public ownership, Herbert Morrison.

Implausible though the idea now sounds, public ownership between the wars was also perceived, like privatization today, as a means of increasing economic efficiency. And, indeed, it probably did increase efficiency in important areas of the economy. The economic historian Leslie Hannah has shown that the well-directed reorganization of electricity wholesaling by a new state-controlled national grid company, the Central Electricity Board, reduced bulk electricity prices by a third within the space of a decade.[1] The transformation of the gas industry after the war from a motley collection of run-down municipal and private companies into a national network was probably managed more swiftly and effectively in public ownership than it would have been if the task had been left to private owners. Those who now pour scorn on Herbert Morrison, the architect of Labour's post-war policies to control the commanding heights of the economy, often forget his understandable concern that shareholder-owned companies and indeed municipal companies – the chosen instruments of the Fabians' gas-and-water socialism – could never deliver coordinated national policies in areas such as energy.

Under the Attlee government nationalization was, in effect, a public-sector version of the stakeholder concept. It was designed to offer the public a stake in industries that were expected to become more efficient, while striking a more equitable balance between the interests of workers, taxpayers and consumers. The subsequent history of public ownership was nonetheless one of increasing disillusionment. In the absence of market discipline, the nationalized industries' objectives became confused. The most obvious conflict arose where the political desire to preserve jobs clashed with the industries' financial or productivity targets. Jobs usually won, with the result that the industries' tendency towards overmanning was greatly reinforced. Large economic distortions also arose from the politicians' desire to use the nationalized utilities to control prices and incomes. The further their prices and costs became removed from market reality, the greater the reduction in their economic efficiency.

State enterprise enjoyed access to cheap capital because it could borrow on the basis of the government's guarantee. But the capital was rationed via an arbitrary political and bureaucratic process. Sometimes, as with gas in the 1950s, the industry bosses would persuade the government to back excessive investment in new plant on the basis of overoptimistic assumptions about future demand in what was then a mature industry. At the same time, the growth industries of the public sector had to compete for funds with the government's other political priorities such as healthcare, law and order or education. This meant that British Telecom confronted great difficulties in the early 1980s in financing the replacement of one of the most run-down telecommunications networks in Europe.

Investment decisions in capital-intensive industries like electricity with a time horizon that could exceed 20 years were heavily influenced by the one-year schedule imposed by the Treasury's budgetary procedures and also by the vagaries of the electoral timetable. Decisions were further complicated in electricity by the absence of a free market for the industry's output. There have always been great uncertainties about how to price electricity and calculate investment returns in the industry. Elsewhere, judgements about where to open or close plants could be dictated as much by the need to secure votes in marginal constituencies as by considerations of economic efficiency. This was a Conservative as well as a Labour habit. It was the Tories who insisted that uneconomic steel plants be built at Llanwern and Ravenscraig; and it was the Tories who kept Ravenscraig open, despite huge losses, even after the steel strike of the 1980s had broken the back of the steel unions.

Mrs T second guesses the market

Perhaps the most powerful argument against nationalization was inadvertently demonstrated by Margaret Thatcher herself. In energy she enthusiastically embraced a policy of picking winners, fixing to the point of obsession on the need to expand the nuclear industry. This was understandable in the early 1980s when the world economy was coping with the second oil shock and the British miners were still a force to be reckoned with. But with victory over Arthur Scargill and the collapse of oil prices in the mid-1980s, the policy became inexplicable: nuclear energy was ruinously expensive relative to most other energy sources on any non-alarmist view of the future pattern of energy prices. The catastrophic cost of Margaret Thatcher's dirigiste activity in the nuclear industry became all too apparent when British Energy was privatized for less than the cost of the Sizewell B power station, one of the great white elephants of all time. The paradox is that no one had argued more tenaciously than the former British prime minister that it was madness for politicians to try to second guess the market – especially in energy, where she robustly declared that that a depletion policy for North Sea oil was futile because the market knew best.

In this case management, in the shape of the late Walter Marshall, was on the government's side. In other cases industry leaders resented being second guessed by politicians and bureaucrats whose interests were often remote from any concern for economic efficiency. Alternatively, as in electricity, ministers enjoyed the power to make appointments to the board, but had no power to remove board members. So unless there was specific statutory authority for ministerial requests for changes of policy in the industry, the board would simply ignore ministers. As Leslie Hannah has pointed out, ownership can be weaker than moral suasion based on the coalitions of mutual interest and shared values characteristic of modern Japan. But moral suasion has also had its place in the UK. Politicians used to complain in the 1950s and 1960s that they enjoyed more control over the privately owned Imperial Chemical Industries, or the high-street clearing banks, than over the state-owned electricity industry.

The public ownership framework in which the industry bosses were required to plan their affairs was, then, a peculiarly British muddle. The Treasury's approach to public accounting made no distinction between costs such as capital spending for investment and the normal day-to-day costs of operating the business. Unlike publicly owned businesses in France or Germany, the British nationalized industries were obliged to cope with an inbuilt systemic bias against investment, except in unusual circumstances such as those prevailing in the nuclear industry, where politicians bent the rules. The system was also characteristically British in its adversarial nature. The Treasury invariably sought to control costs and limit the industries' access to the public purse, while the sponsoring ministries acted as advocates for their industries in the battle for funds. If the Treasury sometimes lost, it was because the bosses knew their industries better than the politicians and civil servants and they carefully controlled the flow of information to Whitehall.

Another important failure was that a policy intended to empower workers and give a stake to the people simply spawned giant impersonal bureaucracies in which many workers felt little commitment to owners or customers. The scale and centralized nature of the industries' operations accorded enormous power to the trade unions. Their ability to disrupt national energy supplies and transport was a weapon that could be used both for pay-bargaining purposes and wider political influence. Pay inflation, which had damaging knock-on effects in the wider economy, did not extend to the boardroom, where top executives were poorly remunerated. Employees were paid by seniority rather than merit.

In this the nationalized industries bore an odd resemblance to the most successful Japanese corporations, which embody stakeholder values. But there were important differences. In Japan efficiency is largely confined to those companies that operate in competitive product markets. Contrary to the general perception in the West, much of the rest of the Japanese economy is exceptionally inefficient. And ownership rights in the most successful Japanese enterprises are, for all practical purposes, exercised by the workers, who are closely involved in consensual deliberations about the running of the company. Their unions are enterprise based and supportive of the trust relationships that characterize large Japanese firms.

In Britain's nationalized industries, in contrast, management tended to be autocratic as well as paternalistic. Since the unions were organized by craft, not by individual enterprise, they tended to subvert rather than support the sense of common purpose between management and workers. The ownership function was exercised not by any identifiable group of owners but by politicians, civil servants and industry bosses, who were locked in a perpetual battle over priorities. Among the various stakeholders, the biggest loser in these battles was invariably the consumer. This was Old Labour's experiment in stakeholding; and in its failure to strike a fair balance between the various stakeholder interests, it proved to be a dead end, even if its merits are too often overlooked today.

Monopoly versus competition

A particular merit of privatization was that it introduced market discipline, and in some cases new professional managers, to the public sector, as nationalized industries were prepared for flotation. This exposed grotesque inefficiencies. When Sir George Jefferson was given the job of putting British Telecom on to a proper commercial footing, the company, which had once been part of the Post Office, had little idea of what it owned, what its products cost or where it made its profits. It took time for the market discipline to work and British Telecom remained immensely unpopular with customers for many years after its flotation. In electricity the requirement to put together a prospectus exposed the Central Electricity Generating Board's assumptions about the cost of decommissioning nuclear power stations to critical independent scrutiny for the first time. Almost overnight the estimated bill for decommissioning jumped from £3.7 billion to an astonishing £15 billion.[5] In the water industry nobody had any serious notion of the extent of leakages. The managers simply assumed that it was cheaper to extract more water from the reservoirs than to mend the pipes.

The effect of the market disciplines imposed before and after privatization was to secure huge gains in economic efficiency. Yet the gains were not evenly spread between the industries and between the various stakeholders. This was partly because the privatization process itself was intensely political. Where in the past the nationalized industry bosses argued with Whitehall mandarins about their financing arrangements and investment plans, they now did battle over the terms of privatization. The argument was about the future structure and regulation of the industries they ran, as well as the financial shape in which the enterprises were floated. Perhaps the most epic struggle concerned the fate of British Gas, which was run at the time of privatization by the formidable Denis Rooke.

The task of confronting Rooke over the flotation of gas fell to Nigel Lawson who, as energy secretary, had already forced the corporation to divest itself of many of its peripheral oil and gas interests. The scars of the experience are still visible in his memoirs, where he describes Rooke as a craggy and overbearing opponent who made no effort to conceal his feelings of distrust and contempt for ministers and officials alike. For his part Rooke viewed Lawson as a jumped-up financial journalist who understood nothing about the gas industry. He, on the other hand, had devoted his life to it. As well as having been largely responsible for introducing liquefied natural gas technology into the industry, he had played a central role in switching Britain over from town gas to natural gas from the North Sea, which was a considerable technological achievement. The smooth operations and high safety standards of this network were widely admired around the world, although its cost structure and quality of service to the consumer were less highly praised.

Rooke felt that he knew what was best for the country, British Gas and the customer and regarded critics of the service provided by British Gas under his leadership with the same contempt that he viewed politicians. To this day he believes that privatization has been a disaster, arguing that it has destroyed the sense of community and social service that used to exist in the industry. The only reason that he stayed at the helm through the change of ownership was that he recognized the inevitability of privatization and wished to ensure that as much as possible of the industry was preserved in its existing shape.

Lawson fervently desired to break up British Gas before privatization into separate gas and appliance businesses and into separate regional companies. But his ability to influence the future of British Gas was greatly reduced when he became chancellor of the exchequer after the 1983 election. Despite his departmental interest in raising as much revenue as possible from privatization, he continued to argue that competition was the priority and that British Gas should not be floated as a monopoly, even though this would have maximized the proceeds for the exchequer.

Lawson's successor at energy, Peter Walker, took the opposite view. The new secretary of state surprised his officials by establishing a good working relationship with Rooke. This was possible, in Lawson's view, because Walker was happy to do what he was told. Yet Walker's opposition to breaking up the corporation appears to have been rooted in a desire to grant British Gas as much freedom as possible to manage its affairs in the global energy market.

Unlikely national champions

This reflected an important philosophical divide among leading Tories. Privatization had been promoted by right-wing radicals such as Keith Joseph,

Nicholas Ridley, Geoffrey Howe and Nigel Lawson, with strong support from younger right-wingers like John Redwood. Their beliefs about the nationalized industries and privatization, which were brilliantly articulated in successive books by Redwood, derived from two fundamental ideas.[6] One was that the British people should be allowed to participate more directly in these industries through wider share ownership. This, like the policy of increasing home ownership through council house sales, was intended to give them a real stake in the economy and in society, as we have seen. The other was that one of the keys to arresting Britain's economic decline was to subject cosy cartels and restrictive practices to more competition in a deregulated marketplace. Many of the radicals were instinctively wary of privatizing monopolies intact.

Another strand in Tory thinking, represented by Walker and Michael Heseltine, was similarly sympathetic to popular capitalism, but more permissive in relation to monopolies. These ministers, who had started their careers in small, entrepreneurial firms, were instinctively – and some would argue indiscriminately – pro-business. They remained in tune with the kind of 1960s corporatism that favoured promoting national champions to take on global competition. As Walker put it in explaining his opposition to breaking up British Gas in his autobiography, 'I wanted a powerful British company which could compete around the world'.[7] Where Lawson and others on the radical right believed that preserving British Gas's monopoly at home would ultimately have a debilitating influence on its ability to compete internationally, Walker believed that the monopoly would provide a springboard for international success.

In the short run Lawson lost the battle with Walker and Rooke. In the late 1980s the government was heavily dependent on a steady flow of privatization proceeds of around £4–5 billion or so per year. If such a large privatization had been allowed to fall behind schedule, the chancellor's other political objectives, including tax cuts and the reduction of the national debt, would have been jeopardized. So Lawson agreed to the privatization of a fully integrated gas industry provided that Walker undertook to go ahead post haste. This, says the Tories' David Willetts, was the biggest defeat for the Treasury in the whole privatization programme.

Yet Rooke does not see it like that. For what Lawson omits to mention in his memoirs is that the Treasury did exact a financial price. Rooke still smarts over the terms of the flotation, whereby the Treasury took £2.5 billion from the cash-rich corporation via a debenture – a form of debt which obliged

British Gas in due course to put the £2.5 billion into the government's coffers. He refers to this as 'his' money. Rooke deeply resents having been prevented from using it in what he regarded as the long-term interests of the industry and of the gas consumer. Nor does he acknowledge that the taxpayer had any legitimate claim to the money. At the same time British Gas was also saddled with fixed-price contracts from pre-privatization days which became exceptionally onerous in the light of subsequent movements in energy prices. That was to haunt one of Rooke's successors, Richard Giordano.

The national champion philosophy turned out to be pure hubris. British Gas lost money investing in energy in Canada and failed in its attempt to take control of much of the New Zealand gas industry. The poor outcome of its efforts to diversify overseas was mirrored in other monopolistic industries such as electricity and water. The notion that cosy domestic monopolies could be turned into doughty national champions remains as implausible today as it was when these industries were privatized – although this did not prevent Michael Heseltine from putting similar managerial arguments in his subsequent abortive attempt to privatize the Post Office. The recent history in energy and water, including the fat-cat saga at British Gas, suggests that the urge to engage in international diversification seriously diverted management from its main task of providing high-quality service in domestic utilities. The consumer was a neglected stakeholder. The postscript is that Peter Walker plopped comfortably into a seat in the boardroom of British Gas, whose monopoly profits hc had worked so hard to preserve. In the freewheeling climate of the day, other ministers followed his example in joining the boards of companies that they had helped privatize.

Winners and losers

The more fundamental lesson was that a mere change of ownership could not, in itself, transform the operations of a monopolistic utility or strike an equitable new balance between all the stakeholders in the industry. And despite the determined efforts of the regulators, the quality of the service at British Gas left many customers deeply discontented several years after the privatization. Much the same was true in water, where the large price increases required to finance a big investment programme demanded by the European Union delivered marginal benefit to the consumer at an absurdly high cost. The experience in electricity, meantime, demonstrated the ineffectiveness of regulation in striking an appropriate balance between the interests of shareholders and consumers.

This emerged when the contracting and shipping conglomerate Trafalgar House launched a hostile takeover for Northern Electric. The electricity company suddenly revealed, in its defence against the bid, that there was enormous potential to pay out special dividends to shareholders. The electricity regulator Stephen Littlechild, who had just completed a review of the industry, decided to revise his recommendations on electricity pricing in the light of this new information. This did not prevent a further spate of takeover bids designed to take advantage of the fact that the regional electricity companies (Recs) had been privatized far too cheaply from the taxpayers' point of view. They were, in the City jargon, attractive 'cash cows', ripe for exploitation. Within two years of Trafalgar's abortive bid, nine of the twelve regional electricity companies had been the subject of agreed or hostile takeovers.

With hindsight, it is clear that the Treasury, advised by merchant bankers Kleinwort Benson, allowed the Recs to be privatized with far too little debt in their balance sheets. Against the background of Saddam Hussein's invasion of Kuwait the stock market was nervous and so were the government's advisers. Yet even the tabloid press, with no benefit of hindsight, scented a bargain-basement offer. 'Electricity shares offer investors a sparkling bonanza – Gulf War or not', trumpeted the *Mail on Sunday*. The *Daily Star* declared: 'Sell-off set for jackpot'. But if the failure to float the Recs with more substantial borrowings resulted in poor value for the taxpayer and a bonanza for shareholders, it was partly the government's own fault. For a start, ministers, bankers and brokers all felt that a share issue that flopped with investors was a far greater stigma than an issue in which the shares soared immediately after privatization. And by the time the giant utilities were being privatized, there was enormous impetus behind the programme because the government was raising so much money from the sales.

Margaret Thatcher was urging on her ministers and they in turn were keen to win brownie points in cabinet by doing her bidding. So the timetables were invariably tight; and in the case of the Recs, the timetable was even more tight because an election was looming. Since the industry bosses knew that the privatization proceeds were incorporated in the Treasury's financial projections, they enjoyed immense leverage with ministers through their power to refuse to sign the prospectus. And if the delivery of sensitive information to the government in hugely complex privatizations such as electricity or water was delayed, that leverage was increased even more. So the mechanics of privatization favoured one group of stakeholders – the managers and new shareholders – above all others.

The worst example of how the government became boxed in by its own privatization timetable arose at water, where the formula for the regulation of the industry had to be fixed by 31 July 1989. This was an unusual case, in that the water companies' huge investment programme constituted a big drain on their finances far into the future. So there were pressing questions about how great a financial risk they were running and how the risks should be shared with the taxpayer. No agreement had been reached between the industry bosses and Michael Howard, Secretary of State for the Environment, by the final week of July. The National Audit Office report on water privatization, although couched in the office's usual coded language, reveals a fascinating progression in the negotiations over the water companies' balance sheets.

The bosses initially rejected a deal whereby they would be saddled with debts of £435 million. By 27 July this had been turned into a cash injection into the industry of £700 million of taxpayers' money. In the final discussions between ministers and chairmen, all cumbersomely conducted on a bilateral basis with each individual company, the cash injection had risen to £1.1 billion. Gordon Jones, then chairman of Yorkshire Water, confirmed to me that at the last moment he refused to sign the prospectus because he felt the balance sheet was not strong enough to keep the company solvent through the period of heavy investment. He believes that at least one other water company took similar action.

So hopeless was Michael Howard's position that he was obliged to make further concessions. The cash injection, after various adjustments, ultimately came out at £1.5 billion. So the adverse swing from the government's initial negotiating position amounted to a concession of £2 billion to the industry. No doubt the consequent strengthening of the water companies' finances made them a more attractive prospect to investors. But since the net proceeds of the sale of all 10 companies came to only £3.6 billion, it is hard to believe that the benefit could have outweighed the cost of the taxpayer of the concessions made before the float. Under hard questioning before the Public Accounts Committee, Terence Heiser, permanent secretary at the Department of the Environment at the time, offered what was a vintage stonewalling performance even by the standards of the Whitehall mandarinate. He repeatedly refused to accept that there had been any kind of haggle.[8]

Shock benefits

The best complexion that can be put on these losses to the taxpayer is to acknowledge that the exchequer subsequently derived huge benefit from the efficiency gains achieved in the privatized industries. Some of these gains came from the introduction of new technology; others from the regulatory formula known as RPI minus X, whereby all the industries except water were forced continually to reduce their overall prices to the consumer in real terms. Perhaps the most impressive case in point was that of British Telecom, which has succeeded in making both substantial cost reductions and great improvements in the quality of its service.

At the time of privatization in 1984 this involved huge risks for the government since it was the biggest stock-market flotation that the world had ever seen. Patrick Jenkin, the minister who gave the go-ahead, felt that the risk had to be taken because BT's investment programme could only be financed if it had access to private capital in the private sector. Ironically, BT even surprised itself by going on to rebuild the whole of the British telephone network without making significant demands on the capital markets for funds. The finance came from its own internally generated profits, which proved vastly greater than anyone in or out of the industry had expected.

It is nonetheless true that several of the old nationalized industry problems have returned in a different form. The experience in electricity demonstrates that the managers who run the utilities retain their ability to pull the wool over everyone's eyes. The response of Stephen Littlechild after Trafalgar House's bid for Northern Electric was to upset a regulatory framework that had been intended to provide five years of stability within which the companies would enjoy the maximum degree of managerial autonomy. Such interference amounted to a return to the bad old days of politically inspired short-termism.

In gas the adversarial nature of the relationship between the industry and the regulator has resulted in similar uncertainty. In the privatized environment, the regulators are cast in the role of platonic guardian. They have done better than their detractors would have us believe. Yet their motivation may be coloured by a whole variety of personal considerations, not excluding the desire for honours, which could result in 'political' behaviour. The old gladiatorial combat between the Treasury on the one hand, and the sponsoring ministries and nationalized industry bosses on the other, has simply turned into a battle between baronial regulators and industrial barons.

In due course the introduction of more competition into the utilities will permit much of the regulatory function to wither away. Yet the process is taking far too long. And there are some industries, most notably water, where natural monopoly will probably remain an inescapable reality for many years to come. It is here that the plc structure becomes potentially destructive, because it entrenches a conflict of interest between shareholder and consumer which even the most wise and dispassionate regulator may not be able to resolve. There is also a risk that continued attempts to manage the conflict through a regulatory cap on prices could lead beyond the release of inefficiently used resources to needless redundancies – especially when the managers are motivated by incentive schemes that encourage them to look for short-term cost cuts and a disaffected public, egged on by the tabloid press, makes angry demands of the regulators for lower prices.

In lieu of the plc

Indeed, the boardroom pay scandal stems partly from the unquestioned assumption of the privatizers that the forms of accountability that apply to a plc operating in a competitive product market would be appropriate for the delivery of monopoly services to consumers. The standard response of the privatizers is that there was no alternative. Yet this overlooks a useful precedent that could have provided – and could still provide – a radical alternative to the present ownership structure of the natural monopolies.

Before privatization a quarter of the British water industry was run by companies quoted on the stock exchange. Like the trustee savings banks, these local monopolies did not have conventional owners in the shape of equity investors holding ordinary shares. The capital was in the form of preference shares, which gave the investor the right to a fixed income. Anything that the companies earned over and above this fixed return to the preference shareholders could be used in the interests of the consumer, either by raising investment or lowering prices. The existence of quoted shares provided a modicum of capital-market discipline, since the performance of the companies was monitored by stockbrokers' analysts. And the nature of the capital structure eliminated the scope for conflict between the capitalist and the consumer.

Adaptations of this formula could readily be used to introduce stakeholder principles in the natural monopolies. The water companies, for example, could be required to undergo a capital reconstruction in which ordinary shares were exchanged for preference shares offering either a fixed nominal or index-linked return. Investors would have to be compensated for the loss of growth in future earnings in the form of a slightly higher income. But that is well within the current financial capacity of the industry. The preference capital model is one that John Kay has explored and adapted in advancing proposals for a new corporate format for the utilities that he calls 'the customer corporation'. It is an approach which seeks to restructure the natural monopolies in a way that entrenches cooperative stakeholder values.[9] The attraction of his proposals is that they rebalance the various stakeholder interests in the utilities to give greater priority to the customer, greater freedom to the manager and a much smaller role to the regulator. It is a format that could also be used in the remaining parts of the public sector such as hospitals and schools. But any move in this direction can be expected to run into formidable opposition from those water company bosses who are desperately anxious not to lose their share incentives.

The final verdict on privatization must still be that the policy has immeasurably improved the efficiency of large parts of British industry and commerce. Companies such as British Airways and British Steel, which operate in competitive global markets, have performed far better than anyone would have dared hope when privatization first began – although paradoxically much of the improvement in productivity in these industries took place while they were still in the public sector. Government debt was substantially reduced in the 1980s thanks to the proceeds, even though mismanagement of the public finances has pushed it back up in the 1990s. If political pressures prevented competition from being introduced into the utilities as rapidly as it could have been, the process nonetheless appears inexorable. British Gas, which so firmly resisted attempts to break it up when Denis Rooke was in charge, subsequently decided under Richard Giordano to undertake the task before being required to do so by the regulators. Above all, the utilities operate within a much more transparent environment.

What becomes increasingly clear, however, as the managers and regulators continue to wrestle with large problems in areas such as nuclear power, rail and gas, is that these industries are too complex to be transformed by a one-shot simple solution like privatization. There is no wholly satisfactory answer to the inherent conflicts of interest between shareholder, worker and consumer. Interestingly, some socialist advocates of public ownership such as R H Tawney ended up believing that there was no infallible formula, least of all in the mere transference of property rights, for dealing with such problems.[10] As the privatization process draws to a close in Britain, a similar sense of realism about what can be achieved by changes of ownership is rightly reappearing. Government remains closely involved in the financing of industries like rail, because privatization has, in effect, meant selling a Treasury – i.e. taxpayer-financed – subsidy to the investment public. And because of the political sensitivity in reducing services or closing down lines, politicians have retained the power to step in to over-ride the regulator.

A shortage of legitimacy

Privatization has not been a popular success with the British people. By the mid-1990s, the pollsters Mori were finding – astonishingly – that a majority was actually in favour of renationalizing the utilities rather than leaving them in private ownership. The explanation must be that the vast increases in efficiency in privatized industries have failed to compensate for a perceived lack of legitimacy in their operations. This absence of legitimacy results from their failure to achieve an equitable balance between the various stakeholder interests. This can be perfectly illustrated by the public's reaction to the water industry. In the drought of 1995 the privatized, shareholder-owned Yorkshire Water never reached the point of cutting off supplies. It was nonetheless the butt of national criticism. In Northern Ireland, in contrast, where water was still in the public sector, water was actually switched off. Yet there was no comparable uproar. Perhaps the Northern Ireland water authorities are less efficient than the privatized water companies in mainland Britain. But the lack of a bigger outcry there almost certainly reflects a higher legitimacy quotient arising from a public perception that the interests of the stakeholders are more fairly balanced.

The biggest beneficiaries of privatization have been the managers and shareholders. The outcome has nonetheless failed to deliver on the Tories' aspiration to give the British people a really worthwhile stake in the wealth-creation process. At first sight, the share-ownership tally admittedly looks impressive. From between 2.5 and 3 million shareholders in Britain in 1980 the number of share owners rose, mainly as a result of privatization, to a peak in 1991 of 11 million, after which it fell back to 9.26 million. The striking feature, however, was that 5.7 million of these shareholders held shares obtained exclusively through privatization. In many cases they owned shares in only one company. A mere 200,000 of those who embarked on share ownership through privatization went on to buy shares in non-privatized companies.[11]

It is clear that the British people twigged that there was money to be made by buying privatization issues and selling out quickly. But they also understood that share ownership incurs a fiscal penalty when compared with tax-privileged forms of ownership such as occupational pensions. Throughout the period of privatization, in which the stock market saw a phenomenal rise, private individuals were in fact net sellers of company securities to life assurance companies and pension funds. In other words, the biggest benefits of privatization accrued to people in their capacity as policy holders and members of pension schemes – paternalistic forms of ownership conveying little sense of a stake in rising share values.

This serves as a reminder that the real litmus test of any government's commitment to wider share ownership lies in its readiness to change the tax system to put private share ownership on an equal footing with institutional ownership. The Tories flunked the test. Wider share ownership has merely been a byproduct of the urge to privatize. As an exercise in bringing capitalism to the people, the Conservative version of stakeholding has flopped.

Where privatization has achieved some limited but welcome success on this score has been in increasing the level of employee share ownership. Nearly a million have become owners as well as earners at the company where they work, which is a stake worthy of the name. But this cannot have been a great consolation to those in privatized industries like electricity generation, where around two-thirds of the employees in National Power and PowerGen have been made redundant.

Other jobs have, of course, been created elsewhere as competitors have come in to former monopoly markets. The increased efficiency in the utilities also means that the rest of British industry and commerce carries a lower burden of costs and is thus more competitive. The paradox is that the jobs that remain are more sustainable as a result, but do not make people feel secure. Indeed, the sense of insecurity that afflicts the British workforce is partly a legacy of the great upheavals wrought by the privatization programme. The time has now come to consider what the welfare state has done to remedy the problem of insecurity and to look at its contribution to stakeholder values.

Part Four

From Welfare to Well-being

10

Back to Bismarck

*W*hen a newly unified Germany confronted growing social unrest in the Great Depression of the nineteenth century, Bismarck responded by inventing the welfare state. His compulsory social insurance plans, enacted in successive statutes in the 1880s, were part of what modern politicians would have called a twin-track strategy to arrest the rising socialist tide. A legislative assault on the political activities of the workers was tempered by welfare provisions that were intended to buy off opposition to the ruling class. Then as now, welfare was seen as a way of legitimizing the operations of the state and establishing a more 'inclusive' society.

In Britain the people had to wait until 1908 for the introduction of the old age pension and 1911 for national insurance. But it was the experience of the depression in the 1930s that created the impetus for the unprecedented post-war growth of welfare spending, driven on the one hand by the influence of Keynes and on the other by William Beveridge's *Report on Social Insurance and Allied Services*.[1] The reforms of the Attlee government after 1945 provided a model of social reorganization that was widely adopted across the world. Today the objectives of the welfare state extend beyond the relief of poverty to include social insurance, redistribution and smoothing out the level of income over the lifecycle. The welfare budget in Britain amounts to more than a quarter of national income and takes over two-thirds of all government spending.[2]

Western politicians no longer confront an ideological challenge of the kind faced by Bismarck. The collapse of the Berlin Wall has seen to that. But they do have to cope with the consequences of levels of unemployment on a scale not seen since the 1930s and, in the English-speaking economies, the all-pervasive sense of insecurity in the workforce. Yet far from buying anyone off, governments are engaged in a heated debate about how, and how far, to prune the welfare state. The commitment to provide comprehensive protection against sickness, poverty and unemployment – or, as Beveridge put it, the evil giants of Want, Disease, Ignorance, Squalor and Idleness – has come to be regarded as the problem, not the solution. And despite the fact that more and more of the population now receive some kind of welfare benefit, there appears to be an inverse correlation between the growth of welfare spending and the general sense of security. Enormous outlays on health, education, housing and social security no longer seem to enhance the values of an inclusive society.

The new pragmatic political consensus is for the fiscal hair shirt. In Britain the remnants of Keynesian orthodoxy were formally done to death in Geoffrey Howe's budget of 1981, which tightened fiscal policy in recession in the interests of orderly public finances and lower inflation. In continental Europe it took another decade and a half before governments followed suit. There, fiscal policy was tightened during the economic slowdown of the mid-1990s to satisfy the convergence criteria of the Maastricht Treaty. The two great 'isms' with which the West sought to counter the communist threat – Keynesianism and welfarism – are out of fashion; the sound of beleaguered politicians breaking implicit social contracts is to be heard all across Europe. The fiscal crisis of the state now extends to solidaristic stakeholder societies like Germany; while Sweden, for long regarded as the ultimate example of enlightened welfarism, is enduring an economic crisis that will not be resolved in the twentieth century.

The demographic squib

The most potent critique of the welfare state thus comes not so much from libertarian thinkers who have ideological objections to the state disposing of ever-higher proportions of national income as from good housekeepers who claim that the whole apparatus is no longer affordable. The viability of the stakeholder approach to welfare, it is suggested, is being undermined by a demographic time bomb: the number of elderly people in the population is growing in relation to those in work. This pragmatic case derives particularly strong support from lobby groups that stand to gain financially from the further privatization of pensions. As far as Britain is concerned, the demographic argument is misleading.

It is true, certainly, that all the populations of the developed world are becoming older and that the elderly lay a bigger claim than most to healthcare and social security spending. In many countries in continental Europe the costs will be especially high because the state operates generous, unfunded pay-as-you-go pension systems which rely on solidarity between the generations rather than on a pool of investments to guarantee the payment of retirement incomes. In Britain the number of pensioners will undoubtedly increase in relation to the working population in the very long run. The Government Actuaries' figures suggest that the ratio of working people to retired people, known as the support ratio, will fall from 3.3 in 1991 to 2.5 in 2060. But virtually all this decline takes place after 2020 because the population is already relatively elderly.[3] And the demographic strains will be much less in Britain than elsewhere. The Department of Social Security has forecast that the ratio of working people to pensioners will be higher in 2040 than in most other developed countries apart from Ireland.[4]

In addition, the British state pension system is one of the least generous in the industrialized world. Successful social insurance systems are a characteristic of consensual rather than individualistic societies. In the absence of a shared vision of social welfare in the 1960s and 1970s, British politicians of left and right failed to establish bipartisan consensus on generous state pension provision. No sooner had Barbara Castle brought about a modest overhaul of the state pension system in the Labour administration of the late 1970s than the Thatcher government started to undo her work. As one of the more rigorous right-wing Tory intellectuals, David Willetts, has pointed out, the cost-cutting amendments made to the basic state pension and to the state earnings-related pension (Serps) since 1979 have, in effect, defused the demographic time bomb.[5] To the extent that Britain has a demographic problem, it chiefly concerns the expansion of the very elderly in the population. Between 1979 and 1992 the cost of support for the elderly in residential and nursing care homes rose from £10 million to £2.5 billion; and the over-85s are projected to rise from 1.5 per cent of the population in 1991 to 2.4 per cent in 2011.[6]

Making Robin Hood redundant

An alternative attack comes from those who claim that the welfare state is a middle-class racket.[7] Beveridge's principle of universalism, a conscious departure from the poor law tradition, means that the rich receive child benefit, free healthcare and free education if they so choose. And since the rich live longer than the poor, state pension schemes often redistribute income from the poor to the rich. Public choice theory, which derives from the work of James Buchanan and others at the University of Virginia, asserts, meantime, that the welfare state is manipulated for the personal ends of politicians and bureaucrats. If state pensions are vulnerable to the ageing of the population, it is because the politicians used them to win votes: pension benefits were set high in the early years when the costs were low, without regard to the potential increase in future financing costs as the population aged. As for the bureaucrats, they are alleged to be more interested in providing the services that enlarge their empires than those which best meet the explicit objectives of the welfare state.

There is an element of truth in the public choice argument, especially in the countries of southern Europe and in the developing world. But the critique is exaggerated in relation to the UK. And those who worry about the payment of benefits to the middle classes often fail to look at how those benefits are financed through the tax system. What matters is the net effect of benefits and taxes; and in practice the biggest redistributive task of the welfare system in the UK is smoothing income across individuals' lifetimes. In effect, the state operates as a savings bank. As John Hills of the London School of Economics has shown, most welfare benefits are self-financed over people's lifetimes rather than being paid for by others; and the system does redistribute quite successfully from the lifetime rich to the lifetime poor. Nor should it be forgotten that benefits are of much greater relative importance to the poor than to the middle-class recipients; or that Beveridge's advocacy of universalism was rooted in the belief that the middle classes would not be happy to contribute to a redistributive welfare system unless they themselves were beneficiaries – an inclusive criterion.

A third attack comes, interestingly, from the left-leaning Tory Chris Patten, whose period as governor of Hong Kong has induced a bout of revisionism on the appropriate size of the welfare state. Patten has come to believe that the lower levels of public spending in the dragon economies of Asia are part of the explanation for their very high growth rates; and that Britain would benefit from reducing the share of public spending in national income by a significant amount. This boils down to an argument about competitiveness; and while academic evidence suggests that there is no direct relationship between a country's level of taxes and public spending and its ability to compete in world markets, there is a common-sense logic to the idea that if companies are required to carry an excessive burden of social overhead they will either lose out in global markets or move their operations out of the country concerned.

Sweden, where the state allocates two-thirds of national income – the highest proportion in the developed world – offers strong circumstantial evidence. Its standard of living fell from the third highest in the world in 1970 to 17th place in 1992, while national income grew by only 1.5 per cent, compared with 2.6 per cent for the rest of the OECD area over the same period. No net private-sector jobs have been created there since the early 1960s and, with the highest paid age group (45–49-year-olds) receiving only 6 per cent more than those of the lowest (20–24-year-olds), there are powerful disincentives to the formation of human capital: the most productive workers are reluctant to acquire new skills and absenteeism is high. All employment growth during that period has been in services provided by local government and all the jobs created have gone to women. Professor Sherwin Rosen of the University of Chicago has remarked that 'in Sweden a large fraction of women work in the public sector to take care of the children of other women who work in the public sector to care for the parents of the women who look after their children'.[8]

No doubt the culture shock that takes place when a free-market Chicago liberal is exposed to the full blast of Swedish social democracy results in an element of provocative hyperbole. But there is a hard kernel of truth in the professor's diagnosis. The attempt to counter unemployment by creating public-sector jobs has contributed heavily to the fiscal crisis that has troubled Sweden since the start of the decade.

Yet at 50 per cent of national income Sweden's tax burden remains the highest in the OECD. Not surprisingly, the country's 25 largest companies have moved their activities offshore, taking 75 per cent of their employment, production and sales away from the domestic economy. And the share of the competitive sectors of the economy in gross domestic product has halved over the past 40 years.

Britain's slimline welfare state

So Chris Patten has a point. But whether it applies to Britain is another matter. For Britain not only has a lower level of public spending than Sweden, Germany, France and Italy; it has the lowest level of welfare spending in the European Union apart from Portugal. Within Europe Britain is also a relatively cheap labour country. And while the Swedes and the Germans are busy exporting jobs around the globe, Britain, although it invests heavily in the rest of the world, manages to attract the highest level of inward investment in Europe. At the end of 1994 the OECD estimated that the total stock of foreign direct investment in the UK amounted to $219 billion, compared with a total of $273 billion in Germany, France and Italy combined.[9] This hardly suggests that competitiveness is being undermined by an oversized welfare state.

Moreover, the comparison with the Asian dragons needs to be carefully examined. The impressive Asian rates of saving that have contributed to high investment, and thus to rapid economic growth, are often attributed to Confucian values. This is ironic. Growth rates in Asia since the start of its industrial revolution have been the slowest in the world apart from Africa; and the reason that used to be advanced in the pre-dragon era for this poor performance was that Confucianism was inherently hostile to values supportive of economic growth. In fact demography is one of the most powerful influences on the level of saving. And if Britain has seen low rates of household saving in recent decades while the dragon economies' savings have been high, this is partly because the Asians have had proportionately more people in those age groups that normally save a great deal in preparation for retirement. This will change, because Asia is ageing very rapidly. More than half the world's old people, who consume rather than save, will be in Asia by 2030.[10] That means that Asian household savings ratios will soon be tumbling; and, to the extent that services such as pensions, healthcare and education are provided by the state in Asia, public spending will be going up.

As it happens, Patten's announcement of his conversion to lower public spending was not accompanied by detailed advice on how public spending might be cut. This will have disappointed his right-wing colleague Peter Lilley – no less thoughtful a politician, outside the party conference season – whose efforts to roll back the boundaries of the state at the Department of Social Security had been notably unsuccessful. Despite constant reductions in the levels and coverage of unemployment benefit, the erosion of the state pension system and a big shift towards the means testing of benefits, public spending in Britain remained obdurately high under the Tories. General government expenditure excluding privatization and lottery proceeds stood at 42.75 per cent of gross domestic product in 1994–5, which was marginally higher than when the Thatcher government came to power in 1979 and well above the levels that prevailed in the 'socialist' 1960s.[11] While the Tories succeeded in reducing the role of state enterprise within the economy through privatization, the right-wing notion of a 'night watchman' state remained a very remote prospect. The state is still Britain's biggest employer. And the striking feature of spending on welfare since the mid-1970s has been its stability as a percentage of national income.

The Sorcerer's Apprentice on welfare

This brings us to the real problem – and the real paradox – of the welfare state. Despite public spending having risen to very high levels in absolute terms, it fails to satisfy the perceived needs of the people or to make its full contribution to social solidarity. This reflects both the nature of the demand and the way in which provision is financed. In advanced countries the demand for publicly provided goods such as education and healthcare tends to rise disproportionately in relation to incomes. And because there is limited scope for productivity improvement in the public sector, the prices of public goods tend to rise faster than those in the private sector. Such is the in-built buoyancy of public spending that no sooner does a minister plug one hole in the dyke of public finance than another leak is sprung. It is a measure of the intractability of the problem that a right-wing radical like Peter Lilley could make no significant inroad into the bill for welfare. He was immobilized with all ten digits in the dyke. The much trumpeted success of the Tories' privatization programme needs to be seen in this context. Selling off state assets was a great deal easier than making inroads into inexorably buoyant state spending.

But there is, to change the metaphor, a democratic tripwire that subverts the spending process. There comes a point where voters tell pollsters that they would be happy to pay more taxes for better public services, but refuse to vote for higher taxes when they go into the polling booths. Such behaviour stems from an understandable concern about giving a blank cheque to free-spending politicians who work within a Whitehall system that is hostage to the demands of the more vocal lobby groups and special interests. It is also a response to the inability to pick and mix our public services. Even where services such as pensions are provided more efficiently and cheaply by the state than by the private sector, there is a problem in financing them out of a growing national income because of the perceived lack of legitimacy in the way taxing and spending decisions connect.[12]

Higher unemployment since the mid-1970s has increased the burden on the welfare state to a degree never conceived of by Beveridge. It has been made worse because the corporate sector has been reducing an important part of its contribution to the national welfare system. The shift away from stakeholder-type paternalism towards incessant downsizing in industry and commerce has proved expensive for the state: the taxpayer now foots the bill for job insecurity where previously large private employers made a substantial contribution. The decline in civic commitment and the breakdown of the family make similar additions to the cost of welfare as people push on to the state tasks such as caring for the elderly or disciplining unruly teenagers that have hitherto been regarded as obligations of community and family. There has thus been a big change in the composition of welfare spending, in which social security has taken a much larger share, while education and housing have been the most notable losers. And the shift is more than a purely cyclical phenomenon reflecting the state of the economy.

All of this imposes a traumatic strain on social cohesion and on the tax system. While our demand for the public goods provided by the state continues to increase, the sense of social solidarity and common purpose fostered in wartime has steadily eroded. The decision of John Major's government to set up a national lottery is one of many symptoms of the resulting fiscal stress. It is impossible to prove that Britain has reached the limits of taxation. But the fact that every country in the developed world since the early 1980s has seen public spending outstrip tax receipts, and a consequent slide into structural budget deficit, suggests that there is indeed a generalized fiscal crisis of the state. The difference between stakeholder societies and the more liberal English-speaking countries is simply that the latter confronted fiscal crisis earlier because they wanted to reduce taxes. Those on the left who argue that Labour politicians should honestly admit to the electorate that they wish to increase taxation in order to spend more have failed to grasp the nature of this problem.

The risk is that the process becomes self-feeding. If every developed country runs a structural budget deficit, there is increased demand on the global pool of savings. So savers and investors demand higher real rates of interest in exchange for supplying funds; and their demands are further heightened when they seek compensation for the increased risk that governments will default on their spiralling debts. The outcome is a vicious circle whereby higher real rates of interest on government debt put further pressure on budget deficits, making them harder to cut. They also restrain economic growth, which in turn adds to the fiscal strain because unemployment is higher than it would otherwise be. In a world of disinflation and debt-financed welfare the chief winner is the private rentier, who enjoys a bonanza from the high real interest rates. Yet the gains are hollow, because few of us are pure rentiers. Most savers and investors also have a stake in the labour market, whether directly or through offspring and grandchildren. Even for those who are pure rentiers, the party stops from the moment governments give up the budgetary struggle and default on their obligations either directly or through inflation, of which more in Chapter 11.

Work didn't pay for the prodigal's brother

The other side of the welfare state paradox is that its mechanisms increasingly subvert its role in providing the glue that holds society together: they exclude people at the bottom end of society from participation in the labour market and the capital market. The problem stems from the side effects of welfare arising from 'moral hazard', a phenomenon that afflicts all forms of insurance. Moral hazard can best be understood by reference to the story of the Prodigal Son. The prodigal's brother stayed at home and behaved in a morally responsible way, but no one slew any calves for him. Not only was this unfair; it reduced the incentive to work and save, since the rewards were shared by the brother who lived riotously. The practical manifestation today arises where the incentive for unemployed people to move back into the workforce is minimal because a combination of increased income tax and the removal of benefits – the poverty and unemployment traps – ensures that there will be little or no improvement in living standards. For almost everyone on benefit, a majority of job vacancies will look unattractive because they are caught in a bind that imposes very high marginal tax rates on taking up a job.

This, too, is an area where the stakeholders and libertarians part company. In Germany the belief in universalism dies hard. If there is a budgetary crisis, as with pensions, the social partners discuss cuts in provision while hanging on to the principle of universalism for all they are worth. In Britain, in contrast, a Conservative government has opted to target more spending through means testing. This sounds like good housekeeping. Yet universal benefits are already targeted on the less well off and the disincentive effects of means testing are often counter-productive.

The problem is exacerbated because Beveridge's original design was tailored for a world in which the male was the breadwinner and the female the home-based carer. Today the response of unskilled households to declining relative and absolute levels of pay has been for the female partner to go out to work. The interaction of unemployment and other benefits with means-tested income support results in the returns from work for the wives of unemployed men being low. There is thus a growing polarization in the labour market into two-earner and no-earner couples: work-rich and work-poor families. The share of jobless households among all non-pensioner households has risen from 6.5 per cent in 1975 to 19 per cent in 1994. At the same time, in nearly 60 per cent of households every adult is in paid work.[13] Government spending on these households without work has been rising sharply in every economic downturn since the late 1970s and failing to fall much in the upturn. The trend cannot go on indefinitely, since the ratchet effect will ultimately lead to those in work becoming more reluctant to finance the workless households via increased taxes. We are back, in short, to the fiscal crisis of the state. Few things illustrate more clearly how welfare no longer operates to reinforce stakeholder values of inclusion. In this instance it is both divisive and unsustainable.

For lone parents the unemployment and poverty traps pose comparable dilemmas. Since more than 90 per cent of single-parent mothers are estimated to have had unplanned pregnancies, the claim that teenage girls become mothers simply to jump the housing queue is far-fetched.[14] But only a minority of such women can hope to find jobs capable of covering childcare costs. It is no coincidence that the numbers of lone parents is highest in areas where general unemployment is high. This is where it is most difficult for an unmarried mother to raise her standard of living by marrying. Nor is this the only way in which the benefit system is at odds with the conventional values of community. Frank Field, an outspoken Labour critic of means testing, has pointed out that the system is also morally corrosive in that it provides a powerful incentive to conceal income and to cheat the authorities. The problem is common to all systems involving means testing.

Thrift doesn't pay for the poor

A similar set of issues is raised by the disincentive effects of means tests on saving. This is particularly important in relation to the state pension system, which has been substantially eroded as a result of the decision in 1982 to increase basic pensions in line with prices instead of earnings. When the Rowntree Foundation published John Hills' authoritative study on the future of welfare in 1993, the basic pension was worth about 15 per cent of average gross male earnings, lower than at any time since 1971. The change to price-related pensions means that if earnings grow by 2 per cent, the pension will be worth a mere 7.5 per cent of average earnings by 2030. Taken together with reductions in the value of Serps, this amounts to a deliberate policy of shifting provision away from state pensions towards means-tested income support.

The rules for income support penalize those with capital of more than £3000, making membership of occupational pension schemes a waste of time unless the resulting pension is quite large. John Hills found that it was actually a disadvantage to have savings that produced investment income of between £5 and £47 a week. So where Beveridge saw the basic pension as something for the individual to build on, the modern state pension involves serious disincentives to saving, especially for blue-collar workers. Increasing resort to means testing is expensive to administer and the take-up of benefit is lower than with universal benefits because of the stigma that attaches to means testing. It is therefore perverse that the Tories should have chosen to concentrate their cost-cutting efforts on the basic pension rather than on Serps. The outcome is growing inequality, even though pensioners as a group have seen an overall increase in incomes. The Institute for Fiscal Studies has found that, while the richest pensioners at the start of the decade were 50 per cent better off than in 1979, the poorest were only 10 per cent better off.[15] The changes in the state system mean that many in future will be excluded from a worthwhile stake in the growth of the economy. This underlines the point that in individualistic societies such as Britain the crisis of the welfare state is not so much about finance as about need.

It is clear, then, that something is seriously amiss with the mechanics of the welfare state, which no longer contributes to 'inclusive' values as it used to. And on the central issue of the growing inequality of incomes, the state now appears powerless to alter the trend. As Hills has pointed out, the welfare system managed to blunt the impact of the increase in labour-market inequality on the gross incomes of the least well off up to 1985. Thereafter changes in the benefit rules have resulted in an overworked system running out of capacity to cope. Means testing and the linking of benefit to prices rather than earnings mean that income inequality both before and after retirement are now increasing regardless.

It is hard to escape the conclusion that the Tories' first answer to the crisis of welfare – seeking to target benefits more effectively through means testing – has failed. What, then, of the second answer, the privatization of welfare?

Pensioners mugged

Pensions are the biggest single item in the social security bill. They represent the ultimate test for any government that seeks to reform the welfare system. And at first sight, privatization sounds an attractive way of relieving the fiscal crisis of the state. But people who worry about demography should be clear at the outset that privatizing pensions cannot provide a general solution to the problem of an ageing population, because the rise in the numbers of retired people relative to those in work inevitably means that the elderly will be making a bigger claim on the resources of the economy. Changing the financing of pensions cannot alter that basic truth. What the privatization of pensions can do is to legitimize the way in which resources are shared between working and retired people.

The state scheme is run on a pay-as-you-go basis, which means that today's pensions are paid out of today's government revenue. Despite the widespread belief that national insurance contributions go into a fund to pay for benefits, this is a myth. National insurance is simply taxation by another name, which means that pensions are caught up in the legitimacy problem that affects taxing and spending. Part of the case for privatization, then, is that it provides a more transparent mechanism whereby personal savings are invested to produce a pension on retirement. Funding pensions in this way does not permit redistribution from the better off to the less well off. But it does pre-empt inter-generational conflict and avoids political battles over the allocation of tax revenues, which means that it is generally perceived as legitimate. Yet legitimacy was the very opposite of what the Conservative government actually achieved, whether in relation to its promotion of personal pensions in the 1980s or in its longstanding support for company pension schemes.

Consider, first, the personal pensions campaign, which was spearheaded by Norman Fowler with assistance from John Major. This had a superficial logic. If the state pension scheme is being deliberately eroded, some other form of pension provision is required for the less well off. In fact more than two-thirds of the average income of retired manual workers comes from the state pension and other state benefits. What Fowler and Major failed to recognize was that personal pensions usually involve costs of selling and administration which make them uneconomic for anyone earning much less than £10,000 a year.[16] In effect, many people who took the government's tax bribes to opt out of Serps and invest in a personal pension will receive a poor return from the insurers because the return on their very low contributions will be substantially eroded by costs. At the same time the Financial Services Act failed to provide ordinary people with adequate protection from fast-talking salespeople who were paid commissions on the pension plans they sold.

These were true children of the American New Right – greedy individualists who were prepared to push commercial practice to the limits of the legitimate without regard for the interests of their customers. In what was still, then, a self-regulatory framework, many salespeople cynically advised miners, nurses, teachers and others to leave good pension schemes and opt into more expensive personal pension plans with poorer benefits. Egged on by the government, the insurance companies were only too pleased to go along with this ambush of the innocent. The result has been a blight on the lives of thousands. Compensation for the victims is taking an unconscionable time to secure and the whole fiasco will contribute to inequalities of income among the retired population for years to come. Part of the cost of this unrestrained pursuit of individual profit falls on other personal pension plan clients of miscreant companies, who are involuntarily forced to pay for the compensation out of their own plan's funds. To the extent that compensation fails to cover all the gaps, the bill will fall on the taxpayer as those with inadequate retirement incomes turn to the state for support.

Paternalism goes off the rails

When it comes to company occupational pension schemes, the private-sector contribution to welfare has been more positive. More than 10 million people are covered by these arrangements, which put a substantial amount into the retirement incomes of the British workforce. In many respects such schemes represent one of the best aspects of corporate paternalism, which is why they enjoy the support of all the main political parties. But they also embody a fundamental snag. The main form of provision – the 'defined benefit' scheme which pays a pension related to length of service and the level of pay before retirement – is designed for a world of stable, lifetime employment and low inflation. That is the very opposite of what we have experienced over the past quarter-century.

One result is exclusion: growing numbers of part-time or casual workers, particularly women, are not eligible for pension scheme membership. Another is that the absence of adequate protection against inflation in most private-sector schemes has resulted a heavy financial penalty for so-called early leavers – a euphemism for people who have been made redundant or moved to other jobs. An additional penalty is usually incurred because the pension rights are calculated on the early leaver's pay at the time of leaving the job. So for early leavers whose earnings grow over the course of their career, benefits will be lower than for those who stay in the same job. The result is that they end up subsidizing the pension fund of their former employer. Very few people actually receive the full benefits, normally two-thirds of final pay, promised in the pension scheme trust deed.

The whole system, then, is based on the principle of robbing downsized or delayered Peter to pay timeserving Paul. From the employer's point of view the rape of the early leaver has made it much easier to meet the cost of bigger pensions for expensive long-stayers. While the worst features of the penalty for premature departure have been mitigated since the government introduced legislation in 1986 to enforce inflation proofing up to a ceiling of 5 per cent, this has only provided partial protection. It is striking that in each 20-year period ending in the years between 1970 and 1990 the increase in retail prices averaged 7.7 per cent.[17] So defined benefit schemes are liable to hinder job mobility without any evidence that they are accompanied by improvements in productivity to compensate. And since employers retain substantial control over the schemes, they have used them to help finance generous redundancy packages, thereby softening the downsizing pill in the restructuring of the past two decades.

Given that older employees have bigger pension entitlements, the employer can offer them larger pay-offs which help guarantee harmonious labour relations. Older workers are also more likely to be unionized than are young ones. These factors lead to a bias towards shedding older workers regardless of their productivity and skills. That bias is now being reinforced as employers are becoming more aware that the actuarial cost of employing older people increases as they come closer to retirement.

Stumping up for the elderly dropout

For many white-collar workers, these redundancy packages may be welcome, opening up the prospect of a longer and more enjoyable retirement on a decent income. But for the majority, it is another matter. Older workers, however able, are the ones least likely to find new jobs. Many give up hope of finding a job and fall out of the workforce. Here lies part of the answer to the question of why the participation of older men in the workforce has fallen more sharply in Britain than in most countries in the OECD area. We have created a new form of social pariah: the elderly dropout. Nearly 1.25 million men in the 50–65 age group are not looking for jobs. They are neither retired, nor conventionally unemployed.[18] In 1977 the proportion of people in work in the decade before normal retirement age was 86 per cent. This has declined progressively and David Willetts expects it to fall to 60 per cent before long.[19]

The cost to the welfare state is large. Sympathetic doctors have adopted a flexible approach to certifying older unemployed men as eligible for invalidity benefit, which is more generous than unemployment benefit. So numbers claiming invalidity benefit have soared from 600,000 in 1979 to more than 1.5 million today, despite an improvement in the nation's health.[20] And there is a wider cost in that services of experienced and productive workers are prematurely lost to the economy. Tim Congdon of Lombard Street Research sees here a potential explanation for the failure of the great productivity improvements in the British economy since 1979 to be reflected in much higher employment.[21]

The conventional wisdom that early retirement for these older people makes room for more youth employment is based on a misunderstanding known as the 'lump of labour' fallacy. This refers to the mistaken assumption that there is a fixed amount of work available in the economy. In practice younger workers are usually imperfect substitutes for older workers because they have different skills. Experience around the world suggests that many vacancies created by early retirement are never filled. So in the modern global marketplace the outcome of pension-fund-financed early retirement in the UK may even be to create jobs in foreign countries where other employees have skills available to fill the gap. The exclusion of many older workers from the labour force is thus needless.

More holidays for bosses

Another problem with occupational pensions is that the original paternalistic impulse has been abandoned by many large companies in favour of the ideology of shareholder value. The pension fund has become a profit centre rather than a way of enhancing a stakeholder relationship with employees. Large surpluses have arisen because actuaries overestimated pension fund liabilities: they did not foresee the extent of the redundancies of recent years which helped shrink pension liabilities. They also underestimated the high returns earned in the stock market in the 20 years from the mid-1970s. Since 1987 the government has insisted that pension funds should not be allowed full tax relief if they accumulate funds much in excess of their pension liabilities. The pension funds have therefore distributed their surpluses indirectly: companies have stopped or reduced contributions into the fund – a practice known as taking a contribution holiday.

Employees and pensioners do not have an automatic right to a share of these surpluses. A defined benefit pension scheme gives its members no tangible stake in the pension fund's investments. It is a nebulous form of property right which consists of no more than a promise – which turned out to be very nebulous indeed in the case of the Maxwell pension funds – to pay a given level of benefit. The investments exist simply to guarantee that promise. Scheme members may nonetheless be granted some additional financial benefit. Yet there is no question as to who takes the lion's share. Data from the Pension Schemes Office accumulated between 1987–8 and 1993–4 reveal that, while companies received more than £100 billion in contribution holidays, pension scheme members were given just £8 billion in improved benefits.[22]

The resulting inequality no doubt reflects a legally correct apportionment of the spoils. But it is thoroughly inequitable, since little has been done to restore the real value of the pension rights of the redundant scheme members whose entitlements had been whittled away by the great inflation of the 1970s and 1980s. The greater part of the payout simply went into company profits. All pension scheme members were thus excluded from a commensurate share in the huge rise in the stock market. The members were also usually required to continue making contributions to the pension fund when the company itself had stopped.

The trustee-directors were, of course, involved in a potential conflict of interest in deciding how to split the surpluses. Their jobs were partly dependent on continuing growth in the company's profits and they stood to gain from contribution holidays as their bonuses and share-incentive schemes reflected the improved profitability. Many also enjoyed privileged access to the pension fund because they could raise their own salaries just before retirement in such a way as to enjoy disproportionate and undisclosed increases in their own pensions – a practice discussed in Chapter 9. This was one of the more grotesque examples of the values of paternalism and community being hijacked by the new individualistic ethos. All in all, the occupational pension system embodies inequalities similar to those that afflict the welfare state and the wider labour market. While it has delivered worthwhile benefits to some, it does not deliver the kind of stake that would strike any fair-minded person as equitable. And its legitimacy has been further eroded by the abuse of the conflict of interest inherent in the position of trustee-directors.

How to pay for a welfare solution

What, then, is the stakeholder alternative to the Tories' approach of more means testing and more privatization of welfare? The approach that best fits the criteria of inclusiveness and avoidance of disincentive effects is that of the basic income, which is at the opposite end of the spectrum from means testing. This offers unearned flat-rate benefits to all at below the normal wage, but above subsistence level. The benefits are then subject to redistribution, or targeting, through the tax system. The idea goes back, in effect, to the citizen's income proposed by Tom Paine, described in Chapter 1. Its merits are simplicity, the reduction of the unemployment and poverty traps, high levels of take-up (unlike means-tested benefits) and, more arguably, the reinforcement of social solidarity. It also offers more choice by changing the relationship between paid work, unpaid work and free time. Flexible working arrangements become much easier to adopt.[23]

This has marked advantages over a minimum wage, which suffers from several flaws. If set at a level that makes a significant difference to the living standards of the low paid, the minimum wage risks putting them out of a job by making them more expensive to employ. At lower levels it will not take people off benefit. Equally important, it is also an ineffective way to target poverty, because the poor rarely derive much of their income from wages: more than 70 per cent of the bottom fifth of households with children are either one-parent families or couples without full-time earnings. Moreover, a single male breadwinner with a large family receives no more than an employed male with a working wife and no children. In contrast, a basic income varies according to family circumstance.

Yet it has to be acknowledged that for all its attractions, a basic income would entail marginal rates of tax significantly in excess of present levels. In other words, a basic income approach is unlikely to command assent in today's circumstances. So for the moment, the welfare state's contribution to solving the problems of unemployment and income inequality will continue to be one of make do and mend. The interface between the tax and benefit system and the labour market is a complex area which goes well beyond the scope of this book. But it is worth saying, in passing, that where the jobless are concerned there is a strong case for shifting the balance of welfare towards subsidizing employment rather than unemployment. This can be done through payments to employers who take on unemployed workers and through back-to-work bonus schemes, as in Japan and the United States. The size of the subsidies can also be varied according to the length of time a person has been out of work.

Education and training are also vitally important. The problem here is that no one knows what is likely to be required in future against the background of a rapidly changing global economy. It is striking, too, that many of those who have founded and managed the world's most technologically advanced companies were ill-qualified educational dropouts. Bill Gates of Microsoft and Scott McNeely of Sun Microsystems are obvious examples. Neither of these two innovative entrepreneurs had any formal training for their chosen careers.

This is not to argue for policy inertia. It simply suggests that it is more important to focus on the basic qualities of literacy and numeracy than on specialisms where the educationalists would be trying to second guess the development of industrial and commercial markets. There is, in addition, a wealth of evidence to suggest that those who stay at school longer receive more training over their lifetime. Those who receive least are the ones with low levels of basic education. Once again, the focus should be on work-related training in the company, because government schemes appear to have done very little to help the unemployed.

As the deputy governor of the Bank of England, Howard Davies, has argued, companies may not be able to offer lifetime employment any more but they can offer employability. This is the thinking behind the continuous training promoted, for example, by Unipart's in-house university, known as

Unipart U. The innovative motor parts concern is a dedicated follower of stakeholder principles. Davies also argues for tax relief for individual learning accounts to pay for training and retraining, a form of expenditure which has the merit of leaving it to the individual to make the choices and judgements about what skills are likely to be relevant in future.[24]

The question is, how are such measures to be financed? Labour's traditional instinct is to squeeze the corporate sector, a risky move in a country that relies so heavily on inward investment and which Labour itself believes to be underinvesting in plant and machinery. It would only make sense in the context of a wider review of the taxation of savings and investment. More sensible, in the short term, would be to recognize that the Tory attempt to give people a stake has been excessively biased towards ownership as against employment, and to look for savings which redress that imbalance.

One potential source of revenue which fits that criterion would be a levy on the proceeds of demutualizing building societies and insurance companies. The moral case here is strong. Wealth built up by earlier generations of savers is being blown on a single generation, partly to satisfy the desire of the directors for share options. A levy on the abandonment of stakeholder forms of ownership would be a particularly harmless way of transferring some of the flotation proceeds back to the community if it were earmarked for investment in human capital such as education and training.

Another candidate might be the abolition of tax relief on mortgage interest. As well as costing nearly £3 billion a year, the relief achieves precisely the opposite of what its supporters claim for it. Instead of helping first-time buyers, it provides a subsidy to existing owners. This is because banks, building societies and the buyers themselves estimate their ability to meet mortgage-servicing costs by reference to income after tax and tax reliefs. So buyers who naturally tend to borrow to their maximum capacity bid up the value of the housing stock in favour of existing home owners.

Some will immediately object that this would be an act of political folly when the housing market is depressed and negative equity afflicts some of the least well off. But the housing market has improved; and as we saw in Chapter 2, the negative equity problem is illusory because nearly 80 per cent of the mortgages taken out in the housing boom in the late 1980s were attached to endowment policies. These will now be showing good returns after the sustained stock-market surge. The insurance companies could be encouraged to give borrowers easier access to the equity in these policies and to reduce the surrender penalties for people who wish to switch to a repayment basis. The moral case for applying pressure to the insurers is strong, since the proportion of endowment mortgages sold in the 1980s was absurdly high in relation to most people's need for flexibility. The figure reflects the way in which commission-hungry salespeople bludgeoned potential home owners into taking out endowments regardless of personal circumstance. It was the housing market's equivalent of the personal pensions fiasco.

Nor should the £21 billion defence budget be overlooked. While defence expenditure has come down as a percentage of national income, it remains extraordinary that the real level of military spending has still increased in absolute terms since the collapse of the Berlin Wall.[25] The end of the Cold War threw up a classic opportunity for the management technique known as zero-based budgeting, whereby the merits of each spending project are reexamined from scratch. Such a discipline would force the military to confront very basic questions. What, for example, is the point of the costly European fighter aircraft in the post-Cold-War world? Against whom will it be deployed? And is it really impossible to tackle these putative new threats from non-superpowers without new and more expensive hardware? The Tories have resolutely refused to confront such questions. There must be a cost-cutting opportunity here for any incoming government.

The enormous upward pressure on public spending will nonetheless remain, which implies that efforts will have to be redoubled to ensure that taxpayers' money is deployed more efficiently. Those like Frank Field who see no escape even for a Labour government from greater reliance on private provision are undoubtedly right. There will have to be more partnership arrangements with the private sector which should aim to avoid the corrosive disincentive effects and inequalities that have been allowed to creep into the system. More private-sector financial discipline will be needed, too, in the provision of public goods, although such discipline cannot be allowed to undermine the basic integrity of the services.

A real stake in pension fund prosperity

In state pensions there can be no return to earnings linking because of the legitimacy problem referred to earlier. The radical solution must be to move to a more generous single-tier basic pension, while the second-tier job now undertaken by Serps is given exclusively to the private sector. In the occupational sector, meantime, there is a need to acknowledge that for the great majority, lifetime employment is a thing of the past. That points to an alternative form of provision which gives people a much greater sense of involvement in the workings of the economy, while eliminating most of the injustices of the defined benefit system: the 'money-purchase' or defined contribution approach to pensions. In essence, the employees receive back all the contributions into the fund, plus the return on the money, and invest it in an annuity for their pension when they retire.

There can be no cross-subsidies in such a system from job changers to the company and to the job stayers, because everyone has an identifiable pot of money of their own which they can take with them to another employer. The management of the funds can be more democratic: since the company does not guarantee the solvency of the pension scheme, it does not need to retain majority control of the board of trustees. The pension fund cannot be used as a slush fund for the directors. And money-purchase arrangements would not require regulatory arrangements of such complexity as defined benefit schemes, because there is no need to police the solvency of pension funds to ensure that there are enough assets to meet the liabilities.

The most common critique of money purchase is that the employee ends up shouldering the investment risks instead of the company. The level of the pension depends on the state of the stock market at the time the individual retires. Yet it is possible, in today's sophisticated capital markets with a very wide variety of financial instruments on offer, to offset most of the risk associated with the timing of the purchase of an annuity. Moreover, money-purchase schemes provide far better insurance against unforeseen job changes and reduced earnings. Research by the Institute for Fiscal Studies has shown that the conventional belief among pension experts that defined benefit schemes are superior is probably wrong.

In a detailed statistical exercise assuming the same rate of investment return for both types of scheme, based on 3500 people in the 1988–9 official retirement survey, the IFS found that a majority of both males and females would have been better off in a money-purchase scheme.[26] Its work demonstrated very clearly that the distribution of returns in the defined benefit scheme was heavily skewed to a minority of members because of the substantial redistribution from short-stay employees to long stayers, and from low earners to high earners. It concluded: 'At the most basic level, a majority of plan participants, via their contributions, subsidise a few. This privileged minority will exhibit longer tenures and higher salary profiles (especially final salary). They will typically be better off and male.'

Volunteering for compulsion

Companies are moving slowly towards money-purchase occupational pension provision, partly because the financial and regulatory burden for them is less than with defined benefit. Among the attractions of money purchase for policy makers, who have to worry about the big gaps in pension provision in the UK, is the fact that such schemes lend themselves well to the principle of compulsion. Under defined benefit schemes the existence of coercive hidden subsidies meant that the practice of making membership of the company pension scheme a condition of employment was oppressive. It was not unlike the trucking practices of the nineteenth century whereby workers were forced to spend part of their pay on shoddy goods at the company store. The Conservative government's decision in the 1980s to make the practice illegal was based on libertarian principle.

No doubt some Tory politicians would continue to feel hostile to compulsion, even in a money-purchase scheme which eliminated inequitable cross-subsidies and undesirable penalties for job mobility. Yet it is a perfectly legitimate role of the state to address the problems that arise from short-sightedness on the part of individual savers. As Frank Field argues, compulsion is a valid option which saves money for the taxpayer who would otherwise pick up the bill when the feckless reached retirement age without a pension. It is already used in countries as divergent in culture as Switzerland and Australia, both of which offer interesting potential models for the future. The money-purchase principle can also be perfectly well adapted to collective pension management outside the company – although putting the investments in the hands of the state is best avoided, since the state may be tempted to reduce the returns, as in Singapore's Central Provident Fund, by tapping the pension fund pot for its own ends.[27]

There is everything to be said, then, for encouraging a shift in the direction of compulsory money-purchase provision in the corporate sector, since it provides a realistic, collective means of giving people some sense of involvement in the risks and rewards of the wealth-creation process. Companies are already moving in this direction voluntarily, because defined benefit schemes are financially burdensome. But there will always be a need for some state involvement in pensions to look after the less well off and provide a safety net in the event of extreme stock-market fluctuations.

There are nonetheless limits to what the private sector can do to bolster the welfare system. This is particularly true of long-term care for the very elderly, where one in four people incur very large medical costs in the final two years of their life. This is an insurance problem, but one which a decade and a half of experience in the United States suggests that the private sector cannot solve on the basis of individual provision. Private insurers cover less than 1 per cent of long-term care in the US because policies are expensive and the insurers feel unable to offer full protection. It is clear that the pooled coverage given by social insurance offered in partnership with the private sector is likely to be cheaper and more effective than pure private insurance.

But that brings us back to the readiness of voters to pay. The need exists, regardless of whether it is satisfied by the public sector, the private sector or some combination of the two. The problem, once again, is the erosion of the legitimacy of the taxing and spending mechanism. The least bad solution may thus be a move towards hypothecated taxes – the earmarking of specific taxes for specific benefits – which has been advocated by Geoff Mulgan of the independent thinktank Demos. Hypothecation is no solution to the overall problem of public spending, but it could make a useful contribution in limited parts of the system.[28]

The one thing that is clear about the welfare state, in all its policy-defying complexity, is that it does not call for demolition. To set about dismantling it when the British people are experiencing the rigour of massive structural changes in the economy would be folly. Despite its problems, it still retains some of its capacity to fulfil the role that Bismarck envisaged for it: to soften the blunt edge of capitalism. And that need has certainly not gone away in today's intensely competitive global marketplace.

11

Europe and the Myth of Globalization

*E*very decade seems to have its own particular nightmare, usually unfounded, about impending economic catastrophe. In the 1960s the French pundit Jean-Jacques Servan-Schreiber was widely believed when he argued that US multinational companies were about to devour their European competitors. In the 1970s the Opec oil producers were generally expected to hold the industrialized countries to ransom for the foreseeable future in a world of disappearing raw materials. There were predictions in the 1980s that the Japanese, who had destroyed the Western motorcycle industry and shaken American and European car producers, were about to polish off Western banking and finance by way of a *digestif*. The equivalent of Servan-Schreiber in the present decade is James Goldsmith, who warns of the threat of globalization and of supposedly unfair low-wage competition from China, India and other emerging economies in Asia. These powerful forces, he argues, are set to destroy our manufacturing industry and wreck what is left of our social cohesion.

The earlier fears did, of course, come to nothing. Servan-Schreiber's guns were pointing in the wrong direction: it was the Japanese, not the

Americans, whose economic might was underestimated in the 1960s. As for his jaundiced view of multinationals, they are now recognized, warts notwithstanding, as the most efficient means ever devised for diffusing technology and skills. The oil producers' reign proved to be brief thanks to the price mechanism, which ensured that a rising oil price provided incentives for conservation and for the development of new sources of energy across the globe. Some producers like Nigeria and Iraq so squandered their windfall gains that they are poorer today than they were before the oil crisis. Indeed, many of the world's most resource-rich countries have frittered away a boost equivalent to the one post-war Europe received from the Marshall Plan.[1] The Japanese, meantime, have demonstrated that their unparalleled ingenuity in manufacturing is mirrored by astonishing incompetence in finance, as their banking system has hovered on the brink of collapse. Note, in passing, that in the 10 years to 1994 they managed to lose a stunning $223 billion on the foreign investments they acquired as a result of the surpluses piled up on the current account of their balance of payments.[2]

Most of the fears that afflicted these earlier decades were rooted in well-known economic fallacies, of which the most important was the age-old mercantilist belief that international trade – in reality a very powerful engine of growth – shrinks the wealth of nations and deprives people of jobs. And the fallacious arguments are now well and truly back in evidence under the rallying cry of globalization or, in France, *délocalisation*, which refers to the loss of control over the location of business activity that results from trade specialization. Economic integration and the free flow of global capital are, so the argument runs, contributing to the impotence of nation states, the insecurity of their citizens and the erosion of the solidaristic values that characterize stakeholder economies.

The Orient express

It is not difficult to see why populist politicians and business demagogues are tempted to foment unease on this score. In the 1970s two-thirds of the global labour force lived in countries that were largely insulated from international trade by self-imposed barriers and controls. Today three giant population blocs, China, India and the former Soviet Union, are entering the global market. Even former opponents of free trade in Latin America have concluded that liberal economics offers the best hope of rapid increases in living standards. They all want a stake in the global economy. And their incentive to acquire one by competing in the global market is huge.

The nature and extent of that incentive can be understood by looking at the global labour market in a very long-term perspective. Before the Industrial Revolution, incomes varied little from one part of the world to another. In a representative sample of countries, Angus Maddison of the University of Groningen has estimated the gap in income per head over more than 170 years. In 1820 the gap between the top- and bottom-performing countries was just three to one. In 1992 it was greater than at any time in history at an astonishing seventy-two to one.[3] In terms of regions, the gap between the best and worst performers has gone from three to one to sixteen to one. Inequality on this scale puts the British competitiveness debate, which is about very marginal differences in per capita incomes in the developed world, firmly into context. It also demonstrates the size of the carrot that now dangles before the developing world.

The dragon economies of Asia, such as Hong Kong, South Korea, Taiwan and Singapore, set an early model for the rest. The logic of economic liberalization and of free access to the global marketplace means that poor but highly motivated and increasingly well-educated people around the globe will now set about closing the gap in incomes per head between the Third and First Worlds in a process known to economists as 'factor price equalization'. While the wages of the unskilled in the West fall, those in China and India rise towards a common level. How far the gap between incomes will close is a matter of dispute between economists. But there is a strong likelihood that in just a few decades these countries will see their share in global income approximate more closely to the size of their populations. We are thus at the start of a huge shift in the balance of economic power in the world. Barring a retreat into protectionism, lunatic policy or war, China and India will become economic superpowers in the twenty-first century, thus reverting to their earlier status in the pre-industrial period as the world's biggest economies.

The caveats should not, incidentally, be brushed aside too lightly: China has, after all, been here before. Within a few years of the Battle of Hastings, it turned out more iron than the whole of Europe did six centuries later. The Chinese also invented spinning machinery for textiles at much the same time. Yet the first industrial revolution in China could arguably be called the most momentous non-event in history, because the Chinese managed to forget the secret of industrialization in the thirteenth century. Collective memory loss on this scale is probably impossible in a world of electronic information flows. But predictable behaviour can hardly be expected of a nation capable of oversight on this majestic scale.[4]

The important point, however, is that the threat posed by Asia to the developed world is overstated. To start with, mercantilists forget that the reason these new entrants into the global market are busy exporting is not that they wish to put money under the bed, but that they need to import. The merchandise imports of the 10 leading Asian developing economies in 1995 were $748 billion, compared with the European Union's imports (excluding its internal trade) of $736 billion.[5] And as far as Asian competition is concerned, the huge disparity in incomes with the West largely reflects differences in productivity. If comparisons are made instead in terms of unit labour costs, the gap between the developed and the newer industrializing countries shrinks considerably: a unit of production in the West requires much less effort from each worker because the huge historic investment in capital multiplies the impact of that effort.

But Western capital is now being exported to the developing world on a huge scale. And the real problem that the West faces as a result is that, when countries trade freely with each other, they tend to specialize more on producing those goods and services where they have a comparative advantage arising from greater relative efficiency. This points to more industrial change in the developed world, with further job losses in the less competitive sectors, while more jobs are created in areas of comparative advantage where the returns to education and skills are high. In this, at least, protectionists such as James Goldsmith are right: the process that economists choose to cloak under the term 'structural adjustment' imposes profound stress on communities as the pattern of employment changes. It is also very unpleasant for the structurally adjusted, since it is impossible for everyone to stay in the same jobs at the same pay rates, even if the overall number of jobs and general living standards go up.

This underlines the point that the biggest loser from globalization is not the nation state but labour, especially unskilled labour as we saw in Chapter 2, which in contrast to capital is not very mobile. Unions are seriously weakened in a world where corporate decisions on the location of plant are substantially affected by the flexibility or otherwise of local labour markets and the level of social costs. The polarization between the classes is further increased because the well educated and well heeled retain the ability to migrate and to travel extensively. Nor is it just working-class solidarity that has been eroded. Culture can be a victim of free trade's tendency to impose norms. The loss of cultural identity is acutely felt in countries like France, where a consequence of trade liberalization and cultural interchange is that the cars no longer look funny, pop music has a rude Anglo-Saxon accent and the language is peppered with Americanisms. French paranoia over cultural identity is sharpened by the absence of reciprocal courtesies. The Americans have yet to acquire a taste for sticky aperitifs or the music of Johnny Halliday.

Yet there is a tendency – especially in the international relations fraternity, for whom globalization has become a rich field of study – to underestimate the role of technology, and domestic factors such as deregulation and privatization, in generating income inequality and unemployment. Indeed, James Goldsmith, like Jean-Jacques Servan-Schreiber before him, is almost certainly pointing his guns in the wrong direction. Technology has been doing more to create insecurity in the job market and undermine stakeholder-type values than has trade with the developing countries, as we saw in Chapter 2. Information technology in particular is bringing about enormous upheavals in the structure of service industries such as air transport, financial services and retailing. You have only to think of the enabling power of the computer screen to sort information and permit people to compare products and prices to see the potential for a near-permanent revolution in services. Many of the tasks performed by broking middlemen, or by functionaries in the professions, will in future be done by the consumer at the touch of a key.

The protectionist non-solution

All these motors of change result in jobs being reallocated within the global economy rather than invariably being lost. Incomes are reallocated too. The overall impact will be beneficial because trade is a positive sum game, bringing mutual benefit to both sides, and technology, at least over the long run, is a net job generator. To deal with the labour-market strain in the developed world, the sensible remedy, consistent with the values of both stakeholding and enlightened liberalism, is to redistribute income towards the losers through the mechanisms of the welfare state. The alternative welfare mechanism provided by protectionism, which imposes explicit or informal tariff barriers which act as a tax on imports, is a less efficient and less equitable way of doing the job. Not only does it increase the prices paid by the consumer. It raises the costs incurred by exporters, making them less competitive, while giving import-competing businesses an incentive to spend on labour-saving investment, thereby adding to the numbers of the unemployed and bringing more downward pressure on the pay of the less skilled.

In the conditions of the Slump in the 1930s, when Britain and the Commonwealth accounted for a sizeable part of world trade, the general tariff, accompanied by Commonwealth preference, was a viable policy. But most economic historians argue that it had only a minor impact on the level of output, although the composition of output may have changed. The high growth achieved in the middle years of the 1930s owed more to the devaluation of sterling. Today, a bigger share of Britain's trade is with Europe and a comparable protectionist policy would have to be conducted through the European Union. A more fundamental difference, however, is that manufacturing, the part of the economy most exposed to international competition, is very much smaller and accounts for less than a quarter of GDP. That suggests that the adjustment in response to international trade pressures cannot have much further to go. Supporting evidence for this assertion comes from analysing the composition of Britain's exports, which are much more science intensive than in the other leading industrialized countries apart from the US; and the proportion of UK exports in low-wage and labour-intensive sectors which are still in direct competition with the developing world is relatively low.

The countries that are more at risk from further structural adjustment in their economies arising from trade specialization are in continental Europe, simply because manufacturing still accounts for a much higher proportion of their national output. They also have more unskilled labour in the tradeable sector of their economies.[6] That suggests that there will be powerful pressures elsewhere in the European Union for trade policies that would be damaging to British interests. And the pressures will be reinforced by the conviction, rife among continental European politicians and some British ones too, that we are all hostage to global market forces which deprive us of our sovereignty and impose a particularly heavy penalty on stakeholder economies.

Markets rule, or not as the case may be

This phobia surfaces not only in relation to the activity of multinational companies, but in response to the supposedly novel powers that have been unleashed in the bond and currency markets. The assumption is that any government that pursues electorally popular stakeholder-type policies which are at odds with the new liberal orthodoxy will be subject to a veto by an army of traders led by hedge fund billionaire George Soros. The most pithy exposition of this thesis came from James Carville, an adviser to Bill Clinton, in the run up to Clinton's first election:

> I used to think that, if there was re-incarnation, I wanted to come back as the President, or the Pope, or a top baseball hitter. But now I want to come back as the bond market. You can intimidate everybody.

Revealing though this may be about the psychopathology of American political advisers, it is at best a half-truth, as is the wider impotence-of-the-nation-state story. There is, for a start, nothing novel either in the constraints that the markets currently impose on policy or in the level of trade integration. As Vincent Cable, the chief economist at Shell International, has pointed out, Japan and Britain are less trade dependent today than they were more than 80 years ago.[7] The world was much more open to both trade and migrant flows before 1914. And under the operations of the gold standard British monetary policy was perpetually hostage to a shortage of gold reserves. Interest rates were constantly having to be raised by the Bank of England in response to out-flows of bullion.

In effect, worries about the impact of economic interdependence on the nation state were put on ice for most of the twentieth century because of the contraction in trade and capital flows that resulted from two world wars and the Slump. Even after the Second World War the Treasury was obsessed, in the Bretton Woods era of fixed but adjustable exchange rates, with the balance of payments constraint. Indeed, the post-war behaviour of sterling has imparted a permanent tic to the face of the British mandarinate; and the fear of sterling weakness has often warped its judgement and reinforced the declinist mentality.[8] This was famously epitomized by the senior Whitehall figure who remarked that the central task of the British civil service was to preside over 'the orderly management of decline'.[9] It follows from this, as Tim Congdon of Lombard Street Research has pointed out, that the post-war British economy was not invariably run according to the principles of Keynesian demand management. Changes in the budget balance were often dictated by sterling and the balance of payments rather than full-employment policy.[10]

Markets have always passed judgements on policy, just as bankers pass judgements about the sustainability of their clients' overdrafts. They also make bad judgements from time to time. In assessing future inflation, bond markets have probably underestimated the extent of the spare capacity in the economies of the developed world; and they have certainly failed to grasp how the increasing flexibility of labour markets has made it easier for governments to keep a grip on inflationary pressure. They may also exert downward pressure, via the location decisions of multinationals, on corporate taxes, thereby making tax systems more regressive as countries are forced to rely more heavily on indirect taxation.

But those who proclaim the weakness of the nation state overlook some fundamental points. Average taxes on corporate income (profits and capital gains) in the European Union have actually increased from 2.5 per cent of gross domestic product in 1980 to 2.8 per cent in 1993. Even the UK, which has gone out of its way to attract inward investment, saw only a marginal fall in corporate taxes as a percentage of GDP during the same period; and that probably reflects other factors such as the increasingly voluntary nature of corporation tax discussed in Chapter 3. These figures hardly substantiate a scare about the erosion of Europe's corporate tax base.[11] Even more striking is that the markets have failed since 1980 to prevent the developed world from running up the biggest budget deficits and government debts in peacetime history.

This is not quite the breakdown in discipline that it seems at first sight, since the bond markets themselves are partly responsible for the size of the deficits and debts. For while markets only rarely punish sovereign borrowers by going on strike, they can impose more subtle, longer-term punishment. In response to the inflation inflicted by sovereign borrowers on savers in the 1970s, the bond markets matched the supply and demand for global funds at a historically high real rate of interest in the 1980s, thereby compounding the borrowers' fiscal problems and contributing to even bigger deficits. This is a stressful discipline. If governments fail to take radical action in response, they dig themselves into a bigger and bigger fiscal hole. In the meantime the higher real rates of interest reduce global economic growth, which makes the budgetary problem even more intractable. So the real loss of sovereignty lies in the way finance ministries and central banks no longer exert much control over long-term interest rates, which are set by the bond markets. Even the short-term interest rates fixed by the mighty Bundesbank do not have the persuasive influence on the behaviour of German bonds that they used to.

All the same, the discipline of the bond markets, such as it is, remains entirely dependent on there being some haven in the system for the funds of nervous investors. At present the world has only one really big creditor country left: Japan. And Japan has been responding to a deflationary economic crisis by running budget deficits on a positively Italian scale. As it happens the

United States is now reducing its budget deficit to less than 2 per cent of GDP – the lowest level in the Group of Seven industrialized countries, at least in relative terms. Because of the rapid ageing of the Japanese population, Japan will probably also revert to a more cautious fiscal policy and a higher national savings rate as soon as economic circumstances permit. So the chances are that the form of bond-market discipline that we now have will prevail for quite a while yet. The real question, which merits a brief digression, concerns the ability of governments to avoid default on their burgeoning debts through inflation.

Debt and the death of inflation

The present level of government debt in the developed world is running at levels hitherto known only in wartime. The traditional response to the problem of wartime debt has been to wipe it out through hyperinflation or to adopt a judicious combination of modest inflation in the immediate post-war years, combined with budget stabilization. These were the contrasting methods adopted respectively by Germany and France after the Great War. Britain, however, took a third route. It sought to honour its obligations to creditors through sound money and fiscal rectitude. These policies were a failure. In 1919 the ratio of government debt to gross national product was 125 per cent, compared with 26 per cent in 1913. By 1938 it was even higher at 141 per cent, having touched a peak of 178 per cent in 1933.[12] The problem was that the real rate of interest on the debt was far in excess of the rate of economic growth, which made debt reduction impossible. After the second world war the debt-to-GNP ratio rose to an astonishing 237 per cent in 1946. The chief reason that the figure had come down to 42 per cent by 1980 was that the government defaulted on its obligations to holders of government stock through inflation. In other words, all legitimate efforts to wipe out the accumulated debt of two world wars made no progress. It took the galloping inflation of the 1970s to do the job.

The United States offers the only precedent during the twentieth century among the big industrialized countries for a successful reduction in the wartime debt burden by reasonably honest means. Between 1946 and 1968 the government debt-to-GNP ratio came down from 134 per cent to 43 per cent. Yet American economic growth, which ran at a historically freakish level of 4 per cent a year during this period, made the task much easier. So did very low real rates of interest. The fiscal position of the developed world today is much more like that of Britain in the inter-war period. Economic growth is sluggish and real rates of interest mostly exceed the rate of economic growth. Attempts to reduce the debt burden, as in continental Europe in response to the demands of the Maastricht Treaty, are proving counter-productive. By depressing demand when monetary policy remains stringent, countries such as France have simply weakened tax revenue while leaving a big burden on social security. France has now been driven to creative accounting in an attempt to meet the requirements of Maastricht.

Perhaps the dynamic Asian entrants into the global trading system will provide a *deus ex machina* by propelling the world back to buoyant rates of economic growth. This is not impossible, because the growth in demand generated by, say, the European Union's exports to developing economies in Asia is now as important for the EU as what happens in the United States. The odds against a generalized default are in any case quite high, in the absence of a shock to the system like the collapse of the Bretton Woods fixed exchange-rate regime, which temporarily undermined monetary discipline. Even so, this is where it becomes difficult to go along with the thesis put by Roger Bootle of the HSBC Group that inflation is dead.[13]

Keynes was surely right when he said that the 'progressive deterioration in the value of money through history is not an accident, and has had behind it two great driving forces – the impecuniosity of governments and the superior political influence of the debtor class'.[14] The laws of human behaviour do not change easily. So there must be a strong chance that the more heavily stretched countries will over the next 20 years or so default on their government debt – not least because inflation provides a way of resolving the battle between a shrinking workforce and a growing number of elderly dependants over their respective shares of national income.

In the modern world, unsound money is likely to be the despairing answer to the fiscal crisis of the state, in which the demand for public services outstrips the readiness of taxpayers to foot the bill, causing social cohesion to break down. These behavioural pressures are particularly intense in Scandinavia and southern Europe, the nordic and southern comfort zones.[15] In countries such as Italy, where government IOUs are of short maturity, it would in fact be difficult to inflate away all the debt by borrowing from the banking system – the modern equivalent of printing money. They would probably have to repudiate debt directly, as Mussolini did in successive forced debt conversions in the 1920s and 1930s. Others with outstanding long-term government debt might take the inflationary route.[16] The picture would be further complicated if the countries concerned were members of the European monetary union, to which we shall come shortly. All countries will, of course, do their utmost to avoid such an outcome, which involves high political and economic costs, even if it relieves the immediate budgetary strain. The point here is rather that governments do retain the power, albeit nuclear, to put the bond markets in their place.

Even though real rates of interest have been high since the 1980s, it remains the case that globalization has allowed governments to raise large sums from foreign investors at a lower cost than they would have incurred if they had been confined to their own restricted pool of domestic savings. That has been one of the chief benefits of the lifting of exchange controls since the late 1970s and it has been particularly helpful to the stakeholder economies in allowing them to put off difficult decisions about welfare spending. Countries have suffered more strikingly from a loss of sovereignty when they have sought to buck the market, as in the case of the Europeans who persisted in pegging their currencies within the European exchange-rate mechanism (ERM). It was the French insistence on turning the ERM into a fixed-rate system that caused the overvaluation of the D-mark to be transmitted across Europe at the time of German unification. Those that stuck it out with Germany became victims of needlessly depressed demand and low growth. For Britain and Italy, the currency markets provided a merciful release by correctly diagnosing and exposing the inconsistency of their policies. The resulting loss of sovereignty was something that most of us could live with very comfortably. All of which brings us to the wider question of how comfortably Britain can live with the European Union in future.

Ever closer disunion

It is tempting for any left-of-centre party to take the view that the social democratic traditions on which the European Union has been built are naturally conducive to a stakeholder society. Up to a point this is true, which is why Labour has been committed under Tony Blair to opting in to the social chapter. Yet the social chapter is largely symbolic. And it pales into insignificance, in terms of the issue of sovereignty and the possible threat to jobs, when compared with the implications of participating in a European monetary union.

A move to monetary union would mean abandoning Britain's ability to operate an independent monetary policy. That implies a very considerable loss of sovereignty, in that the constitution of the new European central bank makes it less accountable than any major central bank has ever been before. While it has a powerful remit to achieve price stability within the union, it has no specific obligation to combat deflation – a significant omission. There is no definition of price stability in the Maastricht Treaty against which to measure the central bank's performance. And its operations will be highly secretive.

That, in the language of the 1930s, is the ultimate bankers' ramp; or, as William Rees-Mogg has put it, a bureaucratic dictatorship. The key point for the moment, however, is simply that a Europe-wide independent monetary policy would rule out for the participating countries any use of the exchange rate as a tool for responding to such shocks as the oil crisis, German unification or the decline of major industries. More of the burden of adjustment would have to fall on the labour market. Yet wages and prices in the European Union, unlike in the United States, are notoriously sluggish in responding to low demand in member states, while domestic labour mobility is poor and the movement of workers across national boundaries is inhibited by language and custom. It follows that there is a simultaneous risk of high regional unemployment in some parts of the union and overheating in others, which could not be remedied by a central bank which is concerned with monetary conditions in Europe as a whole. This could lead to a rerun of the kind of problem that Britain suffered before and after its entry into the ERM, which was a *de facto* single-currency area between 1987 and 1993. When Europe is dealing with unprecedented strains arising from structural adjustment it could also intensify pressure for protectionism and even create the conditions for a resurgence of fascism.

Advocates of EMU argue that the loss of sovereignty is more apparent than real. The fashionable wisdom among economists is that while monetary policy affects real output and employment in the short term, it merely, over the longer run, dictates the rate of inflation. Well, maybe. Yet the lasting political as well as economic damage inflicted on countries throughout the ages by overvalued exchange rates weighs more heavily with me than does the current *bien pensant* economic wisdom. And it is only necessary to consider the short-run pain inflicted on Britain in the ERM in 1992 to be reminded that the economist's lag is not just the politician's nightmare but the people's nightmare too.

In the nineteenth century no one worried about the uneven geographic impact of shocks within the gold standard system because the jobless could emigrate – and did so in large numbers. Today that avenue is closed, but another has opened up. In modern circumstances the natural remedy for shocks that affect only part of the European economy, once exchange rates are irrevocably locked together, is a more active use of fiscal policy. Yet in this respect the European Union will be markedly different from most other monetary unions. Despite the conviction of tabloid journalists to the contrary, its budget is tiny, equivalent to less than 1.5 per cent of Europe-wide gross domestic product. A big increase in the European budget seems implausible for want of a more full-blooded move to federalism than that proposed in the Maastricht Treaty. So the job of taking up the slack in output and employment after a regional shock would fall to national governments.

Fiscal fudge

There is an important political implication here. The balance between fiscal and monetary policy within Europe will dictate the overall exchange rate for Europe in global markets. It will therefore be necessary to coordinate fiscal policy to avoid ending up with the wrong exchange rate. This is to be managed before the establishment of the monetary union by the set of virility tests known as the Maastricht convergence criteria, which include the imposition of ceilings on budget deficits and government debt levels in relation to gross domestic product. These are arbitrary and make no allowance for the point which a country has reached in the economic cycle. Once the union is up and running, the Maastricht Treaty envisages joint discussions on fiscal policy, while the Germans propose to reinforce fiscal discipline through a 'stability pact' which will impose fines and call for interest-free deposits to be made with the central bank where countries fail to come up to scratch.

No one can be entirely sure what EMU will deliver, because we cannot know how the central bank and the individual member states will behave. What we do know for certain is that the fiscal starting point is structurally weak and that the constitution of the European central bank is designed to make monetary policy very strong. When the hard core is established, the bank will have a powerful incentive to establish credibility with the markets and to prove itself to the critics in Germany and elsewhere who have warned that it will preside over 'Esperanto money'. At the same time, those in the initial Franco-German hard core will seek to conform to a rigid fiscal regime. There could thus be a twin deflationary bias in the system.

Since the Maastricht convergence criteria for entry will have to be fudged even by the hard-core countries if the monetary union is to start anywhere near on time, those outside the hard core will have some additional leverage in demanding early participation. So the southern comfort countries, too, will make a fudged entry. If the European economic cycle is likely to dip by the turn of the century, there is a potential nightmare scenario which has been graphically outlined by the economist Brian Reading. It depicts ballooning budget deficits among the weaker second-round entrants in the south, while a 'macho' central bank, unconstrained by any need to take into account employment considerations, would seek to offset profligacy with harsh monetary medicine.[17] Given that there is only one Europe-wide monetary policy, this would penalize the prudent as well as the lax. Worse, a combination of tight monetary policy and loose fiscal policy is a classic recipe for an overvalued currency. So European firms would see their competitiveness undermined as they tried to measure up to the Asian challenge.

There is a worrying potential parallel here with the experience of the gold bloc in the 1930s, when a group of countries led by France insisted on clinging doggedly to their overvalued exchange rates in the face of rising unemployment and mounting industrial unrest. The clamour for protectionist policies could be deafening. And since the stability pact's system of penalties and fines would actually worsen the victim's fiscal position, it would be thoroughly destabilizing unless you believe that good government will invariably triumph over fiscal stress in the southern comfort zone. That is a big assumption, especially if several countries find themselves simultaneously in breach of the stability pact rules.

Italy's dash to curb its budget deficit in order to scramble into EMU is motivated partly by a recognition that its budgetary problems will be eased if EMU delivers lower real rates of interest on the country's public-sector debt. No doubt the present government is driven by the highest motives. But a future government may regard this interest rate boon as an excuse for putting off difficult decisions to raise taxes or curb spending – and spending cuts in Italy still have to be agreed by the unions. So unless Germany seeks to protect the integrity of fiscal policy within EMU by taking control of the Italian budget, which would be difficult, there is a question about how much damage might be incurred before the European central bank gave way, or the weaker countries dropped out of the monetary union and defaulted on their debts.

Stakeholding on the cheap

These are the risks. And they are on a scale that makes worries about any loss of inward investment if Britain stands aside look somewhat academic. But even if we assume that both governments and central banks behave with greater sensitivity than the system is intended to permit, EMU would be a difficult economic proposition for Britain because of its very different demographic profile. The countries of continental Europe have, in fact, been enjoying their socially cohesive stakeholder model on the cheap. Most rely heavily on state pension provision which operates on a pay-as-you-go principle. That is, pensions are paid out of current contributions and taxes; and those contributions and taxes are pitched at insufficient levels to meet the big increase in the cost of pensions and healthcare that will result from the ageing of the continental European population. There are thus huge unfunded pension liabilities which do not appear in the national accounts of the countries concerned and which are not taken into account directly in the Maastricht convergence criteria.[18]

It is possible for governments to renege on these unfunded liabilities. Many are already doing so, but only to a limited extent. In most cases the pain from these cuts will not be felt until well into the twenty-first century. So one way or another, unfunded pension liabilities in continental Europe will mean greatly increased pressure on tomorrow's budgets. Unless Britain were to allow its fiscal position to disintegrate, it would pay a high price for becoming involved in a monetary union where the European central bank may well find itself engaged in a titanic struggle to restrain governments that were having immense difficulty wielding the budgetary knife.

In a monetary union the medicine is shared by all regardless of fiscal vice and virtue. Given that continental European politicians are most unlikely to reduce the fiscal pressure by unwinding the European welfare model, they will make very uncomfortable bedfellows for a Britain in which both leading political parties are committed, at least in theory, to prudent spending and little or no increase in taxes. It is hard to see how, given the lack of convergence between Britain and the other economies on this score, any particular short-term rate of interest that was right for continental Europe would be right for Britain – a rerun under a different guise of Britain's problem when it informally pegged sterling to the D-mark while Nigel Lawson was chancellor.

Whatever the advantages in giving the single market a common currency, it is highly questionable whether Britain should become involved at the outset. In today's low-inflation and possibly deflationary environment, the attractions of being part of an unaccountable central bankers' crusade for price stability are not very appealing, especially if monetary overkill breeds an equal and opposite inflationary reaction in due course. And while monetary union might mitigate trade friction in Europe, it would not mitigate the more worrying potential frictions with the rest of the world if an unbalanced mix of fiscal and monetary policy led to a misaligned European exchange rate.

An alternative scenario is that, after years of low growth and high unemployment, the French lose the political will to persist with plans for a monetary union in which the central bank is required to give Bundesbank-style priority to price stability. Since German public opinion is fearful of a weak euro, there is a chance that French pressure for more political control of interest rates might even stall the whole EMU process. If, on the other hand, Chancellor Kohl concedes on this point, EMU will suffer from a weaker monetary policy as well as a weak fiscal position. While this would make for a more competitive European currency, it would nullify the advantages for Britain of seeking better monetary management by joining EMU. Much hinges on the resolution of Franco-German tensions on this score.

In short, it takes a huge, optimistic leap of faith to see the economic cost–benefit analysis as remotely appealing for Britain. If the currency markets have offered any lesson over the past ten years, it is that flexible exchange rates have operated as a safety valve, enabling countries to release the pressures that arise from ill-conceived policies or divergent economic structures. Global speculation, far from being destructive, has saved Europe from much lower rates of growth than would otherwise have occurred. Attempts at policy coordination, whether in the Group of Seven industrialized countries or within Europe, have in contrast tended to make matters worse. What seems clear is that to abandon the safety valve offered by the currency markets when the world is undergoing huge shifts in the balance of economic activity and big changes in industrial structure would be an act of economic folly, except for the small group of countries in northern Europe whose economies are already so interdependent that unilateral fiscal action has long since ceased to be a useful stabilizing device.

For the French and Germans these are mere second-order issues, because EMU is essentially a political project. Germany regards monetary union as a necessary economic sacrifice on the path to greater political integration. The French see it is a means of pursuing the ambitions of the nation state by other, supra-national means. For the British Labour Party, the French vision is not without attraction. Many on the left in Britain share the French distrust of the market and the instinctive gallic urge to regulate currency and financial markets. They like the European model of social cohesion, with its implicit promise of reduced insecurity. And the presence of George Soros at the demise of the narrow-band ERM blinds them to the benefits that flexible exchange rates have brought, in terms of preventing a further loss of output and employment.

Will the left take the leap?

There will be a powerful temptation, then, for a left-of-centre British government to risk taking the euro-shilling. All the more so, since Britain's poor record with inflation means that it will be paying an interest-rate penalty compared with what it could have if the country submitted to a fiercely independent European central bank. The consequence is that there will probably be a seductive short-term financial bonus to be had on initial entry into EMU – shades of John Major's opportunistic and short-termist thinking as he took his ill-advised plunge into the ERM. Moreover, if sterling is strong before entry, the lower rates of interest will once again be at the cost of reduced competitiveness within the monetary union – shades, too, of the return to the gold standard in 1925.

An additional temptation for Tony Blair could lie in the prospect that a Labour move into EMU would bring about a new polarization in British politics in which Labour's adoption of a 'responsible', mainstream pro-European position would help push the Tories further to the eurosceptic and increasingly loony right, making them unelectable for ever and a day. Yet it is a moot point whether the political and social dividend could outweigh the economic risks – or, indeed, whether the European Union can continue with the inclusive model that has served it so well in the past. Since the enlargement of the original community of six, the union has become a much more cumbersome vehicle for the expression of solidaristic values – and will become more so with further enlargement. The bigger the community, the harder it becomes to use economics as a tool of statesmanship. This was implicitly acknowledged in the Maastricht Treaty's acceptance of the principle of opt-outs and of 'variable geometry', whereby some states can integrate more quickly into a hard core without incurring a veto. And the message was firmly underlined by the very lukewarm endorsement of European public opinion for the monetary union project.

Moreover, if stakeholding is about making democracy work more effectively, there is something inherently odd about borrowing stakeholder values from elsewhere, especially when they come from the social chapter of a European Union which is notoriously devoid of democratic checks and balances – the so-called democratic deficit. A British version of stakeholding could sit perfectly comfortably with the notion of 'subsidiarity' – the idea that legislation should be enacted at the lowest level in the union compatible with full effectiveness. But what Britons of all political complexions need most from their relationship with Europe is growth and jobs. On that score the continental European model has performed very badly over the past decade and a half and it looks more vulnerable to protectionism than a home-grown stakeholder alternative.

It is not essential for Britain to be part of a monetary union, any more than Japan needs to share a common currency with the US or China. Yet there is a deeply entrenched pessimism in parts of the British political establishment which makes people fear exclusion from participation in the mainstream political development of the European Union. There is a hint, here, of the old declinist mentality again. Whitehall is haunted by the memory of the Messina conference in 1955, which Harold Macmillan, foreign secretary at the time, declined to attend because he was, as he put it, busy with Cyprus. A British official who watched the proceedings from the sidelines dismissed the European project as a non-event. After such arrogance, it is hardly surprising that the mandarinate fears a repeat of what is seen by many as the biggest foreign-policy mistake of the post-war period. Yet the risk, in a world where the balance of economic power is shifting away from Europe, could be precisely the opposite: to become enmeshed in an inward-looking political structure with an incipient 'fortress' mentality and an uncompetitive exchange rate just as the economic tide is going out. And the declinist mentality turns into defeatism if we assume that Britain's only hope of achieving price stability is to subcontract the task to central bankers in Europe. There is another, more democratic, domestic means of achieving lower inflation, as we shall see in Chapter 12.

If the risks of early entry to EMU are formidable, the potential benefits should not be discounted. Perhaps the best argument for going in at some point is precisely the defensive one that Britain might be able to do more to prevent a protectionist shift from within than without. Certainly it would be easier within EMU to placate the French, who fear competitive devaluation by the outsiders. That might help preserve the gains of the single market. Yet a question mark inevitably hangs over the extent of British influence, especially in the light of the policy of destructive engagement pursued by John Major in his repeated attempts to placate the eurosceptic right. There is no escaping the fact that monetary union is a Franco-German show in which the Germans have always held the whip hand.

The precedents of history are not all as depressing as that of the Messina conference. There is an instructive parallel with the Latin monetary union of the nineteenth century. This was a project where France was joined in 1865 by Belgium, Italy and Switzerland in its longstanding pursuit of sound money in Europe, inspired perhaps by the vision of Napoleon in St Helena who had declared the need for Europe to have 'a common law, a common measure, and a common currency'. The worries in London were much the same then as they are today. 'If we do nothing, what then?' asked the great political economist Walter Bagehot. 'Why, we shall, to use the vulgar expression, be "left out in the cold".'

At a conference called by the French to coincide with the Paris exhibition of 1867, the self-confidence of Victorian Britain nonetheless triumphed. The British delegate announced:

> So long as public opinion [in Britain] has not decided in favour of a change of the present system, which offers no serious inconvenience…and until it shall be incontestably demonstrated that a new system offers advantages sufficiently commanding to justify the abandonment of that which is approved by experience and rooted in the habits of the people, the English government could not believe it to be its duty to take the initiative in assimilating its coinage with those of the countries of the continent.[19]

British pragmatism proved right on that occasion. The technicalities of the French plan, which was based on a bi-metallic standard, were flawed. And in the aftermath of the Franco-Prussian war the Germans sabotaged the Latin monetary union by adopting a gold standard which was wholly incompatible with the French system. This surely argues for a dispassionate cost–benefit analysis uncoloured by a backward-looking, declinist view of Britain's prospects. EMU may well pose a bigger threat to the social cohesion of Europe and to the 'ever closer union' envisaged by the Treaty of Rome than does either global capital or the Asian challenge. The costs of staying out initially, whether for Labour or the British people, are in some ways less worrying than the risks of going in. There is no need for the outright rejection demanded by the eurosceptic right, any more than we should worry about being accused of wimpish caution for preferring not to join the hard core in the first round. British interests would best be served by a pragmatic policy of wait and see.

12

The Stakeholding Solution

*T*he British political debate has been dominated by the theme of economic decline for so long that it is easy to forget how modest the relative changes in national economic status have been in the course of the twentieth century. Among the countries of the developed world for which valid comparisons are possible only a handful of exceptional shifts stand out; and they are mainly stories of growth, not decline. The most remarkable concerns Japan, where gross domestic product per capita, which is a close approximation of national income per head, grew by more than 17 times between 1900 and 1994. The other big gainers were Norway and Finland in northern Europe, where per capita GDP grew respectively by multiples of 10.4 and 9.1, and Italy in southern Europe, which grew by a factor of 9.4. The growth multiples of most other countries in the developed world during that period were narrowly bunched together between 5 and 7.[1]

The phenomenal growth figures of the leaders are in part a reflection of their relative backwardness at the outset. To take the most obvious case, Japan had been a feudal country until the Meiji Restoration of 1868. By 1900 it was still in the relatively early stages of industrialization, although it was shortly to give the world a hint of what was to come by inflicting a stunning defeat on a great power in the Russo-Japanese war. But the long-run rate of growth experienced by Japan was also greatly influenced by the uniquely impressive showing of its manufacturing sector after the Second World War. The extraordinary economic performance of the Japanese is potentially rivalled only by the smaller-scale economic miracles wrought by the Asian dragons, where industrialization has taken place at a faster rate than ever before in history.

At the other end of the scale, the first and second richest countries by this yardstick in 1900, Britain and New Zealand, inevitably grew more slowly by comparison. Their per capita GDP rose respectively by 3.6 and 3.5 times. Declinists will find grounds for excitement in the lag in performance relative to the United States, the fourth richest country at the turn of the century, which managed an increase of 5.5 times. But the biggest relative losers have been the richer countries of Latin America such as Argentina, which started the century promisingly with GDP per head equivalent to 60 per cent of that of the world's richest country, Britain. Today the comparable figure measured against the top of the table is just 37 per cent.

The other unfortunates are those that started from a low base and simply failed to advance much. Obvious losers here have been the citizens of the former Soviet Union, whose average living standards in 1994 were lower than those of many Latin American countries. Thanks to their disastrous experiment with Marxist economics, the richer countries of Eastern Europe, such as Hungary, Poland and the Czech Republic, were similarly disadvantaged.

Of the countries which most people in 1900 would have expected to end the century at the top of the league, the saddest case is South Africa. Unlike physically impoverished Japan, it is richly endowed with land and natural resources. Yet it has grown by only 2.4 times since 1913 and its GDP per head has fallen to just 15.3 per cent of the US level today. South Africa's performance gives the lie to the nature of the global economic handicap race. In essence, industrialization and trade have produced enormous increases in living standards; and it takes grotesque economic and political mismanagement for countries to fall seriously behind the pack. Mismanagement on the British scale still leaves GDP per head at 84 per cent of the Japanese level, which is hardly something for people to whip themselves into a lather about.

Moreover, the gap is now rapidly narrowing. Britain, unlike the old Soviet Union, is a democracy. Confronted with relative economic decline, it has already shown itself capable of a flexible response. It is no coincidence that Britain and New Zealand, which have seen the greatest relative declines in the twentieth century among the countries of the developed world, have since the beginning of the 1980s been the world's two chief laboratories for radical economic reform. To change the analogy, the message in these estimates of growth in living standards is that it is very difficult for countries to step aboard the fast-moving economic train which is driven by industrialization. But once on board, it becomes remarkably hard to fall off.

Workaholic rabbits versus Samuel Smiles

This raises a serious question about the prominence that politicians and pundits accord to competitiveness in the political debate – especially since the real wealth and well-being of nations are poorly captured by these conventional statistics. What is the meaning of the gap in per capita GDP between Britain and Japan if, as the European trade diplomat Roy Denman once put it, the Japanese are workaholics living in rabbit hutches? This monumentally patronizing verdict – which is, incidentally, no more patronizing than the verdicts passed by many Japanese bureaucrats on Europeans – reflects an important truth which is relevant to the stakeholder debate.

All politicians in the English-speaking world, regardless of party, have long sought to give people a sense of a stake in national prosperity. Where they differed was in their understanding of what constituted a stake and how best to provide it to the voters. In the old left–right debate, right-of-centre politicians placed the emphasis on private ownership as a route to achieving the stakeholding objective. This was matched on the left by a preoccupation with public ownership. Both sides had an exaggerated view of what ownership could actually deliver. And both sides tended to underestimate the role of the workplace in giving people a greater sense of involvement and commitment in the economy and in society. A comparison between Britain and Japan is particularly instructive in demonstrating the relevance of the stakeholder alternative in the post-Cold-War environment and establishing what constitutes a worthwhile stake.

If we start with the Japanese, it is immediately apparent that their chief failure of economic management since the war has been the inability to translate astonishing gains in productivity into tangible improvements in the quality of life. The Japanese model of high savings and export-led growth, in which much consumption is deferred for the benefit of future generations, grinds on regardless of changing circumstances. Yet it would be wrong to regard Japan as nothing more than a gradgrind economy, because the post-war Japanese have found a satisfaction in the workplace and a sense of national purpose which has substantially compensated for the disadvantages of their lifestyle at home. Where the bureaucrats and businesspeople who ran the country succeeded was in giving most ordinary people a sense that they had a genuine stake in society and in national prosperity, even when they were not among the privileged group that enjoyed the benefit of lifetime employment.

As with other countries such as Germany, Switzerland, Norway or Singapore, which are loosely characterized as stakeholder societies, this has delivered not only a place high up on the economic league table, but a high degree of social cohesion and an exceptionally low level of criminality. Even the *yakuza*, the Japanese equivalent of the Mafia, are strangely socialized. They have traditionally operated on the basis of a tacit understanding with the police whereby illegal activities such as prostitution and protection rackets have been tolerated as long as the gangs steer clear of guns and drugs.

If Japan is no longer as cohesive in the 1990s it is the result of inflexible policy which has caused the ownership side of the stakeholder equation to become unbalanced. The vast inflation in land prices has made even rabbit hutches prohibitively expensive for the best paid salarymen. And the low income return on property and shares has raised questions about the solvency of the insurance companies on which the Japanese depend for their incomes in retirement. With land inflation creating great inequalities in wealth, corruption in politics and business increased sharply in the 'bubble economy' period of the 1980s. The money politics of the old one-party democracy, which people accepted as part of the Japanese way of life, degenerated into a level of sleaze that offended against all previous norms.

Even the tacit understanding between the police and *yakuza* became strained, since the gangsters' involvement in shady property deals made them obvious scapegoats for Japan's economic problems. They are now required by law to be licensed to operate as gangsters and are subject to a number of prohibitions, of which exclusion from membership of golf clubs is especially resented by gang leaders.[2] Yet the social cohesion of Japan should not be underestimated; nor should its capacity for change. What history tells us is that Japan takes longer than most other countries to form a consensus for any move in a different direction. But when the change comes, it is dramatic.

In post-war Britain, in contrast, the attempt to give people a stake has been directed more specifically at rights of ownership rather than a working environment designed to encourage a high level of informal cooperation and a wider sense of purpose. This was a reflection of historic circumstance. The unions' entrenched position in the workplace and the class-bound attitudes of British management appeared to pre-empt creative thinking on how to add to the responsibilities and psychological rewards at work. Hence the emphasis on stakeholding through ownership, which was encapsulated in the post-war Tory focus on the notion of a property-owning democracy. The thinking was that of Samuel Smiles, who put the case like this:

> The accumulation of property has the effect which it has always had upon thrifty men; it makes them steady, sober and diligent. It weans them from revolutionary notions, and makes them conservative. When workmen, by their industry and frugality, have secured their own independence, they will cease to regard the sight of others' well-being as a wrong inflicted on themselves; and it will no longer be possible to make political capital out of their imaginary woes.

Smiles was right, up to a point. But his version of the property-owning democracy, which remains central to the Tory vision, does not have much of an answer to the insecurities of the 1990s. The worry for today's industrious and frugal home owners is not revolution but a labour market which provides those who are not home owners with a growing inducement to property-related crime. And there is only a slender likelihood that home ownership will provide as satisfactory an entrée into the prosperity of the British economy over the next 20 years as it did in the past. Now that the baby-boom generation has done most of its house buying, demographic pressure is no longer working so hard to push up house prices. Nor, for all the rhetoric of the Tories in their privatization programme, is wider share ownership a realistic way of giving people a stake.

As we have seen, the great majority do not have enough savings to be able to acquire a prudently balanced portfolio of shares. The Tory readiness to destroy social capital in intermediate institutions such as the building societies and the TSB thus looks extraordinary. These were the institutions which provided the less well off with the next best thing to an ownership stake, in the shape of a secure income which was combined with an indirect form of social insurance that came from modest redistribution within the savings movement. To have pronounced a death sentence on them was an act of vandalism, especially when the redistributive capability of the public sector is under great pressure.

Paternalism, good and bad

In the absence of changes to the tax system, share ownership will be confined for the foreseeable future to big institutional investors. And this is where the greatest obstacle to a constructive Anglo-Saxon version of stakeholding lies. By introducing the values of the hunting field into the capital markets and the ideology of shareholder value into the boardroom, we have killed off what is left of benign paternalism in the workplace. Takeovers govern more and more of our lives. Yet we have retained many malign aspects of paternalism in our pension fund arrangements, which make for inequality and exclusion.

For most of the post-war period in Japan the values of stakeholding were directed at satisfying the needs of both the workforce and the wider population. All were prepared to allow their personal interests to be subsumed in the wider goal of the advancement of the nation. The British form of capitalism, by contrast, incorporates a more atomized view of society. The manager, the worker, the customer, the supplier and the shareholder are all in separate boxes; and their respective contributions are ostensibly directed via the capital market towards the non-nationalistic goal of looking after the supposed interests of the pensioner. The assumption is that society's requirements will best be served by maximizing the return to the shareholder-pensioner, with the interests of other stakeholders (with the exception of the consumer where the company operates in a competitive market) being subservient. The fact that you cannot be the beneficiary of a pension fund without having first been an employee is neither here nor there: the system will see to it that you are insecure while still in employment, leaving the promise of security for retirement.

This narrowly focused form of capitalism is not without its merits. By turning the British into insecure and overborrowed workaholics in an increasingly flexible labour market, it has helped arrest relative economic decline. It is striking, too, that the British have made a more rapid short-term adjustment to the economic conditions of the 1990s than have the Japanese. Yet the chief beneficiaries of Britain's robust but stressful form of capitalism are not really the people in whose name these painful adjustments have been made.

Between 1979 and 1993 the increase in the real value before tax of the equity shares in the average British pension fund, assuming the dividends were reinvested, amounted to an astonishing 477 per cent. That is an annual average real return of 13.3 per cent, reflecting among other things a big increase in the return to capital relative to labour. This belated revenge on

Marx and all his works is an extraordinarily high return by historic standards: the average since the end of the First World War hovered, up to the 1970s, in a range between 6 and 8 per cent.[3] Yet British managers have chosen not to compensate the workers for the shift in the share of profits going to capital by giving them an increased ownership stake in preparation for retirement. They have clung to a form of pension fund paternalism which excludes the majority from a worthwhile share in these supernormal returns.

As we saw in the Chapter 10, the typical company pension scheme merely provides for a guarantee fund, which exists to back a promise to pay a given level of pension, not to provide a stake in future prosperity. The result is that the system ends up being circular. Stock-market and other pressures ensure that executives maximize short-term profitability and pay high levels of dividend in order to keep the share price up and the predators at bay. This then contributes to pension fund surpluses which are ploughed back into the company's profit and loss account via contribution holidays, with only modest and arbitrary amounts going to improve the benefits of present and future pensioners. The circularity of the process helps explain why the mechanism that normally leads from economic growth to a sense of well-being has broken down. Profit has become the end instead of the means. No one has stopped to ask the point of it all.

The divine right of bosses

The collateral beneficiaries of the capital-market merry-go-round are the directors, whose pay and incentive arrangements encourage them to concentrate on short-term profitability. The costs of this focus are high. Morale in the workforce sinks where the gap between pay in the boardroom and the shopfloor widens inexorably. For, despite all the talk about the decentralization of business and the empowerment of individual workers, empowerment does not mean much when the worker lives in constant fear of the sack. And the striking feature of many businesses in Britain today is just how far they have moved from the collegiate, teamwork style of management towards a more autocratic management style. In his recent book *Company Man*, Anthony Sampson remarks that while responsibility has been devolved downwards, power and money have become more heavily concentrated at the top. As companies have become leaner and meaner, he adds, they look less like republics, more like monarchies.

This raises serious questions about legitimacy. Top executives justify their tighter grip on power and their spiralling pay by claiming that in increasingly competitive global markets a single manager can make the difference between corporate success and failure. With information technology, and increasingly transparent markets, it is suggested, these supermen are more readily identifiable and thus have a market value that is independent of the company. Unless they are commensurately rewarded they will go elsewhere. Businesspeople's favourite analogy is with the winner-takes-all system that applies in international sport. No one, they claim, will pay for second best.

Yet the analogy is flawed. The market in top executives is very imperfect. And while there are certainly some companies where success has been associated with the efforts of a single individual, the great majority are led by lesser mortals and draw their strength from harnessing the diverse talents of a wider group. Business in any case lacks the simple scoring system that makes it so easy to identify a winner in car racing or golf. Few fit the description of the stereotypical superman who makes the difference between success and failure. Indeed, many corporate predators argue that the performance of most companies can usually be improved simply by clearing out the boardroom and promoting frustrated executives from the level immediately below.

If business is more unpopular than it has been in decades, the blame does not lie exclusively with top executives. In a period of greatly increased global competition they have been faced with unprecedented challenges which called for measures that were bound to be painful for the workforce. The constant recycling of pension fund surpluses whereby profits have been allowed to become the systemic end instead of the means came about more by accident than design. The British form of pension funding was designed for a world of stable prices, stable markets in goods and services, and implicit lifetime employment. It was the disappearance of that world that perverted the system. Also to blame is the rickety nature of an antiquated accounting framework that regards human capital as a cost instead of an asset, so guaranteeing that the manic pursuit of short-term profit creates an excessive bias towards cost cutting rather than revenue generation. This threatens to debilitate firms in the more advanced areas of the economy where intangible values hold the key to competitive advantage.

In effect, business in the English-speaking economies has hit on a managerial version of the primitive medical practice in which the doctor's response to each and every disease was to bleed the patient. The management gurus who promote this medieval quackery seek to make their prescriptions respectable by using the anaesthetizing language of downsizing, delayering and reengineering. They justify their prescriptions by claiming that the medicine is necessary to prevent an inexorable downward spiral of economic decline.

Yet the reality is that companies are being purged; and as with patients in real life, repeated purging will do serious damage to the corporate victims and their employees. Not only is the remedy worse than the disease; the disease has been misdiagnosed because of the declinist fixation. The problem, as this book has sought to demonstrate, is less one of decline than of how to manage the consequences of structural adjustment and increasing specialization among firms, as economies respond to the twin pressures of technological advance and liberalization in trade and capital markets.

Competitiveness, right and wrong

Just as the yardsticks for gauging corporate performance exert a distorting influence on economic behaviour, the tools for quantifying the performance of the wider economy distort political perceptions. The most obvious example concerns the reliance on gross domestic product, already mentioned in relation to Britain and Japan. GDP is only a measure of those goods and services that are produced specifically for the market sector of the economy. It ignores such services as childcare and care of the elderly that take place in the home. Given that one of the most important labour-market developments of recent years has been the increased participation of women in the workforce, the impression created by the bald economic numbers is potentially very misleading. The expansion in the output of daycare centres that results from this trend is, for example, recorded in the economic statistics without anyone subtracting the related loss in household production that results from the withdrawal of childcare services previously delivered in the home.

The use of GDP as a measure of performance entails countless other flaws. It ignores the capital stock, which in Britain is exceptionally rich, with much historic building and fine Victorian infrastructure still in use. It fails to record the negative investment that arises from environmental pollution, and treats energy depletion as a positive addition to output. And it fails to count in full the vital investment in human capital in areas such as research, healthcare and education. Since these probably make a bigger contribution to future productivity than conventionally measured business investment, this is quite some omission. But the greatest weakness lies in failing to tell us anything useful about the happiness of the nation. What little quantitative research has been carried out on this score suggests that economic progress buys very little extra happiness.[4]

Yet politicians across the world have dedicated themselves to the single-minded pursuit of growth in GDP and have put the notion of competitiveness at the very heart of governmental priorities. This is strange, given that the huge growth of cross-border investment makes the very idea of national competitiveness an increasingly fuzzy one. The preoccupation with relativities, whether at the level of the nation or the individual, is in any case absurd. We cannot all improve relative to everyone else. And the relative differences in living standards between countries in the developed world, as we have seen, remain small. Economists, thinktanks and business institutes have nonetheless pandered to the politicians' obsession by producing more and more yardsticks – often ideologically loaded – of competitiveness. They have spawned league tables by the dozen. Like the managers who so busily generate surpluses for the pension funds, they overlook the point that economic growth is a means, not an end.

What makes this mercantilist concern with competitiveness doubly disconcerting is that it corrupts our values. Consider the arms-for-Iraq affair, where British politicians' focus on improving their country's bilateral trade balance regardless of the nature of the receiving country's regime led ultimately to the abuse of ministerial power. The underlying assumption was the one that sees trade as a zero-sum game and assumes that the purpose of government is to help business accumulate export surpluses. It ignores the fact that a loss of orders to Iraq can, in a flexible market economy, be made good by a shift of resources into other industries and other exports.

The decline in Iraq's real per capita GDP from $3320 in 1960 to $1783 in 1990 – and that is serious decline, at the rate of 2.1 per cent a year – is a remarkable tribute to the viciousness and incompetence of this oil-rich country's rulers. But it is hard to see why the British had to help them in their efforts to impoverish the Iraqi people. Most voters would probably be happy if Britain unilaterally reduced the volume of its international arms trade to the Third World, in view of the dubious morality and the risk that the arms might at some point be used against British troops.

The usual apologia for a hard-headed policy of promoting exports to unsavoury regimes is that jobs would otherwise be lost to competing countries. After the Scott report into arms for Iraq, the excuse sounds hollow – especially so, given that the argument is based on an economically fallacious assumption. In international relations there is everything to be said for the unsentimental pursuit of national interest. But it is not clear how Britain's interests were served by ministers turning a blind eye to the activities of greedy individuals who were prepared to sell equipment to Iraq that was capable of military (including nuclear) application.

Education, education, education – but for what?

Similar questions arise over educational values. There are obvious grounds for concern about future competitiveness here, since Britain spends less of its national income on education than the OECD average and appears by international standards to be underachieving in maths, science and English.[5] The system has been lopsided, in that education has catered well for an academic élite, especially in the universities, while the less bright have been singularly ill served. Yet much of the Thatcher government's educational programme in the 1980s was directed towards mending the part of the system that delivered excellence. All too often its budgetary stringencies and centralizing reforms were carried out in the name of ill-defined 'business' values.

As Simon Jenkins has argued in his powerful polemic *Accountable to None: The Tory Nationalisation of Britain,* higher education before 1979 was not short of faults; but these have not been properly addressed by turning universities into work-oriented, vocational, commercial organizations run more like public corporations than institutions of scholarship.[6] Such perverse educational corporatism has damaged a system whose scientific endowment contributed so much to innovation in Britain's more successful industries such as pharmaceuticals and software.

The fact that it is quite difficult to engineer a serious relative decline in the nation's living standards does not exempt us all from the grind of competing in world markets. But reforms which contrive to do little or no economic good, while undermining the liberal scholarly ethos of the university, are pure philistinism. As with their arms exports to the Third World, the politicians appear to have taken quite literally the economist's textbook convention of *homo economicus* and elevated it to a categorical imperative. Morality is thereby reduced to expediency and scholarship to a commercial overhead.

The risk in Labour leader Tony Blair's pro-education bias is that in emphasizing the importance of education to the economy he will, like Margaret Thatcher, allow corporate values to dictate too much of the shape of education. There is a need to tilt the balance back towards the more humane vision that Matthew Arnold called, in that wonderfully un-Thatcherite phrase, sweetness and light. The Arnold of *Culture and Anarchy* is overdue for a revival. With his assault on the materialistic and rationalistic assumptions of individualistic liberalism and utilitarianism, and his emphasis on culture as the underpinning of political order, the Victorian poet and social theorist has a message for the 1990s.

Unemployment and inequality

The manic pursuit of competitiveness has, paradoxically, been accompanied by a remarkably gloomy consensus about what can be achieved in the way of reduced unemployment. The conventional wisdom is that there can be no return to the low levels of unemployment last seen in the 1960s because the circumstances then were exceptional. Indeed, economists now refer nostalgically to the period between 1950 and 1973 as the 'golden age', since global growth was higher than at any previous point in history. World per capita GDP grew by 2.9 per cent a year, which was more than three times as fast as between 1913 to 1950.

Unemployment in Britain during the golden age averaged just over 2 per cent of the total workforce. Historical figures of unemployment are not wholly comparable with those used by the British government in this period, but as a broad indication of the freakishness of this experience it is noteworthy that in the most widely used historical series, unemployment in the whole period between 1855 and 1945 fell below 2 per cent in only nine peacetime years.[7] We need to understand why circumstances after 1950 were so favourable to employment if we are to make realistic prognostications for the future.

Good policy had a great deal to do with it. A new international order in which the United States played the leading role prevented any return to the beggar-thy-neighbour policies of the 1930s. Trade expanded, in terms of export volume, at a compound rate of 7 per cent, compared with 1.3 per cent in 1913 to 1950 and 3.7 per cent in 1973 to 1992. After the massive physical destruction of the Second World War there was huge potential for reconstruction. Together with technical progress this led to a big upsurge in investment.

In his book *The Unbound Prometheus*, David Landes has argued that the exceptional growth in the golden age reflected the failure of the second wave of the Industrial Revolution in industries such as electricals and chemicals to fulfil its potential because of the two world wars and the Slump. This seems entirely plausible, not least because of the constraints that held back the diffusion of technology by the world's most dynamic economy, the United States. Between 1913 and 1950 productivity in the United States grew at five times the rate of 1870 to 1913 and by 1950 the US economy was bigger than that of Western Europe. Yet the explosive 60-year boom in technical potential was largely bottled up until the world escaped from war and protectionism. Only after 1945 could the US take the natural lead role of the world's largest economy in diffusing technological progress.[8]

If anything marred the economic achievements of this period, it was the failure to remedy the growing inequality between the developed countries and the great majority in the Third World. As we saw in the previous chapter, the disparities in income between these two groups reached unprecedented proportions. With hindsight, it is not surprising that what brought the golden age to an end was a backlash from the developing countries. The two oil crises of the 1970s, together with the associated surge in commodity prices, heralded a world of much slower growth.

These inflationary shocks were exacerbated by the collapse of the Bretton Woods fixed exchange-rate system. The trouble with a combination of free trade and fixed exchange rates is that it simultaneously encourages virtuous and vicious circles. Fixed rates reward frugal nations that run trade surpluses while penalizing the profligates who run trade deficits, despite the fact that the deficit countries make a bigger contribution to international prosperity. The United States, the fall guy of the Bretton Woods system, confronted in the early 1970s the choice of sacrificing growth to keep its overvalued exchange rate fixed or scuppering the whole structure. It opted to scupper, which contributed to the global inflationary shock. And as the world became more preoccupied with the consequences of these shocks, the priorities of economic management shifted from the maintenance of full employment to the reduction of inflation.

A new golden age

For the half-empty-cup school of political economy, the historical uniqueness of the golden age is taken as evidence that there can be no return to the rates of unemployment that prevailed in the 1960s. Yet there is every reason to look forward rather than back. Today's global economic circumstances are astonishingly propitious. Before the collapse of Berlin Wall, the developed world faced the prospect of a depressed twenty-first century, on the basis that savings were going to increase sharply as the population grew older. Too much saving and too little consumption lead to slump – the disaster of the 1930s. With the former Soviet bloc, together with the giants of Asia and Latin America, re-entering the liberal trading system, the problem of excessive saving is deferred. More, and more populous, countries are industrializing at a faster pace than at any time in history. Capital can now be exported to these younger, faster-growing economies to earn high returns for the developed world's pensioners.

There is, in addition, a substantial post-Cold-War peace dividend that will continue to come as a result of the diversion of resources away from the military. This involves more painful adjustment, but the dividend is real. And it is possible that there will be a dividend, too, from the – so far not very remunerative – development of information technology. In the history of technological development it has often taken two or three decades for industry to learn to harness big technological breakthroughs to good economic purpose. If we cannot make another golden age out of all this, something is dramatically wrong. And to suggest that unemployment and inequality cannot be substantially reduced is the counsel of despair.

These, then, are the opportunities. The risks are that the continuing adjustments required in this brave new world will be painful. The golden age phenomenon of lifetime employment in big companies, for example, has gone for the foreseeable future. While the relative economic status of developed countries changes little, that of companies has changed considerably. Of the 10 largest American companies in 1900, only one, General Electric, remains in the top 10 today.[9] In Britain, too, the industrial and commercial landscape has been subjected to much chopping and changing as a result of successive waves of acquisitions and mergers. And now the biggest companies like ICI and Courtaulds have been deconstructing themselves, hiving off parts of their businesses and floating them separately on the stock market.

While there are some big companies, in industries such as oil or aerospace, where size and long-term horizons are an essential requirement for success, corporate giants seem to have lost competitive advantage in the information age. Many of them lack the flexibility that is required to satisfy fast-changing consumer markets and to engage effectively in continuous innovation. Certainly the prospects for big-company employment relative to small look unpromising. The OECD believes that the share of large firms (over 500 employees) in developed world employment is shrinking at the rate of about 1 per cent a year.

In the aftermath of the Cold War, it might be thought that there is unlikely to be a political backlash in response to the pressures of ceaseless economic upheaval. There is no new ideology, in the developed world at least, to help mobilize the feelings of the disaffected. Yet the corrosive impact on Western electorates of high unemployment and income inequality is a potentially dangerous phenomenon. Nor, in Britain, should the fallout from the fat-cat pay story be ignored. Writing in 1923, when businessmen were under attack for profiteering, Keynes pointed with characteristic prescience to dangers that are present today:

> To convert the business man into the profiteer is to strike a blow at capitalism, because it destroys the psychological equilibrium which permits the perpetuance of unequal rewards. The economic doctrine of normal profits, vaguely apprehended by everyone, is a necessary condition for the justification of capitalism. The business man is only tolerable so long as his gains can be held to bear some relation to what, roughly and in some sense, his activities have contributed to society.[10]

Beware of less eccentric protectionists

The public perception of business's contribution to society is, whether justified or not, unquestionably jaundiced. Business lacks what the RSA's *Tomorrow's Company* inquiry calls a licence to operate. It follows that if we cannot find some way of legitimizing the operations of business, there will be trouble. Just as the oil producers of the Third World rebelled in the 1970s in response to a perceived imbalance of global wealth and power, workers in the developed world will find their own way of rebelling against tough conditions in the labour market. As I argued earlier, one threat is simply a further deterioration in the moral and social climate, leading to a growing resort to property-related crime by the disadvantaged. The wider concern is that people will vote for a retreat into protectionism. While this would be a costly irrelevance in today's world of massive cross-border investment, the possibility should not be underestimated. As the economist Harry G Johnson argued, the enduring attraction of protectionism is that it conveys a psychic satisfaction which compensates people for the resulting loss of income by gratifying their taste for nationalism. Odd though this economic jargon sounds, it conveys a serious point about the way human psychology works.[11]

The risk appears especially strong in continental Europe, where nationalism is on a rising tide and the reaction to high unemployment has been timid and introspective. Since Helmut Kohl's bold initial dash for German unification, the European Union's response to the challenge of transition in eastern Europe has been pallid. The technical issue of monetary union has been needlessly allowed to become an immensely divisive political issue. Particularly worrying is the way the French élite talks openly and arrogantly of competition from 'coolies' in Asia, while inflicting low-growth policies on the French people.

In an inward-looking European Union, seemingly bent on low growth, the lure of protectionism is thus magnified. Nor is it easy to be optimistic about the British ability to exert a big influence on the direction of Europe. Moreover, the increase in living standards since the war means that for many, the exercise of choice in consumer markets now seems to provide more freedom than the act of putting a cross on the ballot paper. This can result in increased voter apathy. For those at the bottom of the labour-market pile, on the other hand, consumer choice is limited and the value of the vote proportionately greater. The old nineteenth-century fear of what such stakeless people might do with their vote may yet come back to haunt us.

So far we have been fortunate that the most vocal advocate of protectionism in Europe has been an eccentric billionaire of German-Jewish extraction, with joint British and French nationality, a history of corporate raiding in America and a palatial home in Mexico. A less plausible proponent of economic nationalism would be impossible to conceive than Jimmy Goldsmith. But if we fail to address adequately the concerns of the electorate over security, inequality and jobs, other more effective spokespersons for the nationalist cause will soon emerge.

In place of fear

The great achievement of the British since 1979 is that they have embraced the rigours of this new, insecure economic environment where the continental Europeans have shied away from confronting it. Enormous adjustments have been made in industry and commerce, for which due credit must be given to

Margaret Thatcher. But the macho political and managerial style of the 1980s, which relied heavily on fear as the chief motivator, has outlived its usefulness. The need today is not for slashing and burning, but for building. It is time to restore to capitalism the qualities that make it tolerable for those who will have to cope with the stresses that are still in store.

The argument of this book has been that the stakeholding solution offers a means of legitimizing the tempestuous mechanics of capitalism and of preserving human and social capital in the interests of competitive advantage. What, by way of recapitulation, are its main tenets?

Inclusion

The first must be the concept of inclusion, whether at the level of society or the company. This central criterion of stakeholding makes tolerable the inequalities that are an inescapable characteristic of a vibrant market economy. To some it seems an elusive concept, because it goes beyond the very tangible values of the old left–right political debate in which ownership played a central part. Yet the old debate has lost its force precisely because it overemphasized the tangible and underemphasized the more subtle values that bind society together and underpin the modern economy. In contrast, the language of inclusion has increasing resonance in an age where everything seems to happen too fast and nothing can be taken for granted any more. For the left, it provides a sophisticated alternative to the slogan of equality, although not one which is necessarily at odds with that slogan since it is rooted in the idea of fairness.

Ethical constraints

Another central tenet of stakeholding is that behaviour in markets must be tempered by self-imposed social and ethical constraints. In other words, the exercise of property rights entails obligations that do not begin and end with the property owner, but extend to the wider community. By emphasizing the role of intermediate institutions – companies, unions, churches, clubs, campaigning groups and the rest – the stakeholding concept consciously downgrades the role of the state, at one extreme, and of the autonomous individual at the other. That is not to say that individualism is bad. Clearly it is at the heart of much of what is best in the British political tradition. It also makes a vital contribution to innovation in the economy. The point is rather that individualism can be destructive without the restraining influence of social and ethical norms.

Perhaps the nakedly self-serving individualism of the Thatcherite experiment was a necessary antidote to the corporatism of the 1970s. But it scarcely looks attractive or relevant in the deregulated and downsized 1990s. Moreover, the economic theory of stakeholding convincingly asserts that self-restraint is cheaper than the constant resort to rule books and the legal enforcement of private contracts.

An alternative to market liberalism

The economic case for stakeholding lies precisely in this claim to provide an efficient alternative to the individualistic excesses of market liberalism. This, as we have seen, is because the exercise of property rights in a stakeholder-type economy is influenced by shared values, cooperative behaviour and fairness. Earlier chapters have shown that some British companies can and do manage to strike a productive balance between the different stakeholders and to harness innovative talent in the collective interest. Marks & Spencer, Unipart, the John Lewis Partnership and numerous others have clearly demonstrated that the stakeholder culture does work in a British context. Far from being a fad, or a foreign import, it is a very effective way to run a company, with obvious benefits for the wider economy.

Self-respect

Finally, stakeholding views firms as social institutions in which people aspire to self-respect, as well as to a higher standard of living. This is not on the basis of a woolly-minded appeal to the innate virtues of partnership or cooperation. It reflects a hard-headed acknowledgement that values of loyalty and trust within the organization foster wealth creation and contribute to competitive advantage. The existence of such values within the firm permits management to take a longer-term view, whether in relation to investment or employment. And in the long run the stakeholding ethos is more conducive to corporate success than is a culture in which fear is the main motivator.

The role of the politicians

What are the implications for practical policy? The stakeholder approach is, in fact, a very challenging discipline for the politicians, especially those of the old left, because it potentially shifts the locus of political and economic activity further away from the state towards intermediate institutions. In terms of influencing human behaviour, it asserts the superiority of culture over legislation. This flies in the face of the prevailing political climate, which is one of centralizing interventionism on both the right and the left of the spectrum.

If there is a problem in a particular school, ministers are expected to address it. If the electorate is worried about crime, the politicians' instinctive reaction is to announce that more prisons will be built and more people locked up. If there is a wave of concern over sexual harrassment at work, government examines the scope for tougher legislation in the workplace. Yet these are all problems which reflect failures of leadership and cooperation in the school, the community and the firm. Central government intervention and an ever-increasing body of statute law will never be the best means of handling such things. But that raises a question about the stakeholder alternative. How do you change the culture of a nation?

It can only be done over time, through political rhetoric, intellectual debate and institutional reform. And a central part of such reform inevitably concerns the management of the economy. The politicians' task here is in one respect similar to that of businesspeople. They have to grasp the importance of social capital, foster its creation and avoid its destruction, in the interests of enhancing competitiveness and offering the prospect of individual fulfilment for all in the workplace. And if firms are to deliver on the job promise of the stakeholder idea and focus on the longer term, the politicians' priority should be to provide more stability in macroeconomic policy – the management of money, exchange rates and the national budget.

The overwhelming imperative here is to avoid an overvalued exchange rate for sterling. The biggest losses of output and employment in the twentieth century have usually taken place as a result of such overvaluations, as in the second half of the 1920s, the mid-1960s or the two great recessions presided over respectively by Margaret Thatcher and John Major. This is an area where politicians have a direct and powerful influence over competitiveness, which is why it is so important to make the right decisions about Europe and EMU.

Privatizing monetary policy, preserving social capital

The other requirement of macroeconomic policy is that we avoid the inflationary excesses that have called in the past for such extreme policy remedies. Britain cannot afford to wipe out its smaller businesses in each and every downturn, when these are the main job generators of the future. One solution is a move to an independent central bank. It is interesting that Labour has been edging in this direction, with shadow chancellor Gordon Brown calling for a more open and accountable Bank of England. But the impetus appears to be flagging. The early drafts of *The Blair Revolution* by two influential members of the New Labour hierarchy, Peter Mandelson and Roger Liddle, argued for full independence. By the time the book was published the idea had been junked. The authors judged that it would be unsaleable in the light of the Bank of England's dogged resistance to interest-rate cuts made by the chancellor Kenneth Clarke, which subsequently looked less risky than they appeared at the time. For the radical step of independence was substituted an endorsement for existing Labour policy, arguing that any further moves down the road to independence would depend on the success of moves to reorganize the Bank.[12]

However understandable, this remained an illogical response to what was actually going on – namely that in the summer of 1996 Kenneth Clarke was chancing his arm before an election and turning out to be lucky. The raising and cutting of interest rates is an intensely political business. One of the reasons that countries suffer from inflationary excesses is that politicians have a greater incentive to cut rates than to raise them. This asymmetry means that there is an inbuilt bias against price stability. Interest rates that are oversensitive to the political cycle end up having a destabilizing influence on the economy.

The best of the arguments for an independent central bank is that the removal of control over monetary policy from the Treasury would directly address this problem. Even in a disinflationary world it offers worthwhile insurance against unpredictable inflationary shocks, as well as exerting a countervailing influence against cynical monetary manipulation for electoral gain. But an independent central bank will not work if it is the vehicle for an unaccountable deflationist crusade by a stubborn central banker.

What is needed is a framework of accountability, perhaps along the lines of the New Zealand central bank, whereby the central bank's performance is measured against targets agreed by parliament. The Bank of England would also have to be restructured to ensure that decisions were taken by a suitably qualified group of the great and the good. In normal circumstances such a system would simply aim to deliver a lower rate of inflation than undiluted political management of interest rates would be capable of achieving. Parliament, as the ultimate arbiter, would probably be a more accurate reflection of the nation's inflationary preferences than would either an unfettered chancellor or an independent Bank of England without accountability. Far from being undemocratic, this formula for independence would actually enhance democracy. And it would allow the markets to put greater trust in monetary policy, thereby reducing the need for knee-jerk increases in interest rates whenever the economy shows signs of remotely robust growth.

The prize to be had from a more stable approach to managing the economy is considerable. In the language of stakeholding, it would encourage the preservation of social capital instead of destroying it in bulk whenever the economy turns down. With more stability, it would become easier for firms to retain employees and continue investing through the business cycle because the troughs would be shallower and the momentum less volatile. Businesspeople would cease to worry so much about any upturn being promptly knocked on the head for fear of inflationary consequences.

Make way for the responsible individual

In microeconomic policy, which concerns the structure of markets, the most important priority and a vital determinant of competitiveness is the degree of openness of those markets. Much of the exploration of industry and commerce contained in this book clearly demonstrates how, in a liberal trading environment, entrepreneurial effort in the national economy responds to global profit opportunities as firms play to specialist strengths. The question then becomes one of how to address untoward effects and distortions of the market process.

As I have argued, Britain's hostile takeover habit is a prime candidate for treatment. The frenzied trade in companies, so lucrative to the City, needs to be damped down so that companies can preserve social capital and offer more secure employment. Dividends cannot be allowed automatically to take precedence over jobs and investment whenever the economic cycle takes a turn for the worst. The fiscal sticks and carrots must be rearranged so that the personal as well as the corporate motivation of managers is geared to encourage longer-term investment.

The big investment institutions – the rotten boroughs of the capitalist system – badly need to be democratized and encouraged to conduct a more constructive relationship with the companies in which they invest. They must also be encouraged to recognize that establishing a more honest relationship with their customers is in their own longer-term interest. And we must give people private occupational pensions which introduce them to both the risks and the rewards of capitalism instead of the very arbitrary and unequal outcomes delivered by today's pension fund paternalism.

The welfare system, which must continue to play a central role in any stakeholder economy, needs to direct more of its support towards subsidizing employment rather than unemployment, and towards company training rather than government training.

The erosion of legitimacy in the links between the taxing and spending sides of the welfare equation means that the private sector will have to play a growing part in welfare provision. What matters is that it takes forms that minimize the disincentives to work and to save, and that stop removing skilled workers prematurely from the workforce. In short, welfare, whether administered by the public or the private sector, must respect the values of inclusion.

The future of the left does not lie in the negation of individualism – least of all when flexibility is at a premium in a time of very rapid economic change and when information technology is opening up new opportunities for innovation and self-employment. And the stakeholder critique of economic liberalism is not an inherently collectivist one. It merely highlights the paradox in the Reagan and Thatcher legacy, which manages to combine extremes of unbridled individualism with a one-dimensional form of shareholder capitalism that treats other individuals with extreme disrespect.

The stakeholding solution outlined here is about responsible individualism. It accepts that uncertainty is a condition of life for the foreseeable future and that people who have been used to security in a paternalistic environment will have to develop a more robust sense of independence. And in practice many are finding even in today's less secure and more demanding environment that challenging work is turning out to be more fulfilling than in the more paternalistic environment of the past. Yet the unemployment costs of structural adjustment remain too high and income inequality stays at an unacceptable level. Fear remains endemic, whether it is fear of crime, fear of unemployment, fear of Asian competition or fear that the money will run out in old age.

This book has tried to show how the concept of stakeholding can address those fears, arguing that the principles are such that any country can adopt its own indigenous approach without borrowing wholesale from the statutes and cultures of the Germans, the Japanese or anyone else. To those who object that such principles fly in the face of a centuries-old Anglo-Saxon tradition that rests on the unfettered exercise of property rights, the answer must be that pluralism and the legal concept of trust and trusteeship, which is fundamental to stakeholding, go back a great deal further. For all its merits, today's crude Anglo-Saxon form of capitalism needs refining.

The time is ripe for a more subtle and civilized alternative to the rampant liberalism of the New Right. Stakeholding provides that alternative. It will not deliver a short-term dividend. But in the long run it does indeed promise a worthwhile stake in the future.

Notes and References

Chapter 1

1 Ernest Gellner, 'The rest of history', *Prospect*, May 1996. Addicts of footnotes will soon discover that much of the conceptual debate on stakeholding has taken place in this innovative new magazine.

2 *Labour Market Statistics*, Office for National Statistics, March 1996.

3 For a detailed discussion of the incentives to crime in the US labour market see 'The limits of wage flexibility in curing unemployment' by Richard Freeman in the *Oxford Review of Economic Policy*, Spring 1995. See also Martin Wolf in 'Jobs for the boys', *Financial Times*, April 30, 1996, where he offers a provocative discussion of the plight of the unskilled male. The figure for lone mothers comes from John Hills, *The Future of Welfare*, Joseph Rowntree Foundation, 1993.

4 John Hills, ibid.

5 Quoted by Mark Suzman in a *Financial Times* special supplement on Business in the Community, 1996.

6 Tony Blair, speech to the Singapore business community, January 8, 1996.

7 An excess of Singaporean paternalism is evident in the way the government habitually employs the Central Provident Fund's money for its own ends: the World Bank has estimated that the real return on the fund, which is invested in government bonds, bank deposits and official foreign exchange reserves, was only 3 per cent from 1980 to 1990 – well below comparable returns in the UK. See the World Bank's *Averting the Old Age Crisis*, Oxford University Press, 1994, p.95.

8 Thomas Paine, *Agrarian Justice, The Thomas Paine Reader*, eds Michael Foot and Isaac Kramnick, Penguin, 1987. For a discussion of this aspect of Paine's thought, see John Keane's very readable *Tom Paine: A Political Life*, Bloomsbury, 1995.

9 Will Hutton, *The State We're In*, Jonathan Cape, 1995. Or not, as the case may be.

10 This point is attributed to W A P Manser by Barry Supple in his fine presidential address to the Economic History Society, *Economic History Review*, XLVII, 3, 1994, Blackwell Publishers. My thanks to Forrest Capie of the City University for a copy.

11 Robert Reich in the *New York Times*, January 5, 1996, reproduced in *Prospect*.

12 Paul Milgrom and John Roberts, *Economics, Organization and Management*, Prentice Hall, 1992.

13 See her *Ownership and Control*, The Brookings Institution, 1995. Interestingly, this has received much more attention in Europe than in the US, where the finance school of corporate governance dominates the universities and most thinktanks.

14 Robert Putnam, *Making Democracy Work: Civic Traditions in Modern Italy*,

Princeton University Press, 1993. For his declinist thesis on the US, see 'Bowling alone: America's declining social capital', *Journal of Democracy*, 6, 1995.

15 *The Economist*, February 6, 1993.

16 Alexis de Tocqueville, *Democracy in America*, Vintage Books, 1945.

17 Francis Fukuyama, *Trust: The Social Virtues and the Creation of Prosperity*, Hamish Hamilton, 1995.

18 David Goodhart's paper 'The reshaping of the German social market', published by the Institute for Public Policy Research in 1994, has an excellent account of the German approach to stakeholding, which includes an explanation of the institutionalist economists' position.

19 Mark Casson, *The Economics of Business Culture*, Clarendon Press, 1991. For want of a title like *The End of History* this has not brought the author the popular audience that Fukuyama commands, but it is one of the more thought-provoking economic texts of recent years, algebra notwithstanding.

20 John Kay's thinking on the concept of stakeholding is summarized in a characteristically stimulating essay in *Prospect*, May 1996, on which I have drawn in this chapter.

21 *Tomorrow's Company*, The Royal Society for the encouragement of Arts, Manufactures and Commerce, 1995. The RSA is an interesting example of an eighteenth-century civic association which has rejuvenated itself in the late twentieth century. The chairman of the RSA inquiry was Sir Anthony Cleaver, former head of IBM United Kingdom, and the programme director was Mark Goyder.

22 Samuel Brittan's *A Restatement of Economic Liberalism*, best read in the second edition, Macmillan, 1988, remains a classic touchstone against which to measure all alternatives.

23 See Karel van Wolferen's *The Enigma of Japanese Power*, Vintage Books, 1989, for a fascinating, if jaundiced, view of the way Japan treats its less-favoured children.

24 Figures on real wages are from research by Morgan Stanley. Those on the contraction in employment are from Brian Reading's *The Fourth Reich*, Weidenfeld & Nicolson, 1995.

25 *OECD Employment Outlook*, July 1996, page 94.

26 David Soskice, 'The stake we're in', *Prospect*, April 1996.

27 Anthony Sampson, *Company Man: The Rise and Fall of Corporate Life*, HarperCollins, 1995.

28 For a useful description of the Swiss system see Beat Kappeller's article 'Watching the Swiss' in *New Economy*, Summer 1996.

Chapter 2

1   Figures from *OECD Economic Surveys: United Kingdom*, 1995.

2   News release, Office for National Statistics, May 2, 1996.

3   Hutton, ibid., Chapter 1.

4   Official figures quoted by William Waldegrave, Chief Secretary to the Treasury, in a speech to the American Chamber of Commerce, June 11, 1996. See also the comments of Andrew Dilnot, Director of the Institute for Fiscal Studies, in his

lecture to the RSA, 'Is the labour market working?', *RSA Journal*, March 1996.

5 All figures here from the OECD.

6 Dr Walter Eltis, 'How much of the UK competitiveness gap has been closed?', lecture to the Foundation for Manufacturing and Industry, 1995.

7 High technology accounted for 22 per cent in manufacturing value added in 1994, compared with 16.4 per cent in 1970. This was second equal with Japan to the United States, where the comparable figure was 24.2 per cent, up from 18.2 per cent in 1970. These figures are from the *OECD Observer*, June/July 1996.

8 A problem in discussing slump and depression is a longstanding transatlantic difference in terminology. British historians in the nineteenth century referred to the period between 1873 and 1896 as the Great Depression. Americans use this phrase to describe the period of falling output after the 1929 Wall Street crash. For clarity and consistency I have opted to call the earlier period the Great Depression, while referring to the later period as the Slump.

9 B R Mitchell, *British Historical Statistics*, Cambridge, 1988.

10 Angus Maddison, *Monitoring The World Economy, 1820–1992*, OECD Development Centre Studies, 1995.

11 For figures, see B R Mitchell, ibid.

12 Barry Eichengreen, 'The inter-war economy in a European mirror', in *The Economic History of Britain since 1700, Vol 2*, eds Roderick Floud and Donald McCloskey, Cambridge University Press, 1994. This compendium is an invaluable source on both the Great Depression of the late nineteenth century and the Slump of the 1930s.

13 See Forrest Capie and Geoffrey Wood's essay 'Money in the economy, 1870–1939' in *The Economic History of Britain since 1700*, ibid.

14 See C H Feinstein's figures in B R Mitchell, ibid.

15 Brian Reading, *The Fourth Reich*, Weidenfeld & Nicolson, 1995. A number of thoughts in this chapter were sparked by this fascinating and provocative book on Germany.

16 See W Arthur Lewis, *Growth and Fluctuations 1870–1913*, George Allen & Unwin, 1978. Also P J Cain and A G Hopkins, *British Imperialism: Innovation and Expansion 1688–1914*, Longman, 1993.

17 See Mary McKinnon, 'Living standards, 1870–1914' in *The Economic History of Britain since 1700*, ibid.

18 C H Feinstein's estimates in Mitchell, ibid.

19 The same pattern is unfolding before our eyes today in modern China and other Third World countries as the change from an agrarian to an industrial society takes its toll of community values.

20 W Arthur Lewis, ibid.

21 On employment conditions in the Great Depression, see William Lazonick, 'Employment relations in manufacturing and international competition' in *The Economic History of Britain since 1700*, ibid.

22 David Cannadine, *The Decline and Fall of the British Aristocracy*, Yale University Press, 1990. A contemporary estimate by the Essex squire John Bateman found that less than 1700 'peers' and 'great landowners' owned two-fifths of the total area of England and Wales in the 1870s. This is quoted in Cormac Ó Gráda,

'British agriculture, 1860–1914', in *The Economist History of Britain since 1700*, ibid.

23 Cannadine, ibid.

24 Quoted in Cannadine, ibid.

25 Cormac Ó Gráda, ibid.

26 Current figures from the Council of Mortgage Lenders. The First World War level of owner occupation comes from Martin Pawley, *Home Ownership*, Architectural Press, 1978.

27 Nationwide Anglia index of house prices, deflated by the retail price index.

28 Rob Thomas, *The UK Housing Market: The Long and Winding Road to Recovery*, UBS Global Research, November 1995.

29 Figures in this paragraph come from Paul Gregg and Jonathan Wadsworth in *Oxford Review of Economic Policy*, Vol 11, Spring 1995 and from *CentrePiece*, the magazine of the Centre for Economic Performance at the London School of Economics, Issue No 2, June 1996.

30 Mitchell, ibid., and *CSO Economic Trends*.

31 See *Labour Market Statistics* from the Office for National Statistics.

32 Institute for Fiscal Studies, *Update: The Changing Face of Inequality*, Autumn/Winter 1994.

33 *Income Distribution in OECD Countries*, OECD, 1995.

34 Figures from David Hale, in a fascinating essay, *How Do We Reconcile America's Economic Success with its New Sense of Insecurity*, Zurich Kemper Investments Inc, March 4, 1996.

35 For an excellent review of the arguments explaining labour-market inequality, see Stephanie Flanders and Martin Wolf, 'Haunted by the trade spectre', *Financial Times*, July 24, 1995.

36 Angus Maddison, ibid.

37 R K Merton, 'Social structure and anomie', reproduced in *Social Theory and Social Structure*, Free Press, 1957. For a helpful discussion of Merton's work, see 'The political economy of crime' by Ian Taylor in *The Oxford Handbook of Criminology*, eds Mike Maguire, Rod Morgan and Robert Reiner, Clarendon Press, 1994.

38 Freeman, ibid.

39 Paul Johnson and Howard Reed, *Two Nations? The Inheritance of Poverty and Affluence*, Institute for Fiscal Studies, 1996.

40 William Waldegrave, ibid.

Chapter 3

1 Hutton, ibid. See also Michael Kitson and Jonathan Michie, 'Britain's industrial performance since 1960: underinvestment and relative decline', *The Economic Journal*, January 1996, for a very clear statement of this case.

2 For the 'gentlemanly capitalist' thesis, see P J Cain and A G Hopkins, *British Imperialism: Innovation and Expansion 1688–1914*, Longman, 1993.

3 It should be emphasized that high inflation is not invariably an indication of low trust. In Japan, for example, a higher rate of post-war inflation than in Germany

or the US was a benign mechanism for spreading the benefits of high productivity in the export sector of the economy to workers in services where productivity was much lower. It thus enhanced social cohesion. For a more detailed explanation of this phenomenon, see Brian Reading's *Japan: The Coming Collapse*, Weidenfeld & Nicolson, 1992.

4　See Brian Reading, ibid., for an explanation of the Japanese liquidity trap, together with an inspired forecast, subsequently borne out, of how the Japanese economy was heading for the rocks.

5　CSO, *Share Ownership*, 1995. Based on a survey carried out for the CSO by Fulcrum Research, this shows that the investment institutions accounted for 60.2 per cent of the £762 billion shares quoted on the London Stock Exchange at December 31, 1994. Pension funds and insurance companies accounted respectively for 27.8 and 21.9 per cent of this figure.

6　Stephen Dorrell, speech to the Confederation of British Industry, 18 May 1994.

7　Trade and Industry Select Committee, *Second Report 1993–94, Competitiveness of UK Manufacturing Industry*, HMSO, 1994.

8　Trade and Industry Select Committee, ibid., *Memoranda of Evidence*.

9　Professor Paul Marsh, *Short Termism on Trial*, Institutional Fund Managers Association, 1990.

10　Trade and Industry Select Committee, ibid., *Memoranda of Evidence*.

11　See, for example, Stephen Bond and Costas Meghir in 'Financial constraints and company investment', *Fiscal Studies,* Vol 15, No 2, 1994.

12　For a discussion of the impact of corporation tax on company dividend decisions, see Stephen Bond, Lucy Chennels and Michael Devereux, 'Company dividends and taxes in the UK', *Fiscal Studies*, August 1995. This is strictly for the more earnest seeker after truth. Others whose algebra is shaky should know that a key conclusion is: 'To the extent that tax-exempt shareholders such as pension funds are now the most influential investors in many UK companies, their tax preference for dividend income is likely to result in significantly higher dividend payout ratios than would be chosen by companies in the absence of this tax bias.'

13　See the article by Andrew Wardlow on investment appraisal criteria in the *Bank of England Quarterly Bulletin*, August 1994.

14　Tim Jenkinson, 'The cost of equity finance: conventional wisdom reconsidered', *Stock Exchange Quarterly*, July–September 1993.

15　Andy Cosh, Alan Hughes and Ajit Singh in *Takeovers and Short-termism in the UK*, Institute for Public Policy Research, 1990.

16　Julian Franks and Colin Mayer, 'Ownership and control', in ESRC project no. W102251003 on *Capital Markets, Corporate Governance and the Market for Corporate Control*.

17　D C Mueller (ed.), *The Determinants and Effects of Merger: An International Comparison*, Oelschlager, Gunn and Hain, 1980, quoted in John Kay's *Foundations of Corporate Success*, Oxford University Press, 1993.

18　Berkshire Hathaway Inc annual report, 1994.

19　John Kay, ibid.

20　Charles Handy, *Beyond Certainty*, Hutchinson, 1995.

21　Trade and Industry Select Committee, ibid., *Memoranda of Evidence*.

22 For an excellent description of how accountants and lawyers engage in creative accounting to beat the regulator, see 'Creative compliance in financial reporting', by Atul K Shah of Bristol University, in *Accounting, Organizations and Society*, Vol 21, No 1. I am grateful to David Tweedie of the Accounting Standards Board for a copy of this article.

23 See John Plender in *Takeovers and Short-termism in the UK*, Institute for Public Policy Research, 1990.

Chapter 4

1   Quoted by Barry Supple, Presidential Address to The Economic History Society, ibid.

2   C H Feinstein, *National Income, Expenditure and Output of the United Kingdom 1855–1965*, Cambridge, 1972.

3   Smith wrote: 'There is one sort of labour which adds to the value of the subject upon which it is bestowed: there is another which has no such effect. The former, as it produces a value, may be called productive; the latter, unproductive. Thus the labour of a manufacturer adds, generally, to the value of the materials which he works upon, that of his own maintenance, and of his master's profit. The labour of a menial servant, on the contrary, adds to the value of nothing...A man grows rich by employing a multitude of manufacturers: he grows poor by maintaining a multitude of menial servants...His [the menial servant's] services generally perish in the very instant of their performance, and seldom leave any trade or value behind them for which an equal quantity of service could afterwards be procured.' Pelican Classics, pp.429–30.

4   Hamish McRae, 'Why we will soon be better off than the Germans', *The Independent*, September 13, 1996.

5   Barry Supple, ibid.

6   Measuring the costs and benefits of empire is a hugely complex endeavour. For a review of the methodologies and arguments, see Michael Edelstein, 'Imperialism: cost and benefit' in *The Economic History of Britain since 1700, Vol 2*, ibid.

7   The figures are taken from an article by Michael Kitson and Jonathan Michie in *The Economic Journal,* Basil Blackwell, January 1996.

8   Figures from GEC's annual report and accounts.

9   *Memoranda of Evidence*, ibid., p.41.

10 See, for example, Geoffrey Owen's article 'Long termism v short-termism' in *CentrePiece*, the magazine of the Centre for Economic Performance at the LSE, Issue 2, June 1996.

11 McKinsey has provided detailed evidence to support this thesis in relation to the US, Germany and Japan in *Capital Productivity*, a research report by McKinsey Global Institute, June 1996.

12 It is worth pointing out, in passing, that the failure to become a big international force in GEC's main markets was not always for want of trying. Some time before the international telecoms group Cable & Wireless was privatized, GEC came very close to buying it from the British government.

13 Figures from Glaxo's annual report and accounts, 1994.

14 Matthew Lynn, *The Billion Dollar Battle*, Heinemann, 1991.

Chapter 5

1 The best sources on this process are Charles P Kindleberger, *A Financial History of Western Europe*, George Allen & Unwin, 1984; and Fernand Braudel, *Civilisation and Capitalism, 15th–18th Century*, William Collins, 1984.
2 For a more detailed account of the growth in the City's international business up to the time of Big Bang, see *The Square Mile*, by the author with Paul Wallace, Century Hutchinson, 1985.
3 Albert M Wojnilower, paper delivered at the Reserve Bank of Australia Conference on Financial Deregulation in Sydney, June 1991. I am grateful to David Hale of Zurich Kemper Investments for a copy.
4 For the most revealing account of the Barings saga, see John Gapper and Nicholas Denton, *All That Glitters*, Hamish Hamilton, 1996.
5 Taken from the BBC Radio Four series *The City*, produced by Colin Wilde and presented by Will Hutton in January 1995.
6 *OECD Economic Outlook*, December 1995, Table 14.
7 De Tocqueville, ibid.

Chapter 6

1 Francis Fukuyama, ibid.
2 See *OECD Economies at a Glance: Structural Indicators*, Table 5.8, 1996.
3 These figures have been taken from DeAnne Julius, *Liberalisation, Foreign Investment and Economic Growth*, Shell Selected Paper, 1993.
4 Figures are from the last published annual accounts filed at Companies House.
5 Facts and figures from the last published annual accounts filed at Companies House and from interviews with the present management and employees.
6 See references to the work of David Guest and colleagues in *Exploring the Economy*, LSE Centre for Economic Performance, 1995.
7 Robert Taylor, 'British workers "the least satisfied in EU"', *Financial Times*, December 28, 1995.
8 This view is advanced by Elaine Sternberg in *Just Business*, Little, Brown, 1994.

Chapter 7

1 Adolf A Berle Jr and Gardiner C Means, *The Modern Corporation and Private Property*, Commerce Clearing House Inc, New York, 1932.
2 The estimate of pre-war equity share ownership is the author's, based on data in the 1959 Radcliffe Committee report on the monetary system. Later figures on shareholding are from the Central Statistical Office's annual report on share

ownership, based on surveys by Fulcrum Research.

3   John Plender, *That's the Way the Money Goes*, André Deutsch, 1982.

4   Figure supplied by US Federal Reserve.

5   Jonathan P Charkham, *Keeping Good Company*, Clarendon Press, Oxford, 1994.

6   Rupert Pennant-Rea, 'Punters or proprietors? A survey of capitalism', *The Economist*, May 5, 1990.

7   For a perceptive account of this episode, and of the original mergers that transformed GEC, see Robert Jones and Oliver Marriott, *Anatomy of a Merger: A History of GEC, AEI and English Electric*, Jonathan Cape, 1970.

8   *The Cadbury Committee Report: Financial Aspects of Corporate Governance*, Gee & Co, 1992.

9   National Association of Pension Funds, *Investment Committee Briefing*, November 1995.

10 The author declares an interest: he is chairman of PIRC.

11 Figures obtained from the company by Pensions and Investment Research Consultants.

12 John Kay and Aubrey Silberston, 'Corporate governance', *National Institute Economic Review*, August 1995.

13 Speech to PIRC's annual corporate governance conference, 1994.

14 All figures here provided to the author by CalPERS.

Chapter 8

1   An alternative intepretation has been offered to me by Richard Reeves, company secretary of British Steel, who says that the PIRC resolution at British Gas did immense damage not only to British Gas but to the wider British economy. While the attribution of so much influence to PIRC is flattering – the author is chairman – it reflects a somewhat exaggerated view of PIRC's power. This is one of many examples of how people in industry seek to deflect the blame for irresponsible and anti-social behaviour: it becomes an absolute necessity for them to shoot the messenger.

2   See Gregg, Machin and Szymanski in the *British Journal of Industrial Relations*, 1993. They found that for the highest paid director at 288 quoted companies between 1983 and 1991, 'the growth in directors' compensation was insignificantly related to corporate performance, whether measured using stock market valuations or earnings per share. They also found that the most significant variable explaining remuneration was sales growth, suggesting that size rather than performance is what matters most.' Quoted in *Just Reward? The Truth about Executive Pay*, by A P Williams, Kogan Page, 1994.

3   This was in *Letters from the Boardroom*, a series of programmes delivered on BBC Radio 4 just before Davies took up his appointment at the Bank of England.

4   Figures from ProShare (UK), *Individual Share Ownership – Facts and Figures*, March 1996.

5   See Brian Reading's *The Fourth Reich* (ibid.) for an account of the shift in the global economy to the so-called Juglar cycle.

6 Michael Brett, 'Rewards for volatility: The LTIP lottery', *PIRC Intelligence*, September 1996.
7 Berkshire Hathaway annual report, 1994.
8 The many ways in which accounting practice can be manipulated have been detailed by City analyst Terry Smith in his book *Accounting For Growth*, Business Books, 1992. Lex of the *Financial Times* frequently comments on the continuing manipulability of accounts – see, for example, the Lex column on July 16, 1996.
9 See the Prudential's annual report for details. Ideas for commutation of salary in exchange for generous participation in profits have also been floated by Allen Sykes in, for example, 'Proposals for internationally competitive corporate governance in Britain and America', *Corporate Governance*, October 1994.

Chapter 9

1 Nigel Lawson, *The View from Number 11*, Bantam Press, 1992.
2 All figures in this section from TSB annual reports and the *Financial Times*.
3 Peter Riddell, *The Thatcher Decade*, Basil Blackwell, 1989.
4 Professor Leslie Hannah, 'The economic consequences of the state ownership of industry, 1945–1990', in *The Economic History of Britain since 1700, Vol 3*, ibid.
5 For a perceptive account of how this came about, see Alex Henney, *A Study of the Privatisation of the Electricity Supply Industry in England and Wales*, published by EEE Ltd, 1994.
6 John Redwood, *Public Enterprise in Crisis*, Basil Blackwell, 1980 and *Popular Capitalism*, Routledge, 1988.
7 Peter Walker, *Staying Power*, Bloomsbury, 1991.
8 Figures in this paragraph from the National Audit Office report, *Department of the Environment: Sale of the Water Authorities in England and Wales*, HMSO, February 1992.
9 See his Institute of Economic Affairs lecture delivered to the RSA on October 31, 1995.
10 This emerges in Tawney's essay *Social Democracy in Britain*, written in 1949, and in *British Socialism Today* in 1952.
11 Figures from ProShare, ibid.

Chapter 10

1 William Beveridge, *Report on Social Insurance and Allied Services*, HMSO, 1942.
2 The main sources of data on public spending, demography and welfare in this chapter are *The Financial Statement and Budget Report 1996–97* (The Budget Red Book), HMSO, 1995; and *The Future of Welfare: A Guide to the Debate* by John Hills of the London School of Economics, published by the Joseph Rowntree Foundation, 1993.
3 Figures quoted in Andrew Dilnot, Richard Disney, Paul Johnson and Edward

Whitehouse, *Pensions Policy in the UK*, Institute for Fiscal Studies, 1994.

4   Hills, ibid.

5   David Willetts, *The Age of Entitlement*, The Social Market Foundation, 1993.

6   Cost figures from Peter Lilley, Mais Lecture 1993, reproduced in *Winning the Welfare Debate*, The Social Market Foundation, 1995. Demographic numbers from Dilnot *et al.*, ibid.

7   The phrase is used by John Gray in *The Moral Foundations of Market Institutions*, IEA Health and Welfare Unit, 1992.

8   Figures on Sweden from the *OECD Economic Outlook*, 1995; *The International Bank Credit Analyst*, January 1996; and Martin Wolf, 'The limits of socialism', *Financial Times*, April 18, 1995.

9   Quoted in Lombard Street Research's *Monthly Economic Review*, June 1996.

10 World Bank, ibid.

11 Red Book, ibid.

12 One aspect of this syndrome was presciently diagnosed by P G Wodehouse in the 1950s, when his butler Jeeves told an American tourist: 'Socialistic legislation has sadly depleted the resources of England's hereditary aristocracy. We are living now in what is known as the Welfare State, which means – broadly speaking – that everybody is completely destitute.' P G Wodehouse, *Ring for Jeeves*, quoted in David Cannadine, ibid.

13 Jonathan Wadsworth and Paul Gregg, *CentrePiece*, ibid.

14 The classic conservative attack on the welfare state in relation to lone mothers came in Charles Murray's *Losing Ground: American Social Policy 1950–1980*, New York, Basic Books, 1984. For the UK facts, see J Bradshaw and J Miller's *Lone Parent Families in the UK*, DSS Research Report No. 7, HMSO, 1991.

15 Dilnot *et al.*, ibid.

16 For a clear analysis of this problem, see *Better Pensions for All*, by Bryn Davies, Institute for Public Policy Research, 1993.

17 Consulting actuaries R Watson & Sons, *Long Term Statistics*, quoted in Richard Disney, 'Occupational pension schemes: prospects and reforms in the UK', *Fiscal Studies*, August 1995.

18 Office for National Statistics, *Labour Force Survey*, Winter 1995–96.

19 David Willetts, ibid.

20 Peter Lilley, ibid.

21 Professor Tim Congdon, Lombard Street Research's *Monthly Economic Review*, May 1996.

22 Figures quoted by consulting actuaries Bacon & Woodrow in their *Pensions Pocket Book*, NTC Publications, 1996.

23 See 'A case for basic income' by the Dutch economist Jan Stroeken in the Autumn 1996 edition of *New Economy* for a detailed exposition.

24 Howard Davies, *Letters from the Boardroom*, ibid.

25 While military spending has declined as a percentage of GDP between 1989 and 1995, it rose in absolute terms from £20,868 to £21,637 over the period, in constant prices. Figures from the *SIPRI Year Book for 1996*, Oxford University Press, 1996.

26 Dilnot *et al.*, ibid.

27 Field has proposed a radical money-purchase pensions alternative in *Private*

Pensions for All: Squaring the Circle, Fabian Society, 1993, and other publications.

28 G Mulgan and R Murray, *Reconnecting Taxation*, Demos, 1993.

Chapter 11

1   See Alan Gelb, *Oil Windfalls: Blessing or Curse?*, a World Bank research publication, Oxford University Press, 1988.

2   The figure is calculated by taking the accumulated current account surpluses for 1985–94 from Table 50 of the June 1996 *OECD Economic Outlook* and deducting the net stock of foreign assets accumulated over the same period. The foreign assets and liabilities are shown in Table 53 of the same publication.

3   Angus Maddison, *Monitoring the World Economy*, ibid.

4   See J M Roberts's *History of the World* for an account of this episode in Chinese history. The shape of the world's present intellectual and physical landscape if industrialization had continued in China is beyond imagining.

5   *Financial Times* leader, 'Changing face of world trade', March 30, 1996.

6   *OECD Economies at a Glance – Structural Indicators*, 1996, Table 4.6.

7   Vincent Cable, 'Globalisation: can the state strike back?', *The World Today*, May 1996.

8   See Philip Stephens' excellent *Politics and the Pound*, Macmillan, 1996.

9   Quoted to me by Sir John Hoskyns, who attributed it to William (Lord) Armstrong, head of the Civil Service in the Heath administration.

10 Professor Tim Congdon, *Gerrard & National Monthly Economic Review*, September 1996.

11 See Keith Marsden, 'There's no need for tax "harmonization"' in the *Wall Street Journal*, May 10–11, 1996, in which this author of a World Bank study on links between taxes and economic growth puts a powerful case against those in the European Commission who claim that globalization is causing fiscal 'degradation' in Europe.

12 The debt figures for Britain are calculated by the author from Mitchell, ibid., taking aggregate liabilities of the state from pages 602–3 and gross national product at market prices from pages 832–5. Figures for the US are those quoted in Alberto Alesina's essay 'The end of large public debts' in *High Public Debt: The Italian Experience*, Cambridge University Press, 1988.

13 Roger Bootle, *The Death of Inflation*, Nicholas Brealey Publishing, 1996.

14 John Maynard Keynes, 'Social consequences of changes in the value of money', written in 1923, from *Essays in Persuasion*, Macmillan and Cambridge University Press for the Royal Economic Society, 1972.

15 The southern comfort zone is, I believe, a coinage of David Roche of the research boutique Independent Strategy.

16 On the Maastricht Treaty definition, Britain's percentage of government debt to GDP is the lowest in Europe, apart from France and Luxembourg, at 54 per cent in 1995 – up from 35.5 per cent in 1991 – declinists please note. These figures are from the *OECD Economic Outlook* for June 1996.

17 Brian Reading, 'After 1999 – What then?' *Monthly International Review* 51,

Lombard Street Research, May 15, 1996. His earlier forecast of a mild, mid-cycle correction in the middle of the 1990s in *The Fourth Reich* (ibid.) has already proved correct. The book contains a cogent analysis of the changing pattern of economic cycles in the twentieth century, which provides a basis for these forecasts.

18 The May 1996 issue of the IMF's *World Economic Outlook* puts the unfunded element of Britain's liabilities at less than 5 per cent compared with more than 100 per cent for France and Germany. See also J B Kuné, Wilfried F M Petit and Aggie J H Pinxt, *The Hidden Liabilities of Basic Pension Schemes in the European Community*, CEPS Working Document No. 80, Centre for European Policy Studies. This puts the accumulated benefit obligations of the UK at 42 per cent of GDP compared with 122 per cent for Germany, 69 per cent for France, 107 per cent for Italy, 137 per cent for the Netherlands and 109 per cent for Spain.

19 For an interesting account of the history of the Latin monetary union, see *In Search of Monetary Unions* by Dr Morris Perlman of the London School of Economics, Special Paper No. 39 of the LSE Financial Markets Group.

Chapter 12

1 Calculations in this and subsequent paragraphs by the author, based on figures from Angus Maddison, *Monitoring the World Economy 1820–1992*, Appendix D, ibid.

2 When I interviewed the head of the fifth largest *yakuza* syndicate in Japan recently, he mused about whether his exclusion from golf club membership constituted an actionable abuse of human rights.

3 Figures for stock market returns are from *The BZW Equity-Gilt Study – Investment in the London Stock Market since 1918*, published annually by Barclays de Zoete Wedd Strategy.

4 For an interesting exploration of the relationship between economic growth and happiness, see the articles by Robert Eisner, Andrew Oswald and Randi Hawkins, Jo Webb and Dan Corry in the Spring 1996 edition of *New Economy*.

5 See A Green and H Steedman, *Educational Provision, Educational Attachment and the Needs of Industry: A Review of Research for Germany, France, the USA and Britain*, National Institute of Economic and Social Research, 1993.

6 Simon Jenkins, *Accountable to None: The Tory Nationalisation of Britain*, Hamish Hamilton, 1995.

7 C H Feinstein's figures, quoted in B R Mitchell, *British Historical Statistics*, ibid.

8 Figures on growth, trade and total factor productivity are from Angus Maddison, *Monitoring the World Economy 1820–1992*, ibid.

9 Anthony Sampson, ibid.

10 John Maynard Keynes, 'Social consequences of changes in the value of money', *Essays in Persuasion*, ibid.

11 Harry G Johnson, *The Economic Approach to Social Questions*, Weidenfeld & Nicolson, 1968.

12 Peter Mandelson and Roger Liddle, *The Blair Revolution – Can New Labour Deliver?*, Faber and Faber, 1996.

Index